IMAGES
of America

SALISBURY BEACH

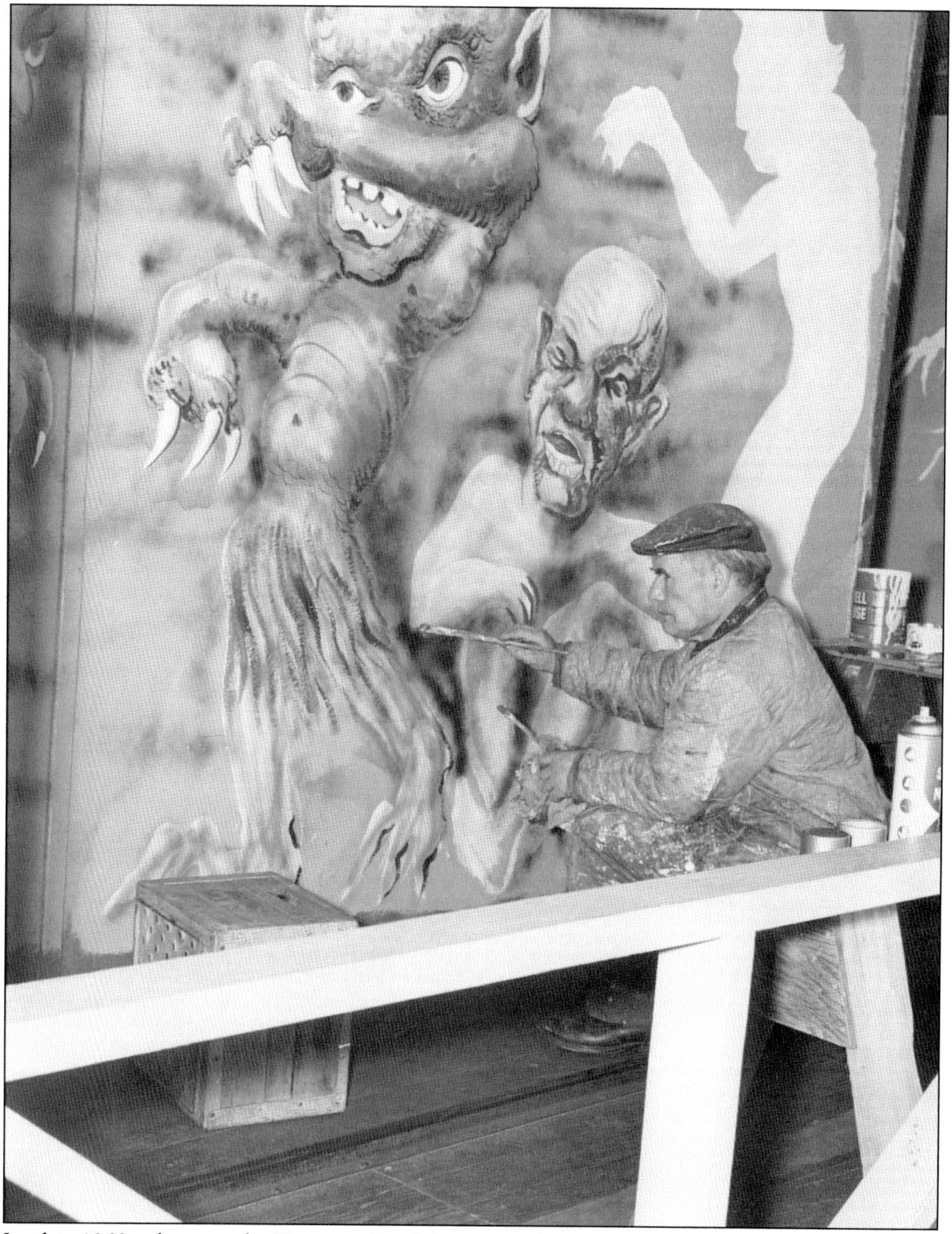

In this 1960s photograph, Dominic Spadola, covered in paint like any true artist, creates a frightening scene on one of the attractions at Shaheen's Amusement Park at Salisbury Beach. Spadola, who painted in Rome and designed scenery for stage shows, painted and constructed characters for the amusement park for many years. (Courtesy Roger Shaheen.)

IMAGES
of America

SALISBURY BEACH

Pamela Mutch Stevens

ARCADIA
PUBLISHING

ISBN 978-0-7385-0444-5

Published by Arcadia Publishing
Charleston, South Carolina

Printed in the United States of America

Library of Congress Catalog Card Number: 00104079

For all general information contact Arcadia Publishing at:
Telephone 843-853-2070
Fax 843-853-0044
E-mail sales@arcadiapublishing.com
For customer service and orders:
Toll-Free 1-888-313-2665

Visit us on the Internet at www.arcadiapublishing.com

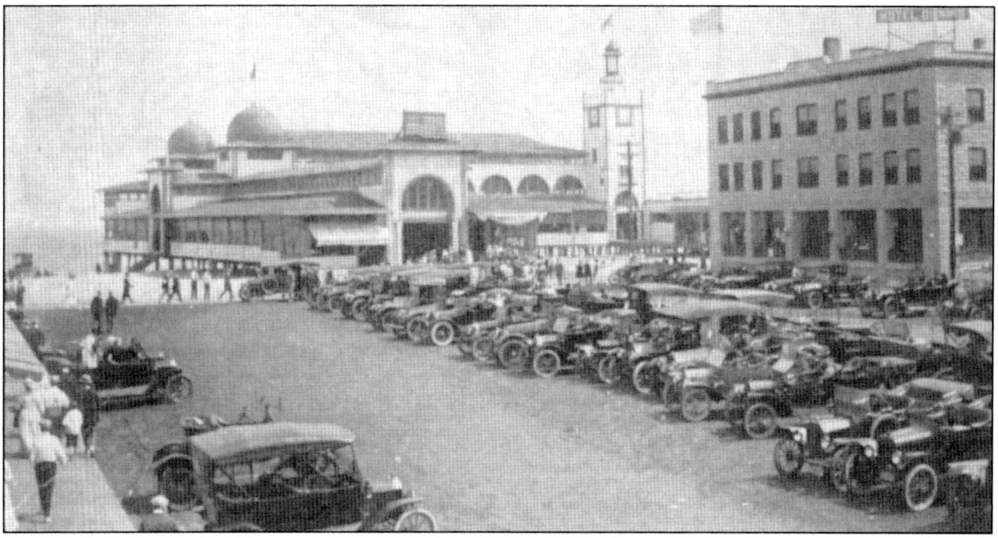

The original Ocean Echo, owned by Michael and Daniel Cushing, was built in 1916, but was completely destroyed by fire on January 5, 1920. The Ocean Echo Pavilion covered more than an acre of ground and jutted into the ocean. It hosted a beacon that was a replica of Old Glory decorated with tricolor lights that blazed above the name on the structure. The Ocean Echo was rebuilt and operated under that name until 1937, when it was auctioned and remodeled as the Frolics. (Courtesy Arnold Marookian.)

On the cover: This photograph shows one of the many families that gathered at Salisbury Beach over the years. The bathing costumes are typical of the 1920s style. The amount and formality of clothing seems to be measured by age. The grandfather is wearing a three-piece suit while one of the younger boys is clad only in shorts. (Courtesy Arnold Marookian.)

Contents

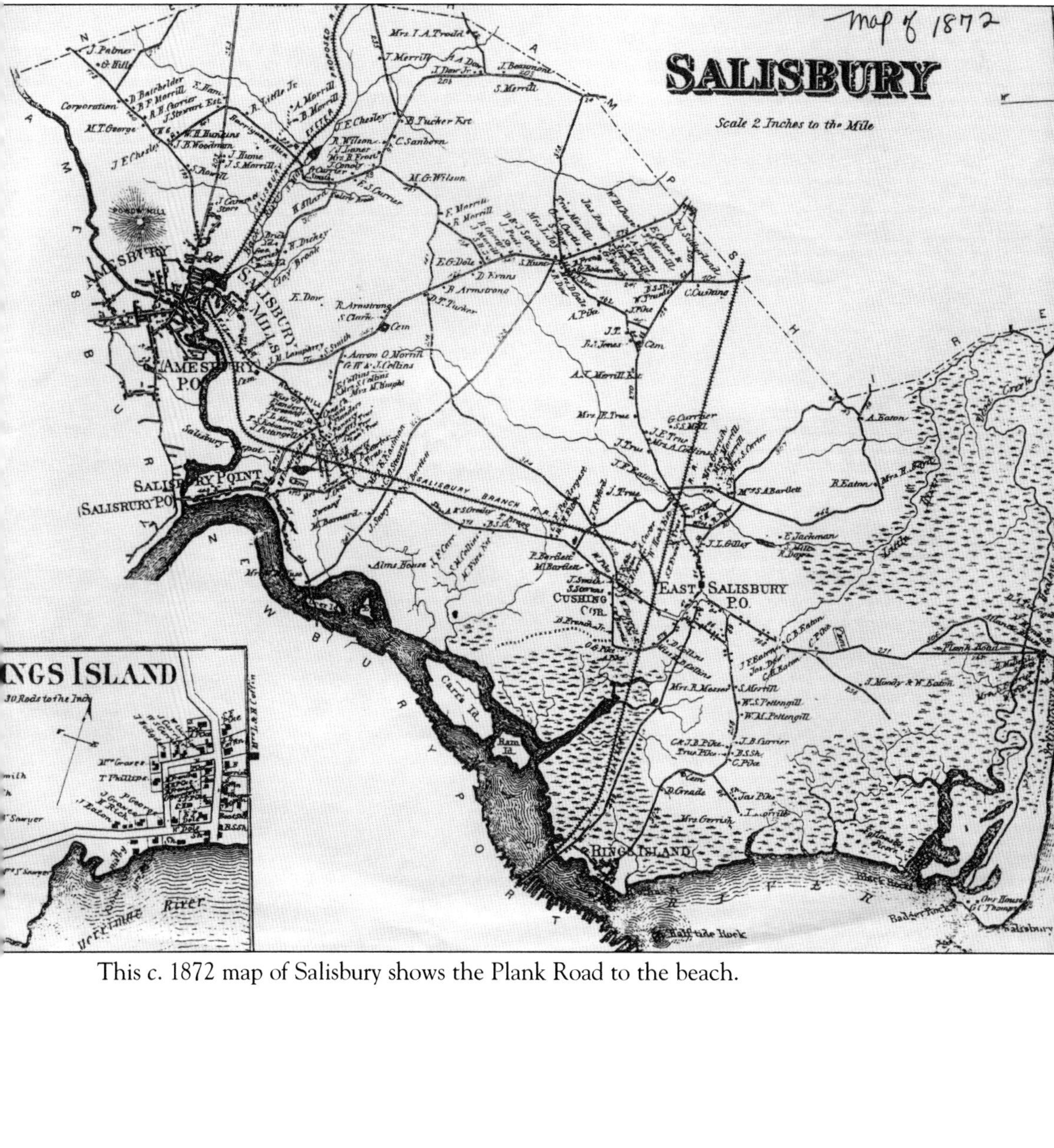

This *c.* 1872 map of Salisbury shows the Plank Road to the beach.

Introduction

Part of the beauty is the fight to keep it,
and that all good things do not come easily
and must be perpetually fought for. Our test is
in our recognition of our love and our willingness
to do battle for it.

—Marjorie Kinnon Rawlings.

Somewhere, for a brief moment in time, there was a magical place by the seashore known as Salisbury Beach. Laughter accompanied the roar of the tide. People came to swim next to the Ocean Echo and dance with the moonlight reflecting off the water. Accompanying the rush of the waves were the tunes of many famous big bands and performers like Lionel Hampton and Frank Sinatra. The ocean and its magnetic force of tides attracted people of all ages. Families came to picnic, to celebrate, and to reunite. Children materialized, frolicking in the surf or searching for a special shell, added to a collection now long forgotten. Adults arrived looking for romance, excitement, or maybe just solace.

The first official "Great Gathering" was held at Salisbury Beach on September 17, 1861. Invitations were sent to all Salisbury natives. Even those natives who had moved as far away as New York and Illinois came to the gathering. All modes of transportation available at the time were used by the crowd of 5,000 people to make their way to the event. Great Gatherings were held every September for many years.

M.D.F. Steere, agent of the Salisbury Mills, had the first cottage built on the beach in 1864, but the property was burglarized and torched in 1908. By 1880, there were 150 cottages on the oceanfront. A hotel, the Blue Fish chowder house, and a wharf were built at the Black Rocks in 1860 at about the location of the current boat ramp. The Black Rocks is at the wide mouth of the Merrimack River, where small tidal streams meet at the south end of the beach. The building of another large wharf in 1870 to accommodate steamboats made the beach more accessible to passengers boarding at different locations on the river. At first, horse-drawn cars, referred to as the "Seaside Railroad," transported people from the wharf to the center of the beach. Steam engines replaced the horses in the 1880s and the line was electrified in the 1890s. A plank road from beyond the square across the marshes to the beach was constructed in 1866.

Salisbury Beach seems to belong to another era frozen forever in pictures, postcards and memories. Many of the amusements are gone, swallowed by the Blizzard of 1978. The plaintive scream of seagulls can be still heard as they perch on deserted buildings shrouding the beach with a blanket of melancholy. The famous carousel adorned with the carved "Looff" horses resides now in San Diego at a shopping mall.

"Writing with light" is the literal definition of the word *photography* from the Greek language. The quality of light at the beach is unique. The sun in summer reflects off the water, creating a shimmering haze. Every object appears distinct and dramatic with an ocean backdrop. Selecting pictures "written" with this special beach light, let us take a brief walk through these images to an enchanted land of childhood, sunburns, and thrilling rides. Close your eyes and imagine Glenn Miller and his orchestra playing their music while couples sashay across the ballroom of a grand hotel in all their finery. Maybe we can find that moonlit path that falls across the ocean and rediscover the magic of our childhood at the once enchanted Salisbury Beach.

One

Seems Like Old Times

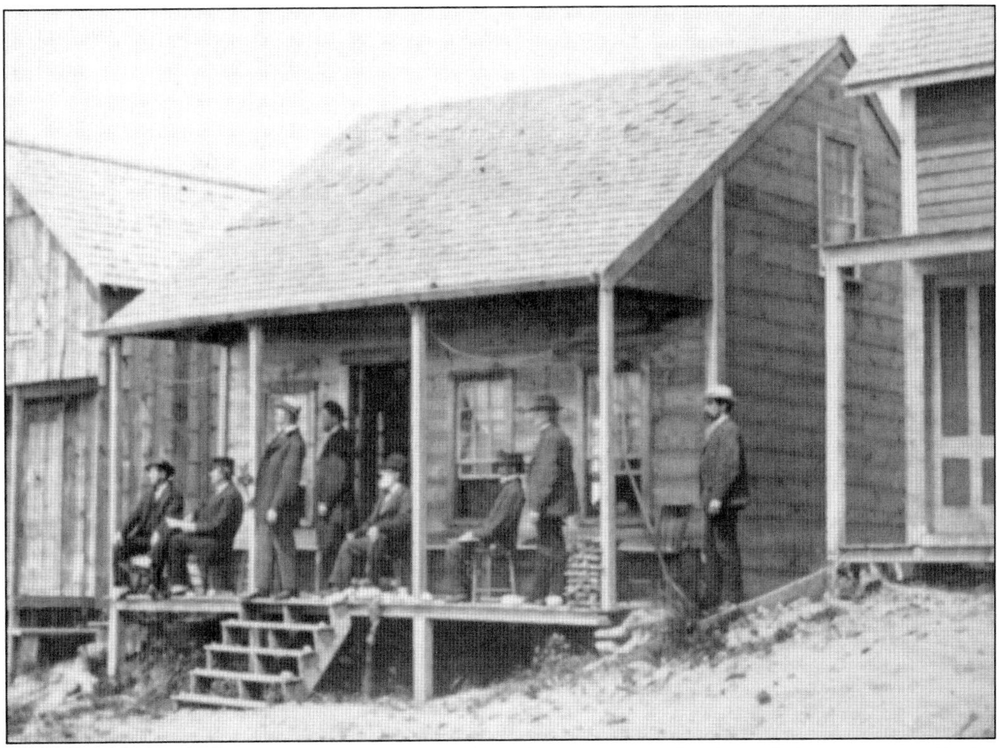

Many cottages were built on the south end of the beach in the late 19th century. All the cottages were later razed or moved to the north end when the south end became a state-owned refuge in the 1930s. Although some cottages were occupied by their owners, most of the early ones were built to be leased. Most had two rooms, one upstairs and one down. The upstairs was often divided by a sheet to separate the men and women. (Courtesy Scott Nason.)

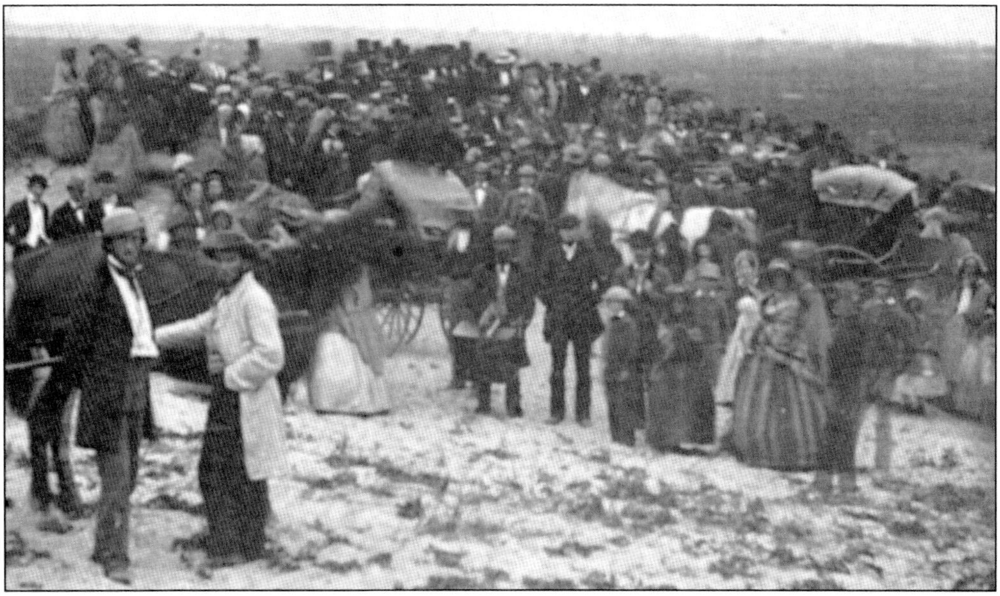

People arrived at Salisbury Beach for the Great Gathering on September 17, 1861, by 48 modes of transportation. The steamship *Clipper* delivered guests from Newburyport, Massachusetts. Invitations had been sent by the Committee on Arrangements to every native son and daughter. Salisbury natives from Illinois and New York City were in attendance. (Courtesy Scott Nason.)

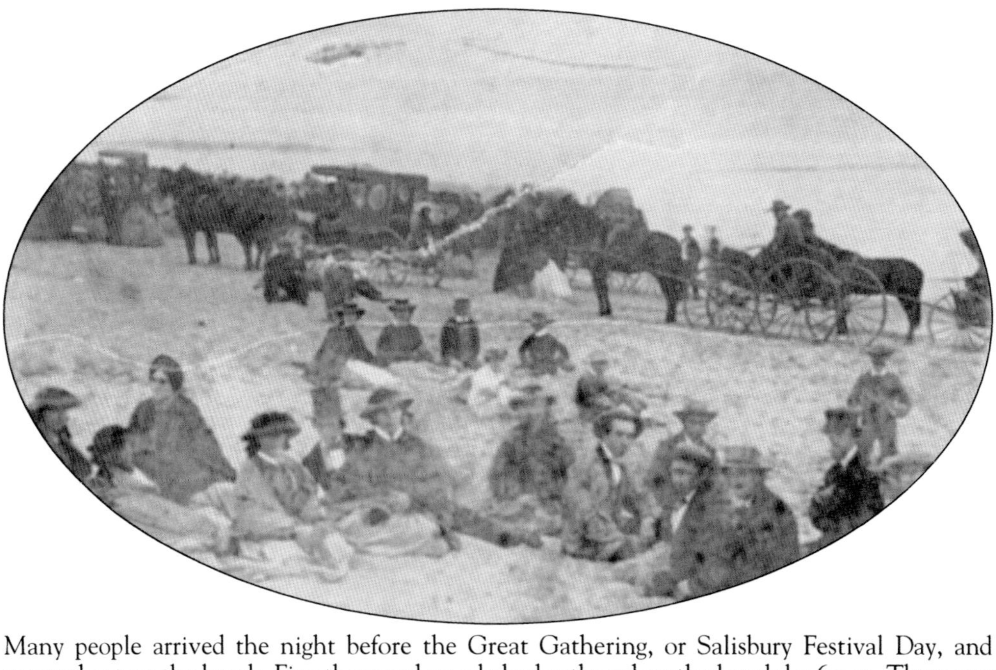

Many people arrived the night before the Great Gathering, or Salisbury Festival Day, and camped out on the beach. Five thousand people had gathered on the beach by 6 p.m. There was spirited music by a well-trained choir and speeches by local orators, including Caleb Cushing, a native son of Salisbury, a diplomat, and attorney general under Franklin Pierce. Clam chowder was served from the Relay House, even though the crowd had brought enough food to feed the inhabitants of Boston. (Courtesy Scott Nason.)

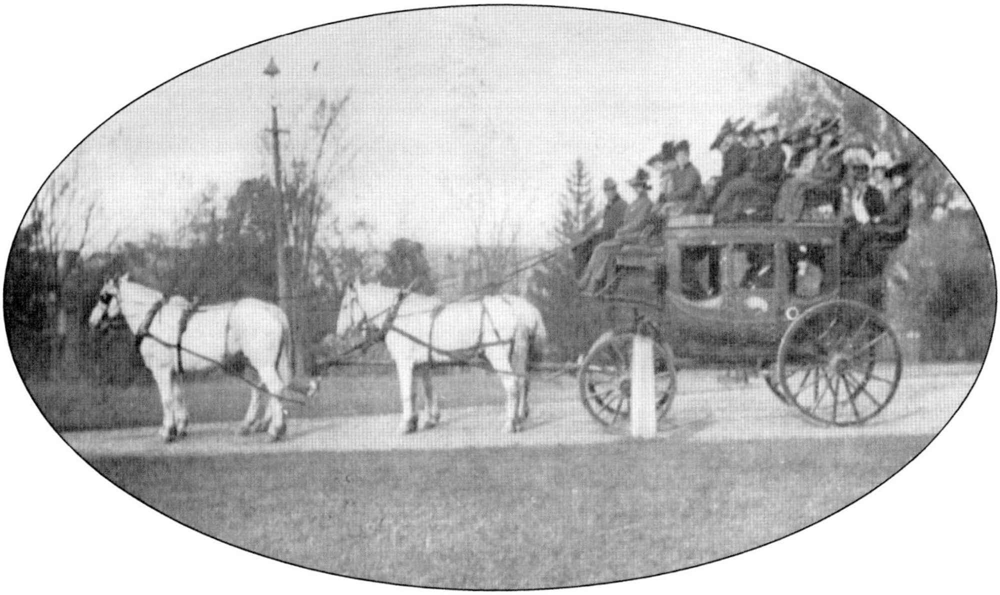

This stagecoach is leaving Bradford College in 1903 to deliver the girls to the dock to catch the ship that will take them to Salisbury Beach for their annual outing.

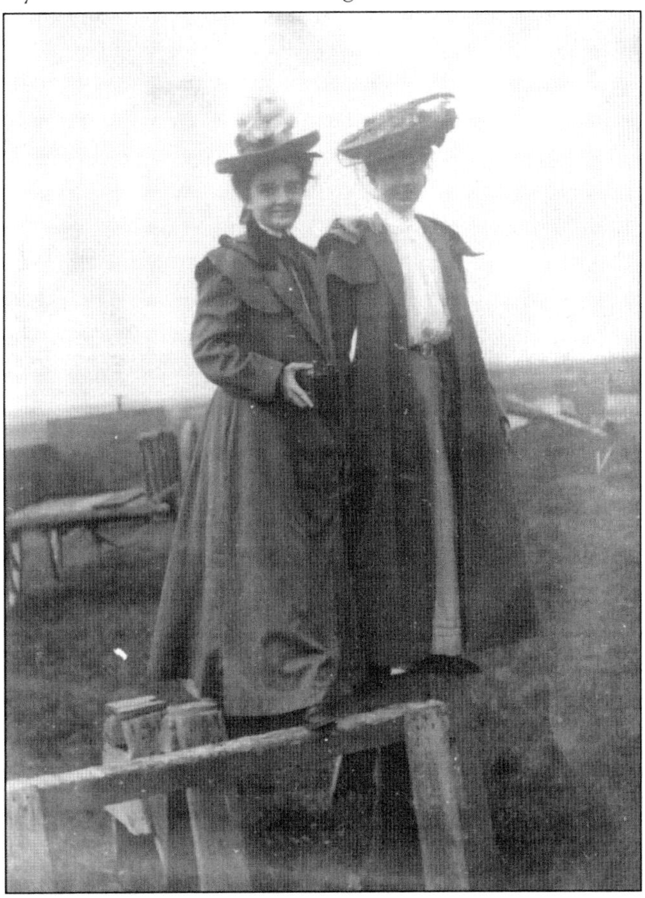

Gertrude Sawyer Morse and a friend, from the Bradford College class of 1903, pose for the camera in full dress near the landing at Black Rocks. They are both wearing fashionable hats, probably "Gibson Girl" blouses (a lot of tucks and lace), completed with a walking skirt covered by a full-length coat.

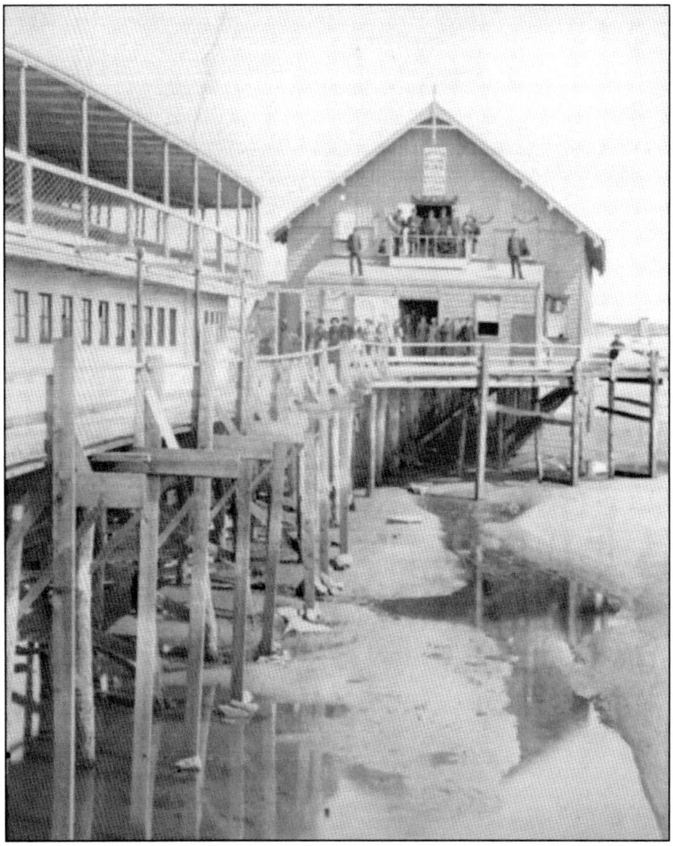

The porch of the Roller Skating Rink accommodates many people possibly waiting for the next boat to arrive at the Black Rocks dock. A sign attached to the rink simply states, "Open Morning, Afternoon and Evening." (Courtesy Scott Nason.)

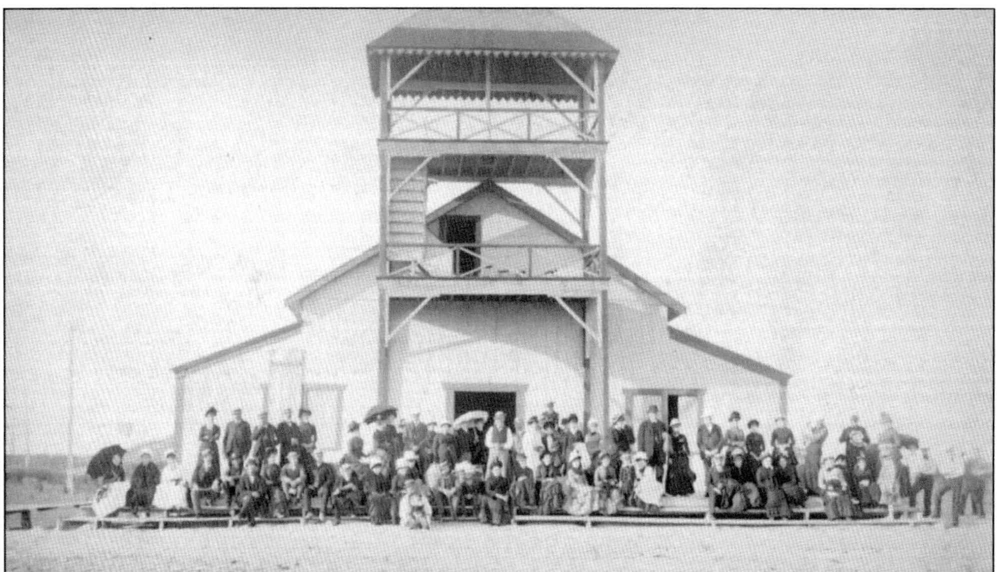

A group poses at the Pavilion at Black Rocks, c. 1880. The atmosphere of true refinement is depicted in this Victorian-era portrait of the beach. The lookout tower must have furnished a wonderful vista of the Atlantic Ocean. (Courtesy Joseph Callahan.)

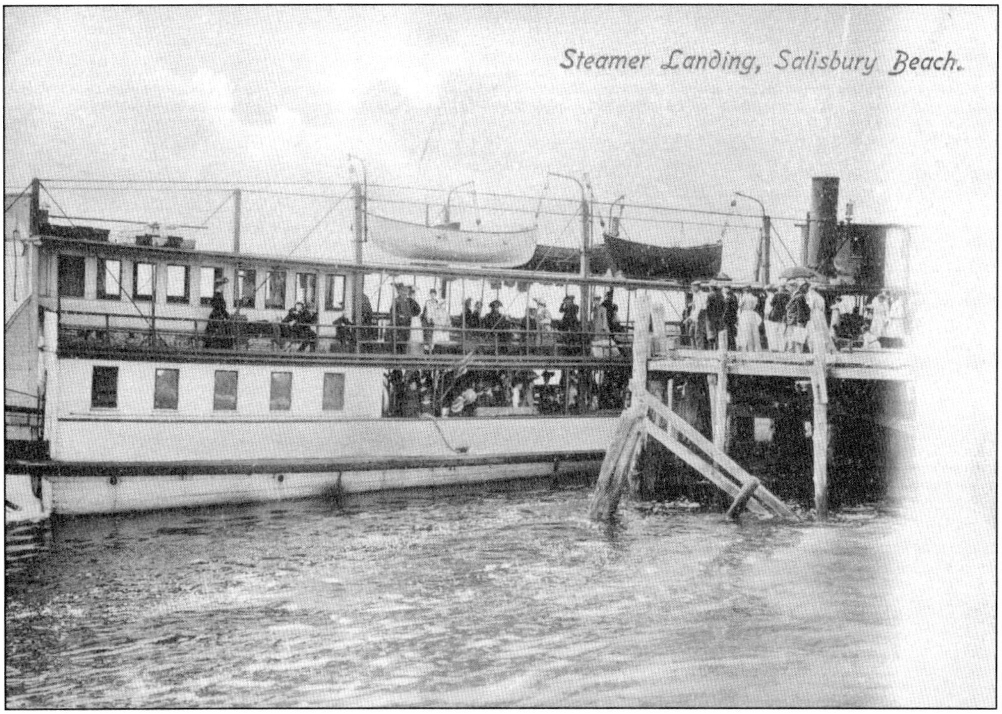

The steamer landing at Black Rocks allowed passengers to catch a transfer ferry. The familiar simmer of the awaited steam engine could be heard by the crowd on the dock. (Courtesy Arnold Marookian.)

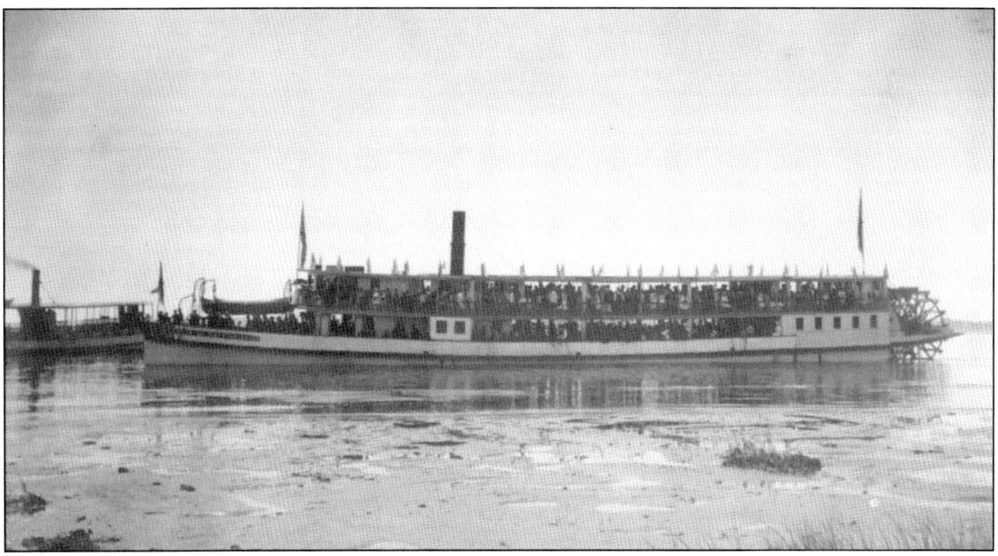

The *City of Haverhill* is docked at Black Rocks landing in 1880s. This 175-ton steamer, a sternwheeler, was a double-decker capable of carrying a large load of passengers. The Black Rocks were a real marine hazard. The famous Capt. John Smith was said to have spent a stormy night anchored off Black Rocks. Several shipwrecks occurred at this location.

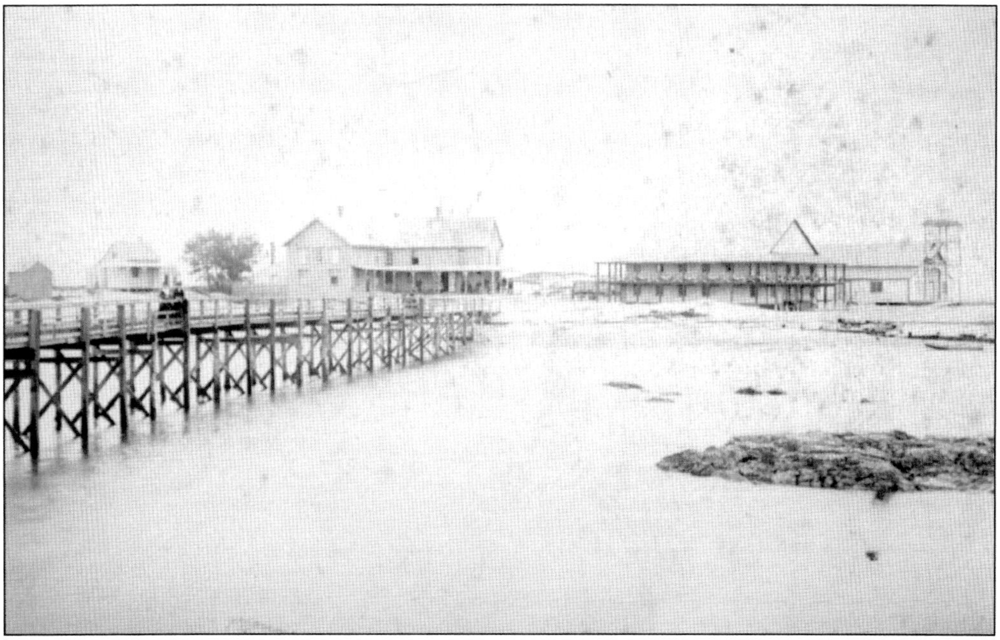

This photograph shows all the buildings and the pier at Black Rocks in 1888. The Pavilion appears at the far right, with the hotel in the center of the picture.

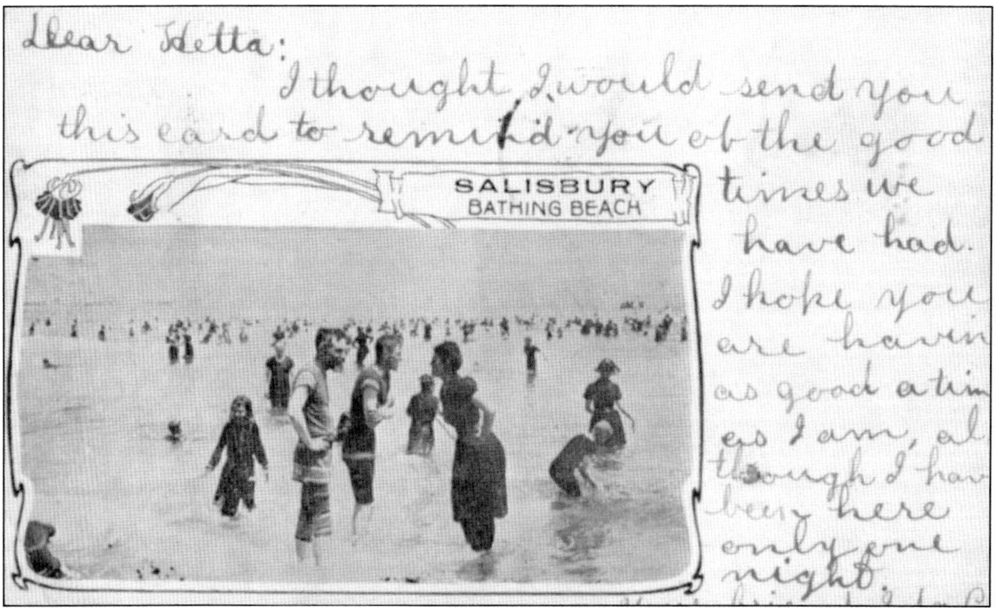

A typical postcard of the era was mailed from Salisbury Beach on August 26, 1904, to Miss Hetta Thompson, Cedar Street, Haverhill, Massachusetts (before zip codes). Ida, the sender, is reminding Hetta of the good times they have had at Salisbury Beach. All the writing was done on the front of the card, with the back saved for the address only.

Students from Bradford College in September 1896, aboard the boat to Salisbury Beach, anticipate a day free from schoolwork. Clockwise from left to right are Margaret Tucker, Maude Cushing, Emily Helmes, Alice Drake, Ann Tomkins, Bess Gaylord, Cora Wolcott, and Sarah Tomkins.

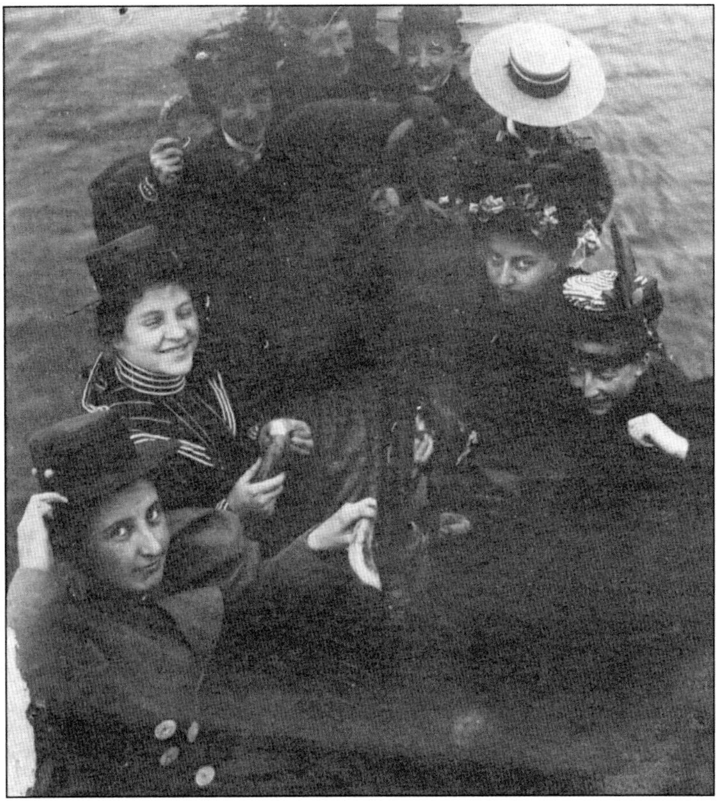

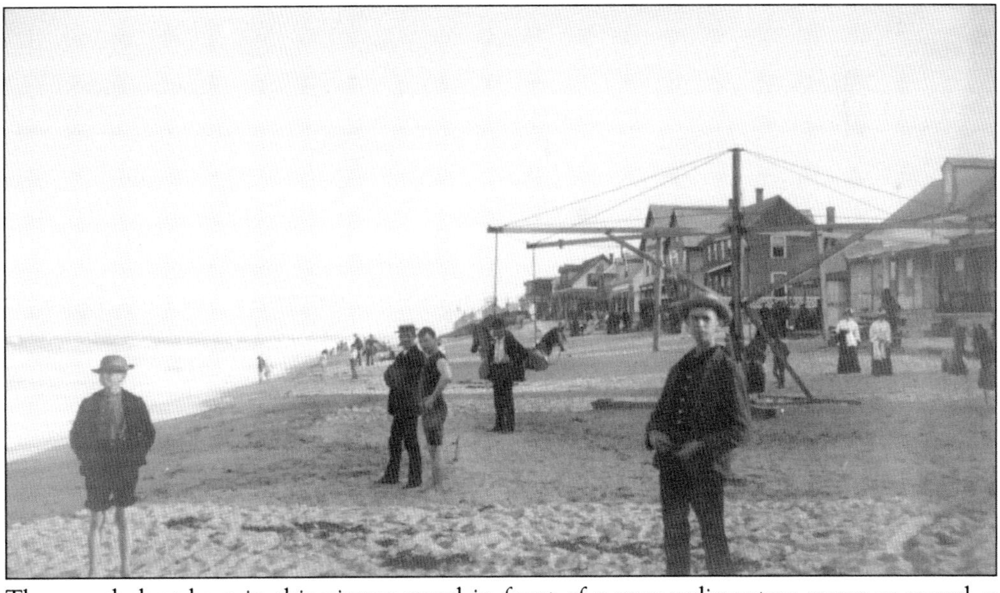

The nonchalant boys in this picture stand in front of a very rudimentary merry-go-round, a precursor to the famous Broadway Flying Horses. This photograph dates from 1888 and is taken at the center of the beach looking south.

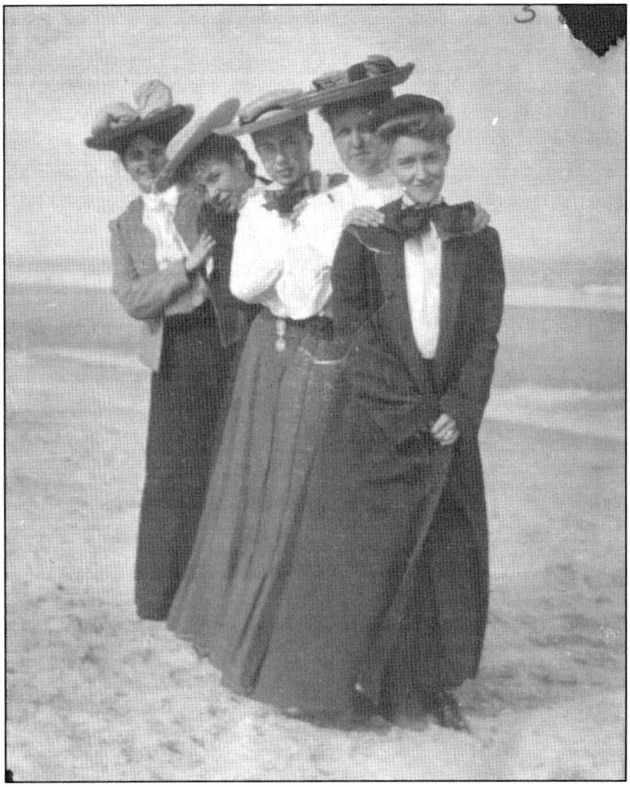

Girls from the Bradford College Class of 1905 form a line on the sand at Salisbury. Included in the picture are Lucy Lindley Fairchild, Laura Williams, and "Belle," noted only as a girl from Alaska. There is no thought of going in for a dip wearing those cumbersome outfits. The last girl in the row is wearing a Spectator jacket, a very tailored garment with cartridge pleated sleeves.

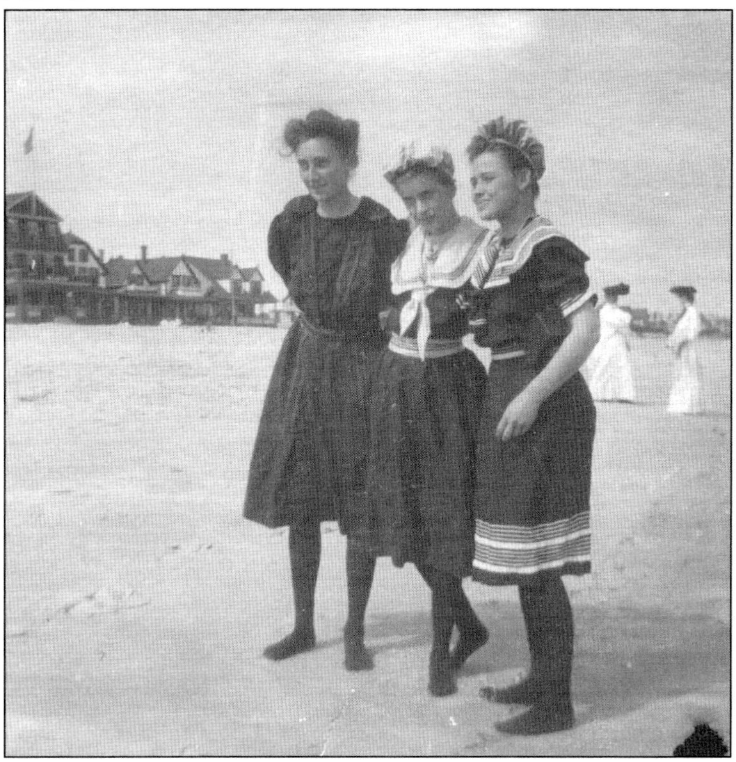

Three bathing beauties from c. 1918 pose for the camera. Swimming does not look like it was an easy feat to accomplish in these outfits, which were usually made of a type of black or navy wool with black stockings that prevented a woman from showing bare legs. One woman stated she was not allowed to take off her stockings on the beach and only went in "paddling," which in today's language would mean wading.

Butler's Toothpick dominates Black Rocks in this postcard. The marker was placed on this dangerous area by the federal government at the instigation of Benjamin F. Butler, a Massachusetts politician and popular Union general during the Civil War. A newer Butler's Toothpick still stands today at Black Rocks.

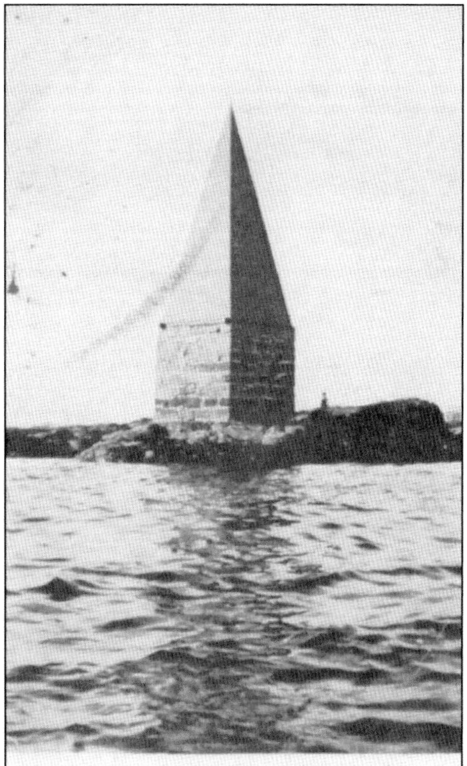

Butler's Toothpick, Black Rocks, Mass.

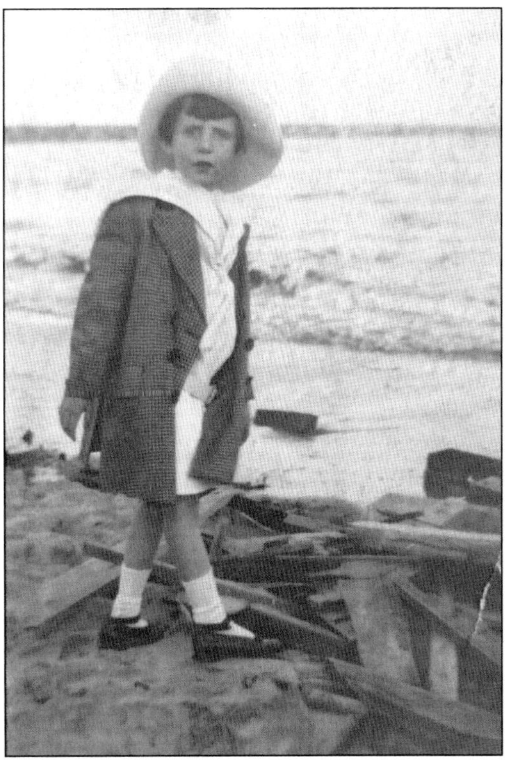

A young child dressed in her Sunday best does not seem to be interested in swimming, but has probably come to the beach to picnic with the family. At the turn of the century, breathing ocean air was thought to be very invigorating to the body similar to a health tonic.

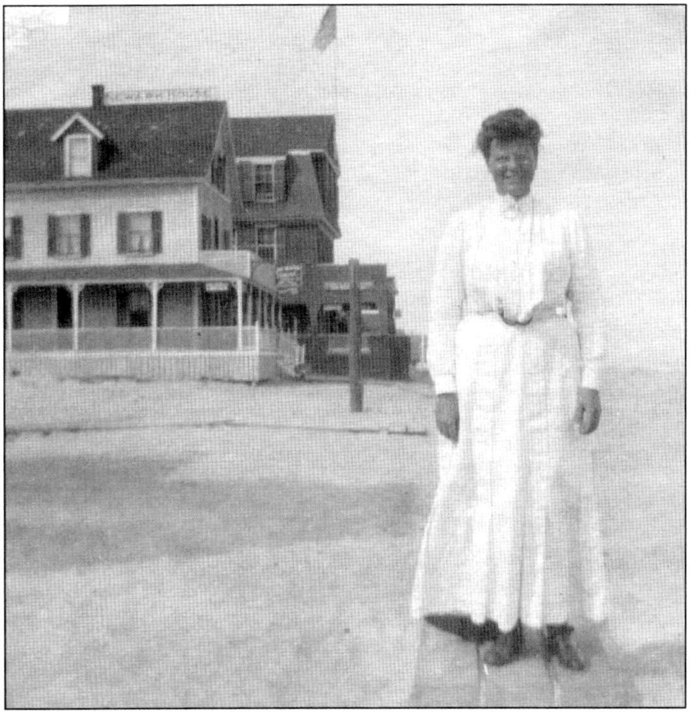

A woman in white strolls on the north shore promenade in front of the Newark and Leighton Houses. Her shirtwaist blouse has shoulder pleats. She appears to be wearing a seven-gored skirt fashionable at the turn of the century. The summer outfits were often made from a lightweight fabric such as batiste (finely woven linen or cotton), voile(transparent loosely woven fabric), gauze, or challis (a fine soft fabric originally of silk and worsted).

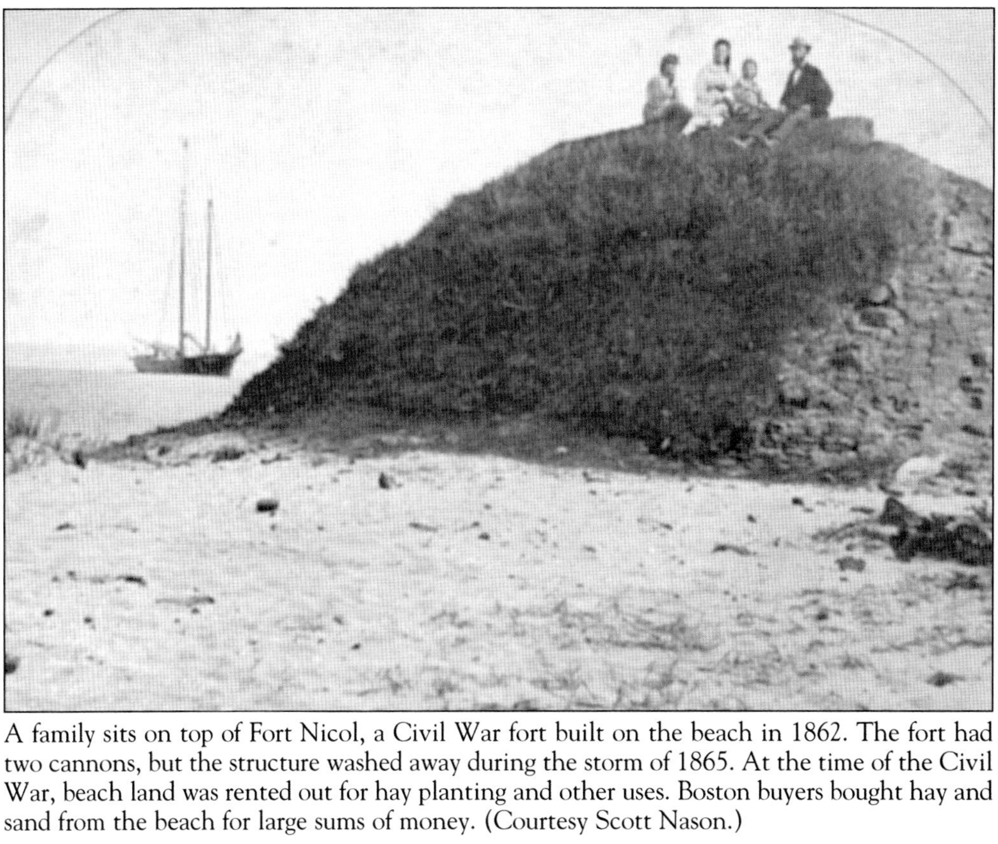

A family sits on top of Fort Nicol, a Civil War fort built on the beach in 1862. The fort had two cannons, but the structure washed away during the storm of 1865. At the time of the Civil War, beach land was rented out for hay planting and other uses. Boston buyers bought hay and sand from the beach for large sums of money. (Courtesy Scott Nason.)

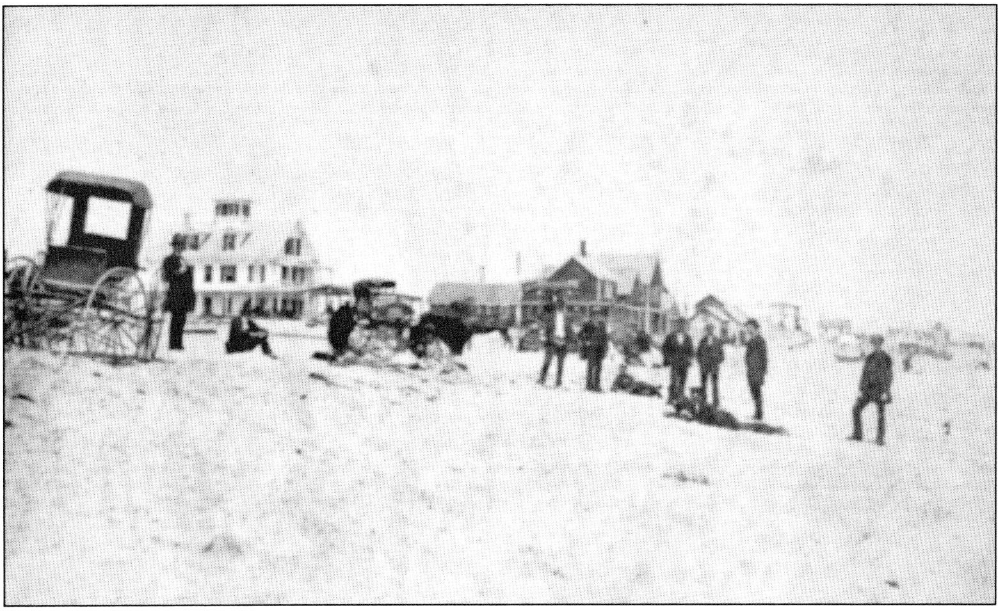

The 1860s were known as "the picnic era," when tenting on the beach was very popular. Crowds set up tents and spent the night on the beach, having traveled great distances to enjoy the sea air. Horses and carriages were driven and parked right on the beach. (Courtesy Scott Nason.)

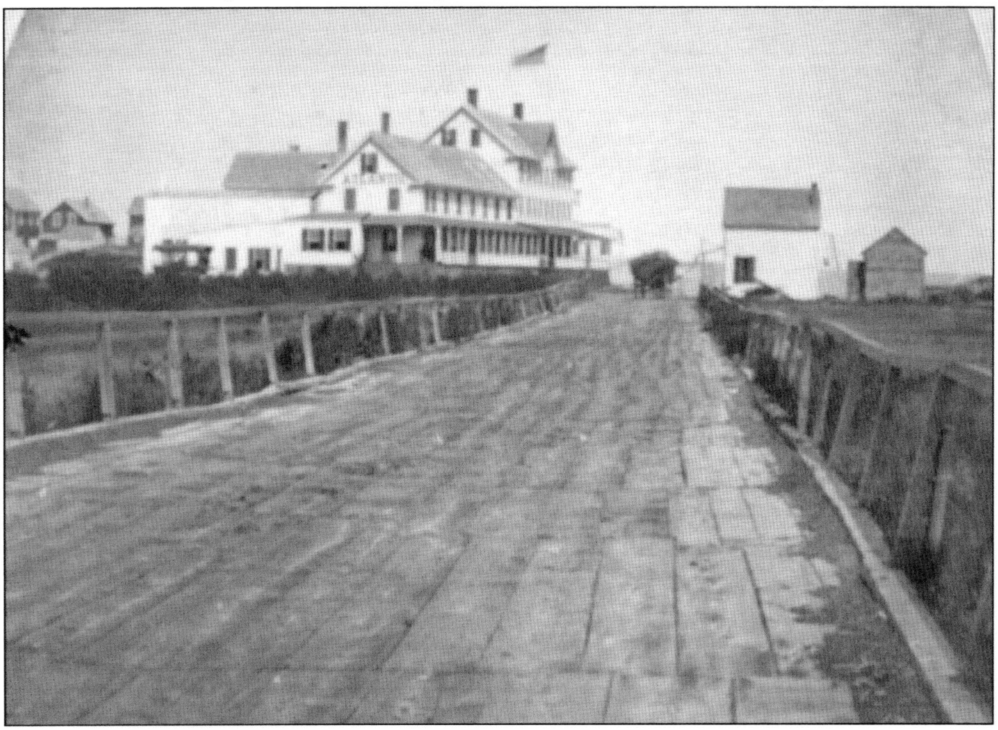

The Atlantic House, situated at the end of the Plank Road, was a hotel that was first kept by Mr. Kimball and later by John Morrill of Newburyport. The hotel had 70 rooms, an icehouse, a beachhouse, and a plank walk to the beach. It was not unusual to see 100 horses and carriages in the stables of the hotel. (Courtesy Scott Nason.)

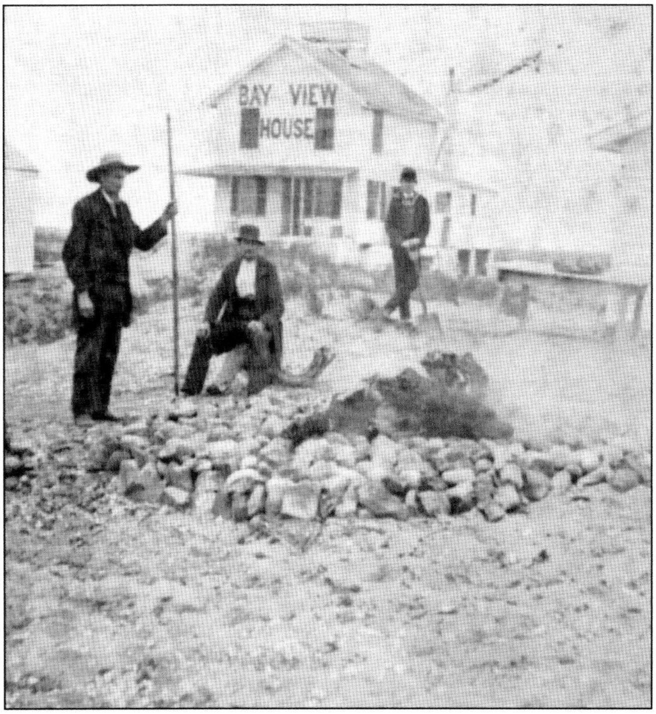

A clambake in front of the Bay View House is being tended carefully by two men and a young boy with a shovel. Usually a large hole is dug in the sand and a wood fire bakes the stones upon which clams, lobsters, and seaweed are layered and steamed to perfection. (Courtesy Scott Nason.)

Our House was named to make its guests feel at home on the beach. These guests appear to be having a party next to a scaffold, which might be some type of swing ride. The only member that seems to be imbibing some refreshment is the fourth man from the left standing up. (Courtesy Scott Nason.)

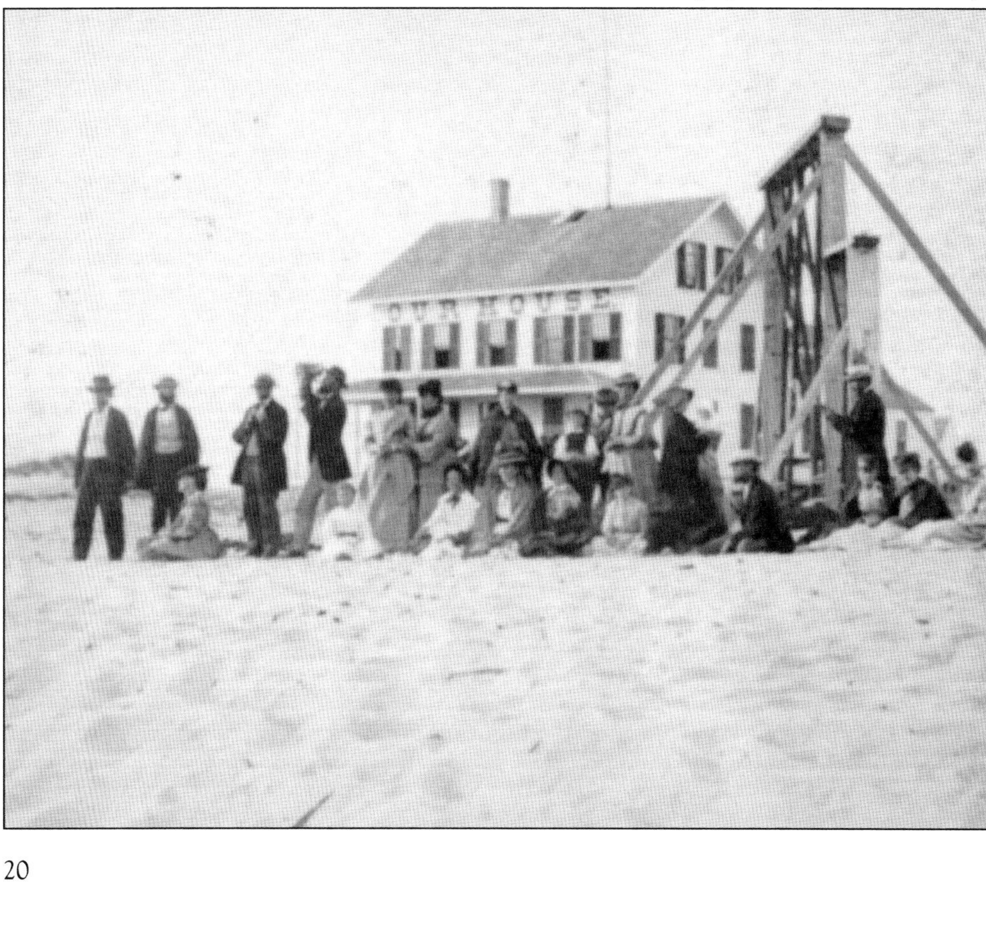

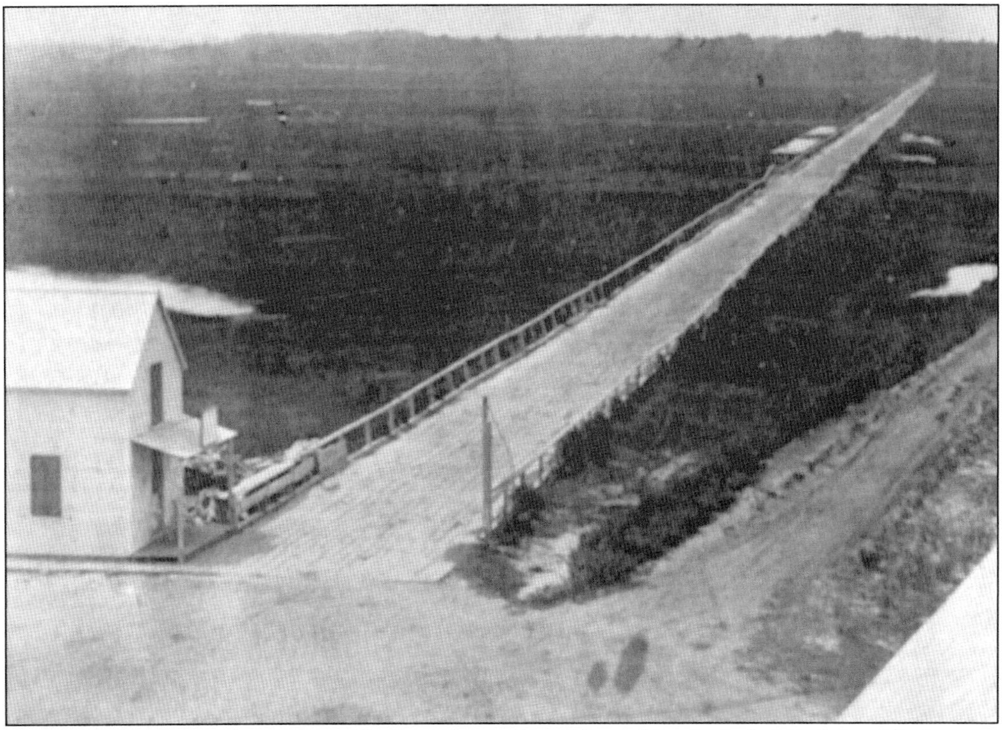

The Plank Road, built in 1866 along with myths of buried treasure beneath its planks, was located to the northwest of the present Beach Road. The road was a rough semicircle that started beyond Salisbury Square and crossed the marshes to emerge on the beach near the old Atlantic House. No effort was made to level the ground before laying the ties and planks, giving the road a washboard effect. The road rose and fell with the ebb and flow of the tides. When the Salisbury Beach Railroad was established, the road was allowed to decay. (Courtesy Scott Nason.)

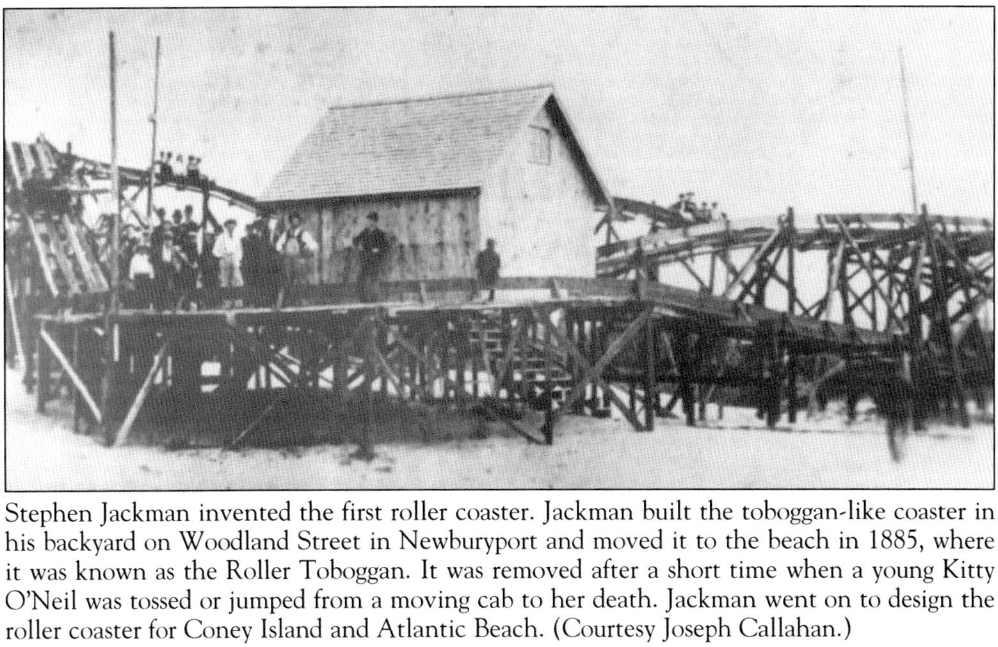

Stephen Jackman invented the first roller coaster. Jackman built the toboggan-like coaster in his backyard on Woodland Street in Newburyport and moved it to the beach in 1885, where it was known as the Roller Toboggan. It was removed after a short time when a young Kitty O'Neil was tossed or jumped from a moving cab to her death. Jackman went on to design the roller coaster for Coney Island and Atlantic Beach. (Courtesy Joseph Callahan.)

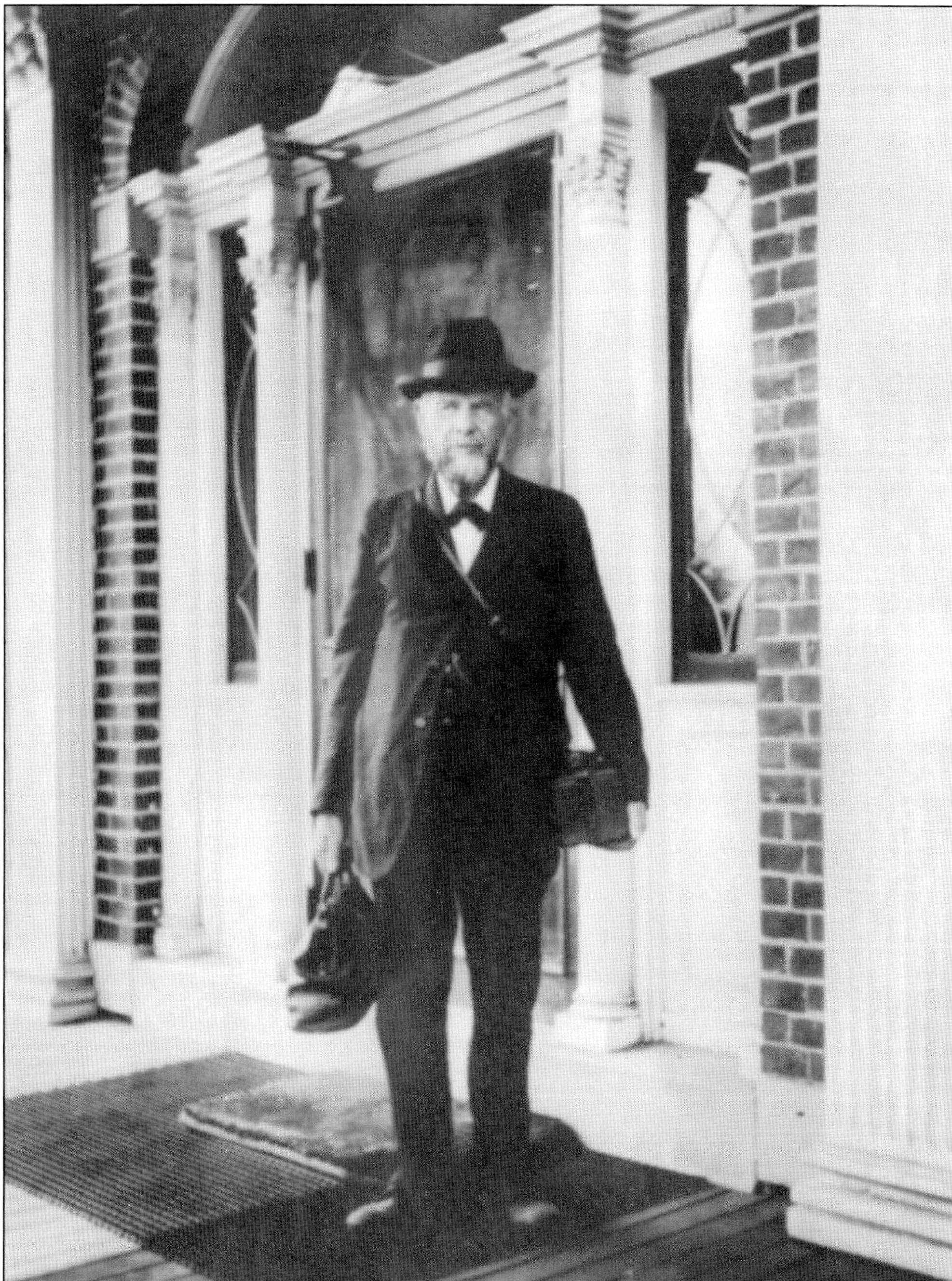

Dr. Jacob F. Spaulding, a Methodist minister with the East Parrish Church, stands with his medical bag in hand. In addition to his clerical duties, he was a highly regarded physician and attended many patients in Salisbury and at the beach in the early 1900s. He was reputed to have lost only one patient during the 1918 influenza epidemic.

Two

In the Good Old Summertime

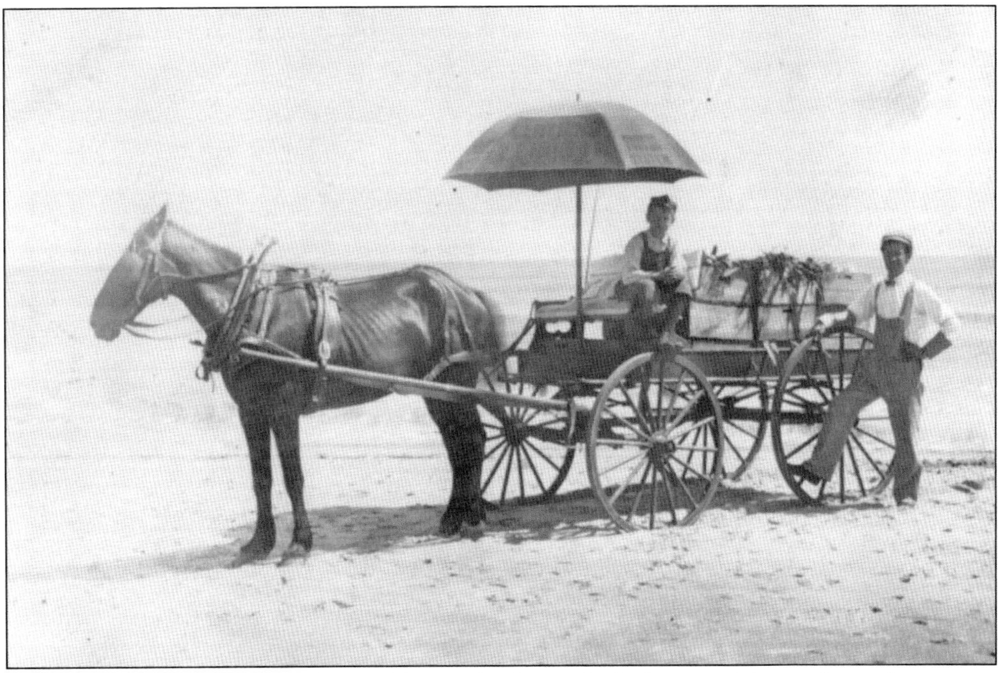

Charles Lamprey, his son Perley, and horse Sarah supply fresh vegetables to the early cottages on Salisbury Beach in 1902. Perley would run to the cottage and take the order and head back to his dad. Charles would weigh the vegetables on a scale. Perley, also the delivery boy, got the most exercise, running back with the produce for the customer.

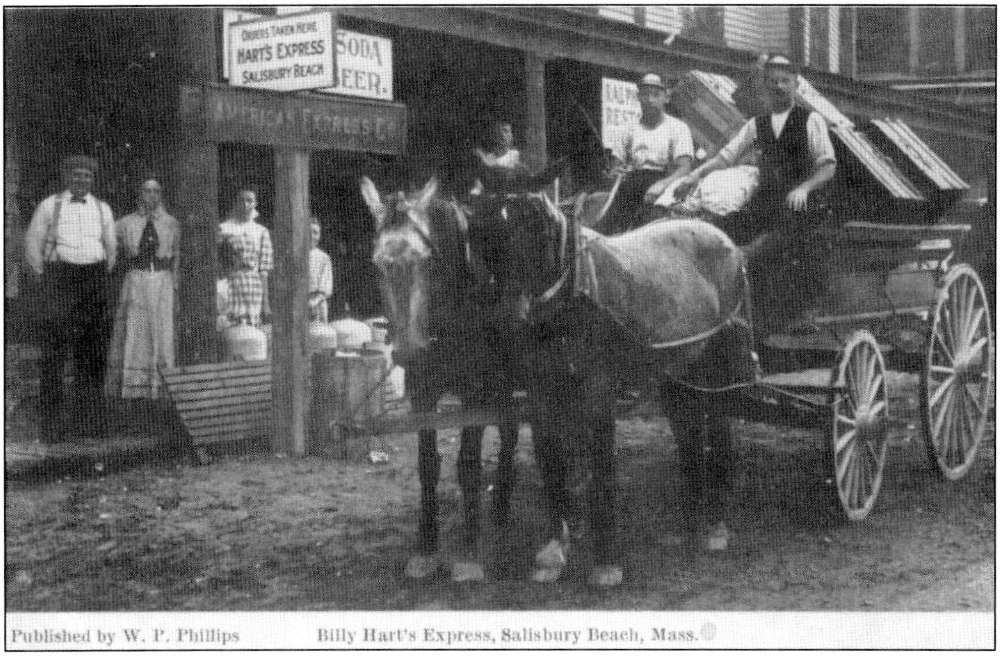

Another wagon used at the beach is parked outside Billy Hart's Express. Orders were taken at the company and then delivered to the customers on the beach. There were several other express companies at the beach including Andrew's and Shaw's Express.

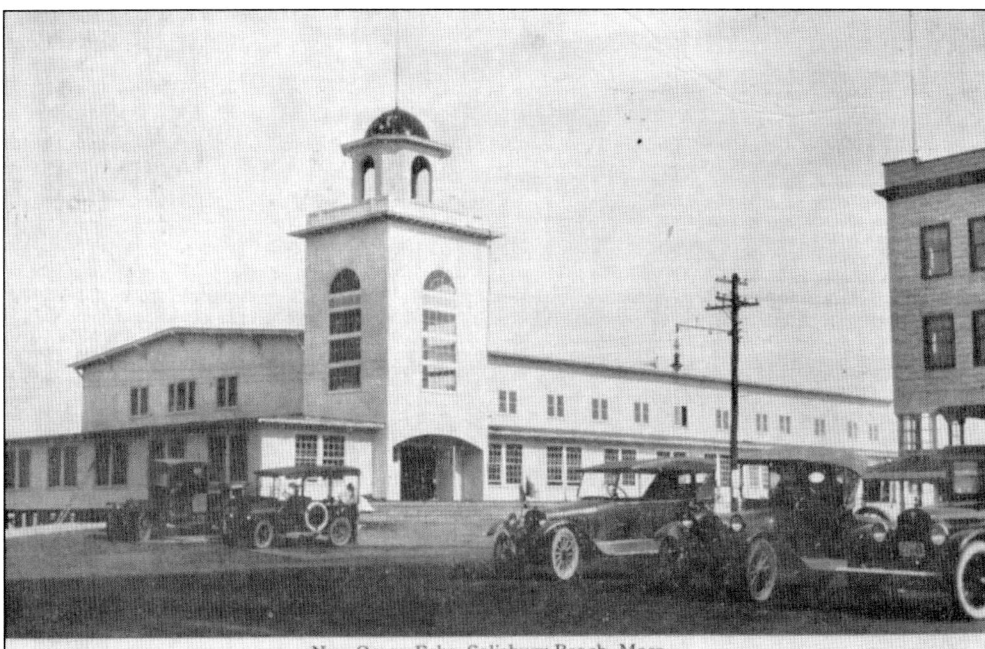

The second Ocean Echo was designed by Lawrence architect James E. Allen. The design included an 850-foot pavilion, but was not as ornate or elegant as the first Ocean Echo that was completely destroyed by fire in the winter of 1920. (Courtesy Arnold Marookian.)

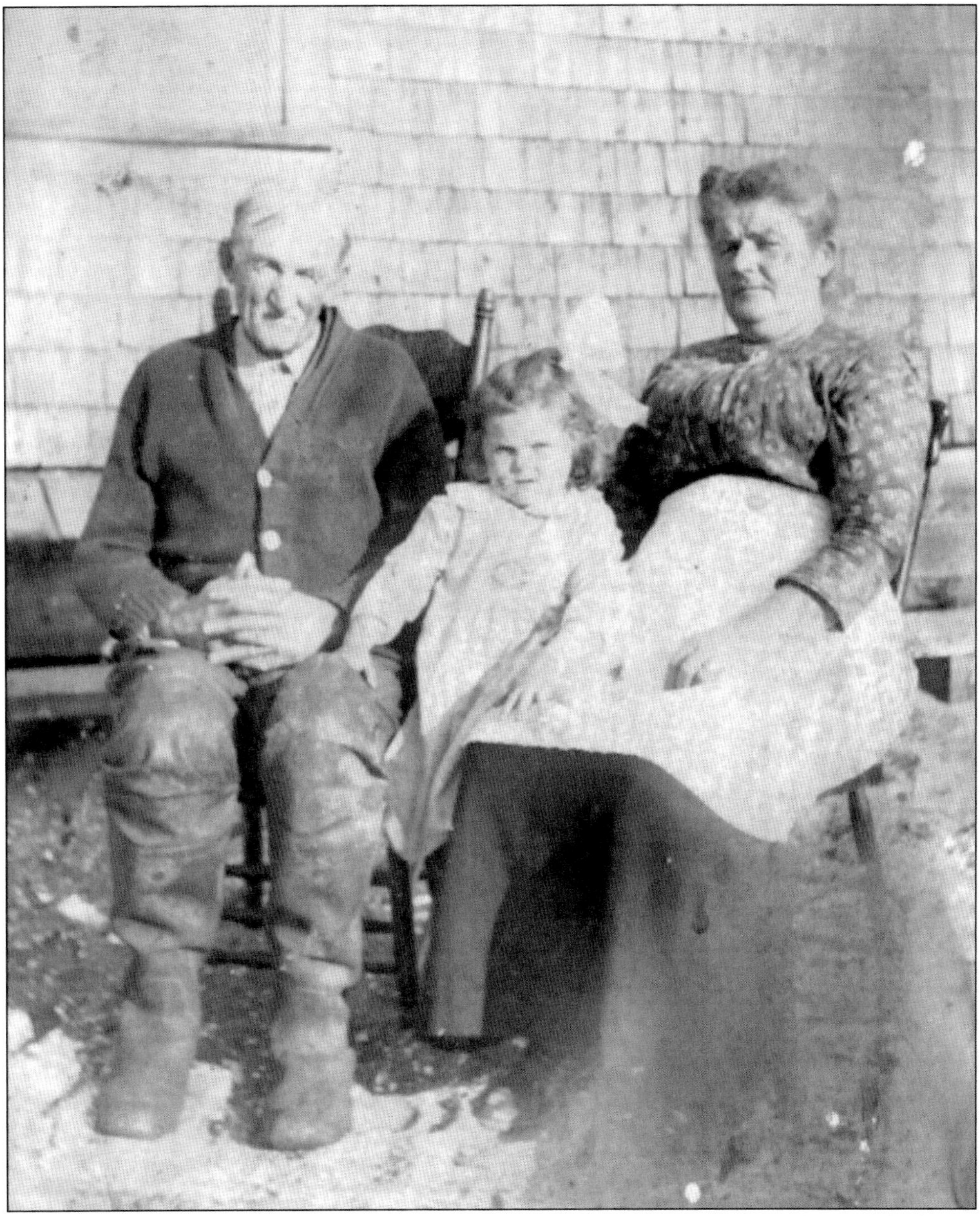

William H. Pierce, his wife Elizabeth, and granddaughter Ethel Merrill, sit in front of the house at Black Rocks. The Pierces moved to Black Rocks in 1888 and became the first year-round residents of Salisbury Beach. William Pierce was employed by the government as the Harbor Range light keeper from 1891 to 1895. He carried the lanterns from the harbor to his home. The government then built him a small house next to the light pole. In 1911, electric lights were installed at the harbor range. The range light was removed from Black Rocks in 1922.

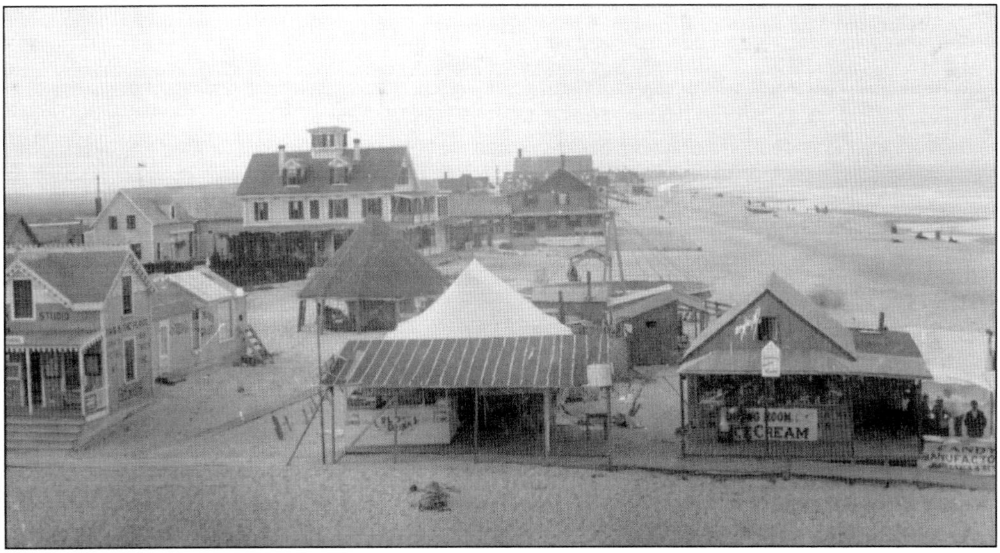

A photographer in 1895 stood at the site of the former roller coaster and aimed toward what is now a food concession stand and arcades. Varney's Union Cafe is on the right with a sign advertising ice cream. Clam chowder was sold at the building in the center.

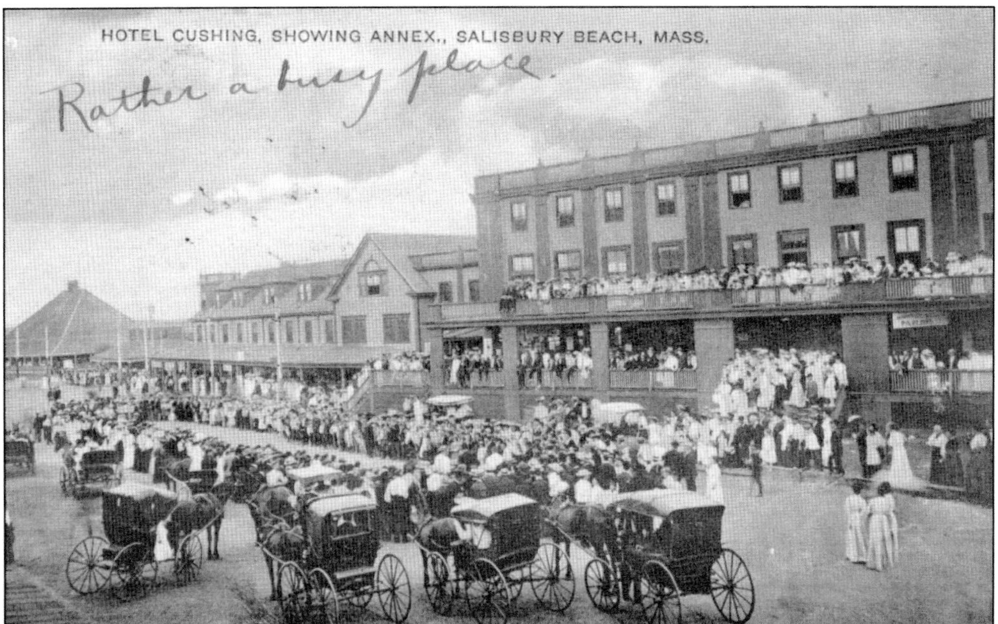

The Hotel Cushing and its annex are shown on a postcard with an understated notation on the front: "Rather a busy place." The hotel, a three-story wooden building with a covered verandah and second story ocean side deck, opened in 1897. The Hotel Cushing embodied the opulence of the Victorian era, with an onyx soda fountain. An annex for accommodating the crowds, an elaborate pavilion for band concerts, a vaudeville theater, and popcorn stand were later additions to the building. The hotel burned down in the famous beach fire on September 9, 1913. (Courtesy Arnold Marookian.)

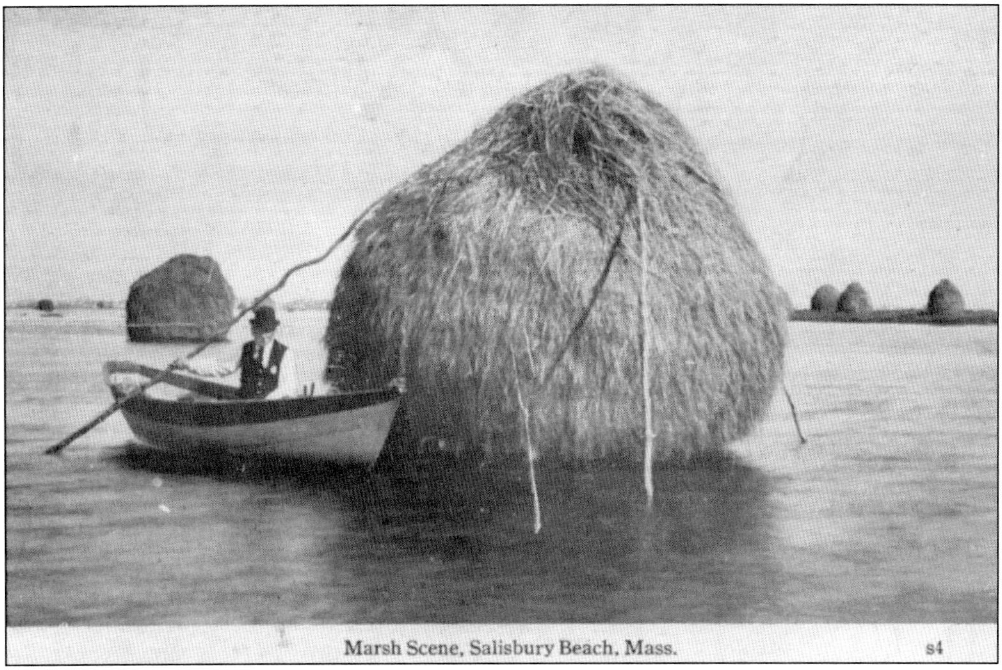

Salt marsh haying was a prime source of income for the citizens of Salisbury. The cattle raised on salt marsh hay produced a rich manure that was highly valued as a fertilizer. The haycock in the picture was poled to straddles (poles made of willow wood) and protected from the elements with thatched grass on top and then tied down to keep the stacks from blowing away. (Courtesy Arnold Marookian.)

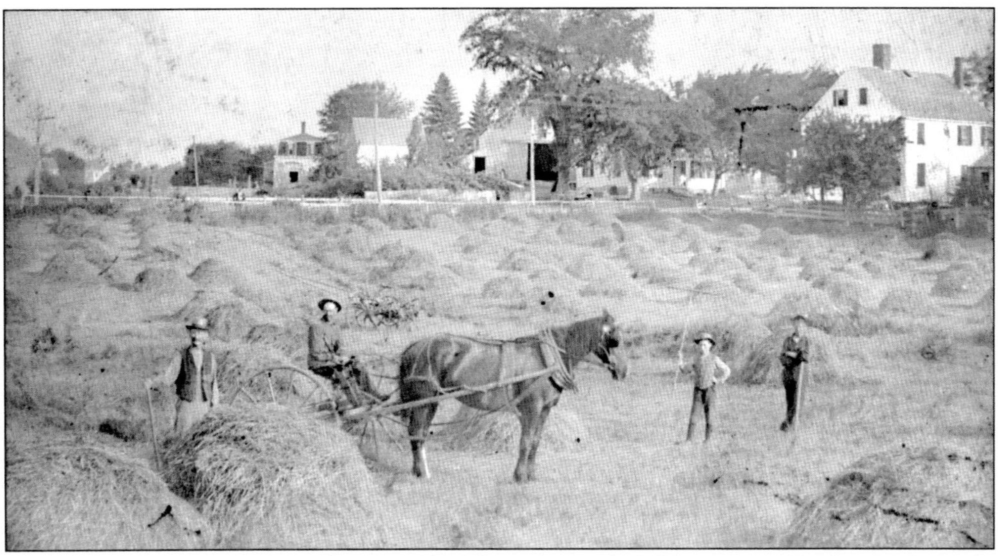

George A. Dow stands in the foreground of this salt marsh field in 1910. The boy to the right of the picture is holding a hay rake used to harvest the hay. There were contests in the town to decide who was the "scythe champion." The horses often had to wear bog shoes strapped to their hoofs to prevent them from sinking into the marsh mud. This work was made easier by the invention of the harvester tractors.

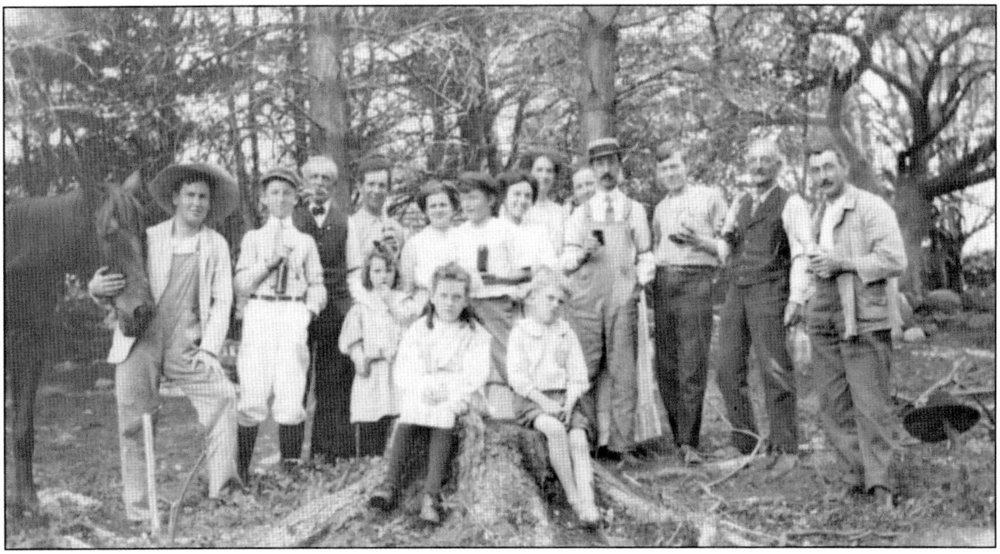

This family picnic took place at Batts Hill in 1910 after a baseball game. Sarah, the beach delivery horse, is shown on the far left. Also in this photograph, from left to right, are the following: Ernest Lamprey (holding Sarah's rope), Maurice Lamprey gripping a bottle of soda pop, grandfather Elisha Tuttle (dressed in a vest and bow tie), Charles Lamprey, Elise Lamprey (age five, in front of Charles), three unidentified women, Jim Beaumont (in overalls), Elise Lamprey Sr. (peeking out from behind Jim), an unidentified man, grandfather Charles Peel (a Civil War veteran), and Buff Benoit. Gladys and Ralph Bowen sit on the stump in front of the group.

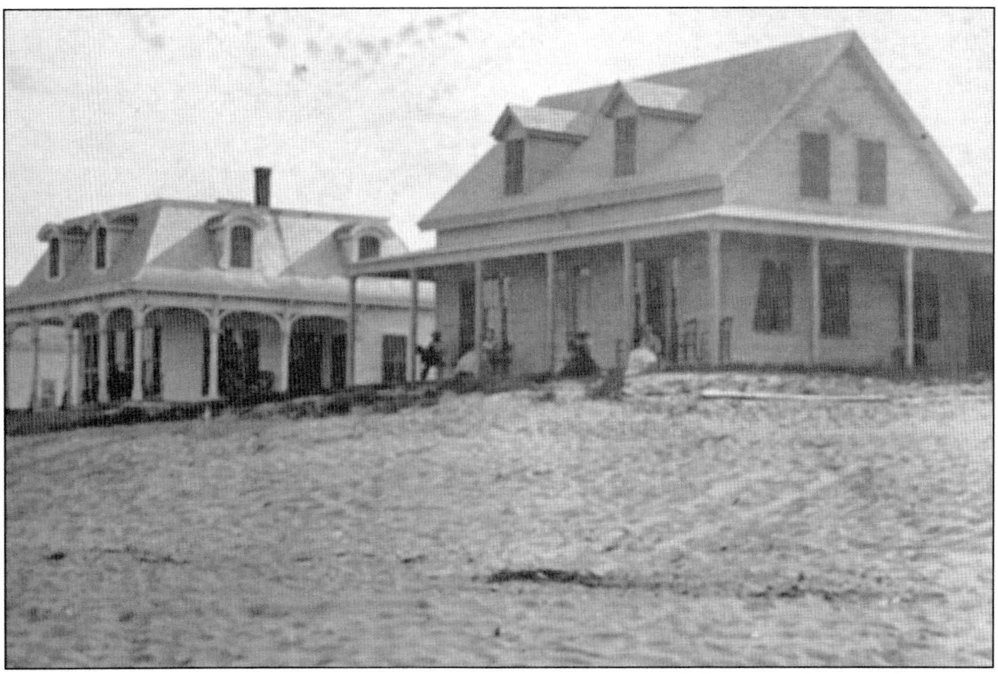

These are two of the more substantial cottages or homes on the Salisbury Beach oceanfront. The house to the left appears to be a Victorian cottage. The house on the right is a much plainer design, but both have wraparound porches that allow the family to enjoy the fresh ocean air. Many of the cottages in the early 1900s were built on long-leased land. (Courtesy Scott Nason.)

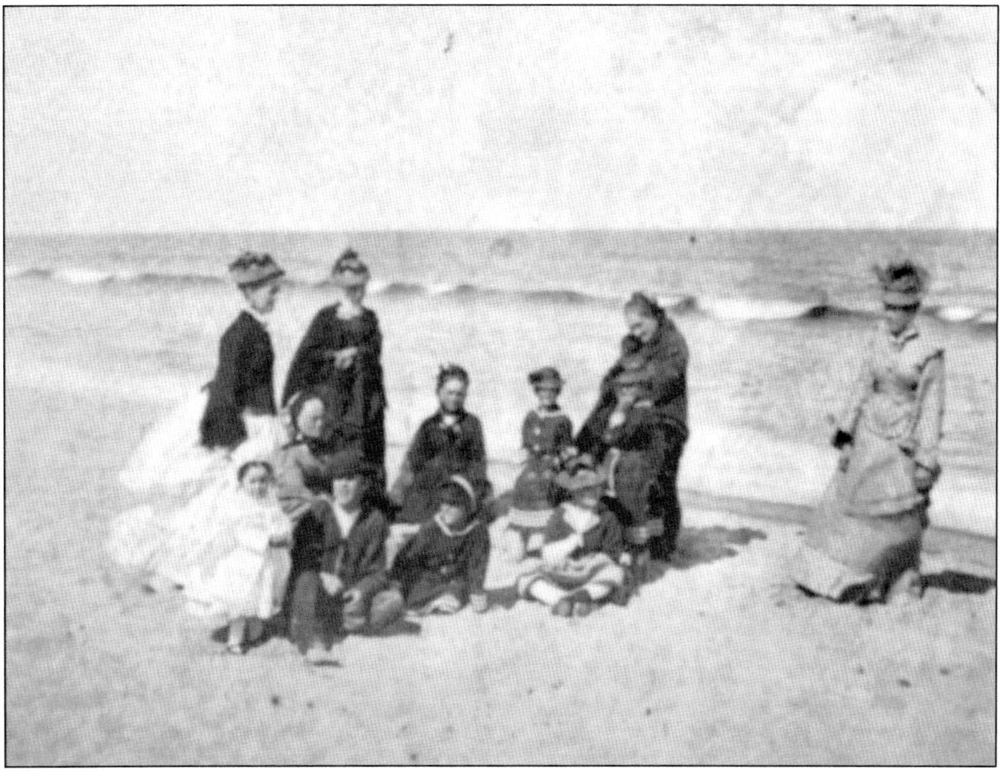

A family stands huddled together, *c.* 1908. One of the women is wrapping her coat around her to avoid the gales of wind. Although some of the children seem to be dressed in swimming outfits, they might just be sailor-style suits, as it does not appear to be even wading weather. (Courtesy Scott Nason.)

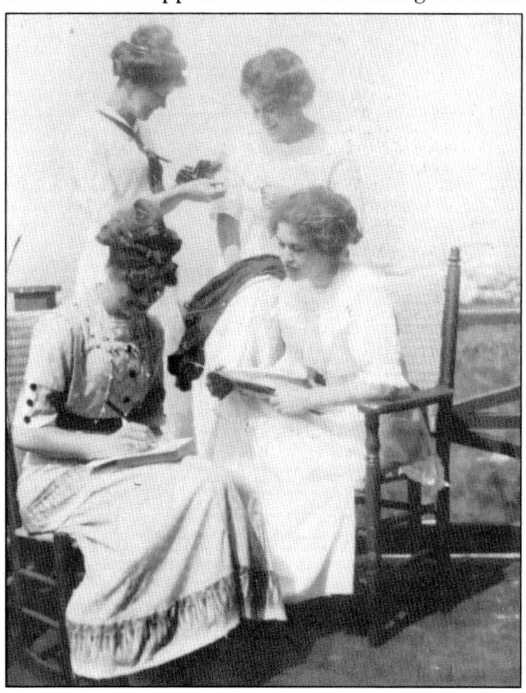

Four officers of the Class of 1911 from Bradford College sit on the porch of a cottage at Salisbury Beach. The woman have their hair in the "Gibson look" that was in vogue at the time. The woman who inspired the hairdo was a passenger and survivor on the *Titanic* and portrayed her own character in the first movie made of this famous sea tragedy. This picture comes from the scrapbook of Jean Ditto Bauer.

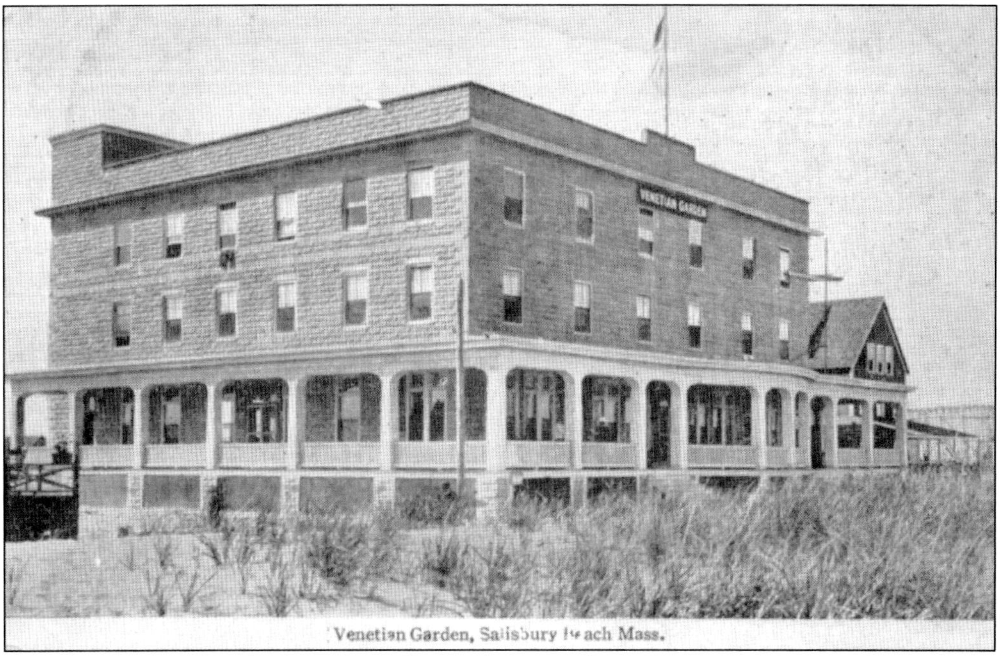

The Venetian Gardens had accommodations for more than 100 permanent guests. Every room had running hot and cold water. The basement contained showers and 150 lockers for the convenience of bathers. Bathing suits could be rented in the lower part of the building. The hotel claimed to have the finest chef that New York offered, with fresh food supplies obtained daily from nearby farms. (Courtesy Arnold Marookian.)

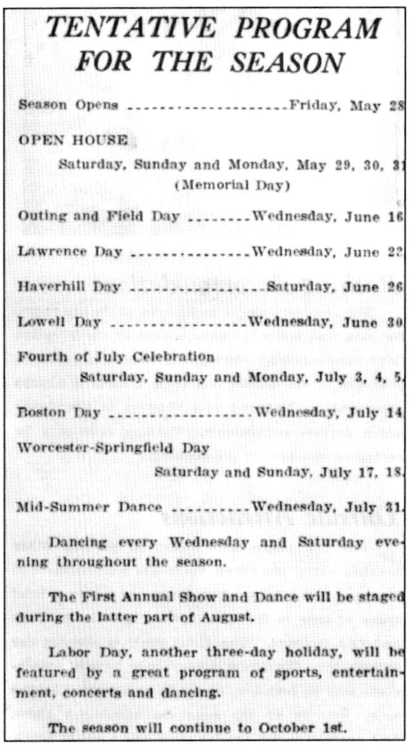

TENTATIVE PROGRAM FOR THE SEASON

Season Opens ....Friday, May 28

OPEN HOUSE
Saturday, Sunday and Monday, May 29, 30, 31
(Memorial Day)

Outing and Field Day ....Wednesday, June 16

Lawrence Day ....Wednesday, June 23

Haverhill Day ....Saturday, June 26

Lowell Day ....Wednesday, June 30

Fourth of July Celebration
Saturday, Sunday and Monday, July 3, 4, 5.

Boston Day ....Wednesday, July 14

Worcester-Springfield Day
Saturday and Sunday, July 17, 18.

Mid-Summer Dance ....Wednesday, July 31.

Dancing every Wednesday and Saturday evening throughout the season.

The First Annual Show and Dance will be staged during the latter part of August.

Labor Day, another three-day holiday, will be featured by a great program of sports, entertainment, concerts and dancing.

The season will continue to October 1st.

This was the tentative schedule for a summer at Salisbury Beach provided by the Venetian Gardens Hotel. (Courtesy Arnold Marookian.)

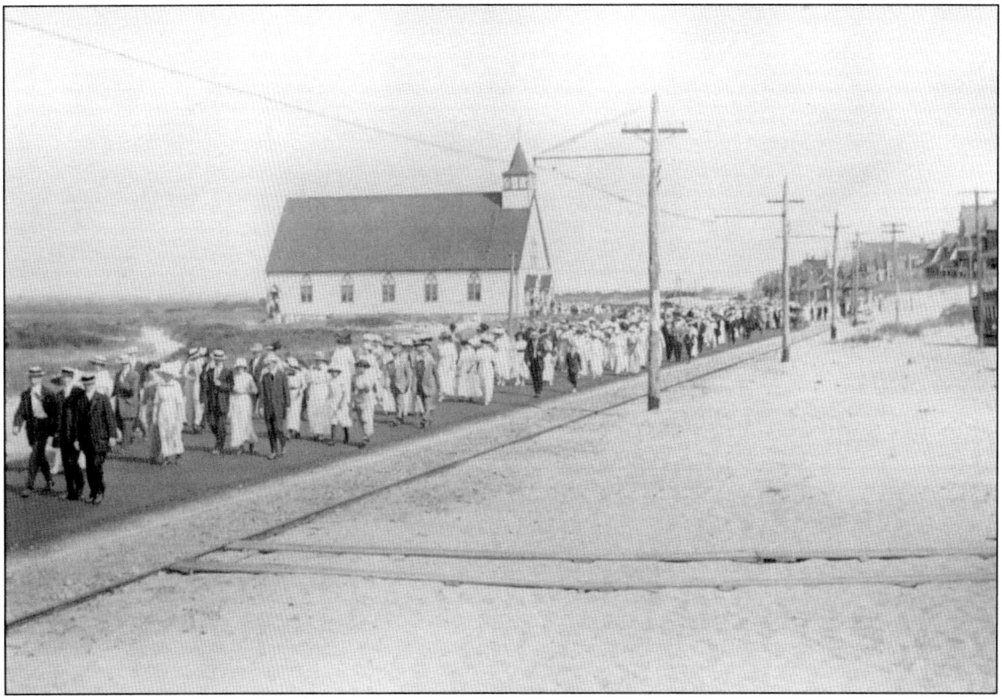

A parade of fashionably dressed people leaves the original Gothic-style Star of the Sea Church, built in 1896 at Salisbury Beach. This could have been an Easter parade. A later church was built at the junction of Beach and Ferry Roads closer to town. The new church was dedicated April 20, 1951. (Courtesy Roger Shaheen.)

Three young women, all seniors at St. James High School in Haverhill, pose on the beach in the latest fashions of 1911. Their annual field day was celebrated at Salisbury Beach. Even though swimwear was available at this time, it appears to be a chilly day and not appropriate for swimming. The Ocean Bathing Suit Company, claiming to have the largest selection in the world, was established in New York in 1883. It advertised bathing wear available by mail order.

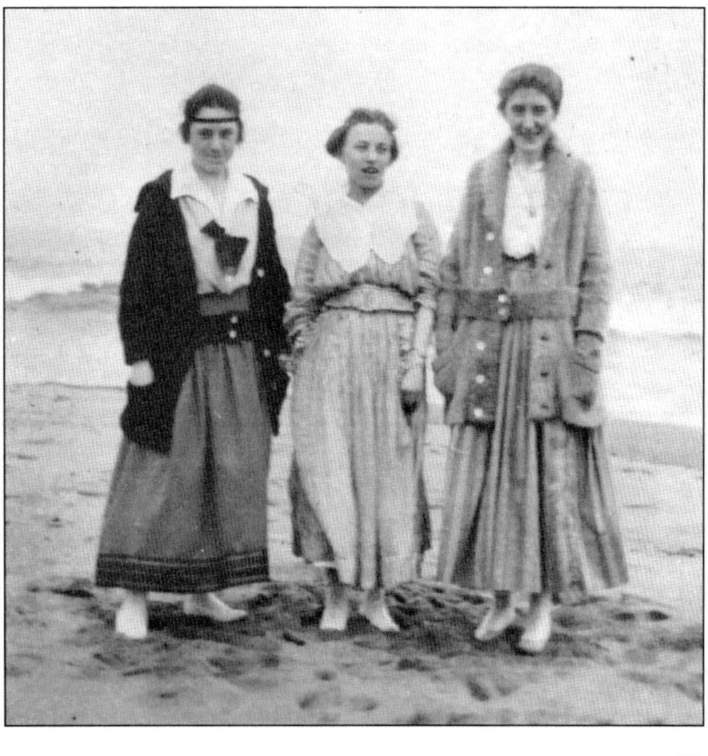

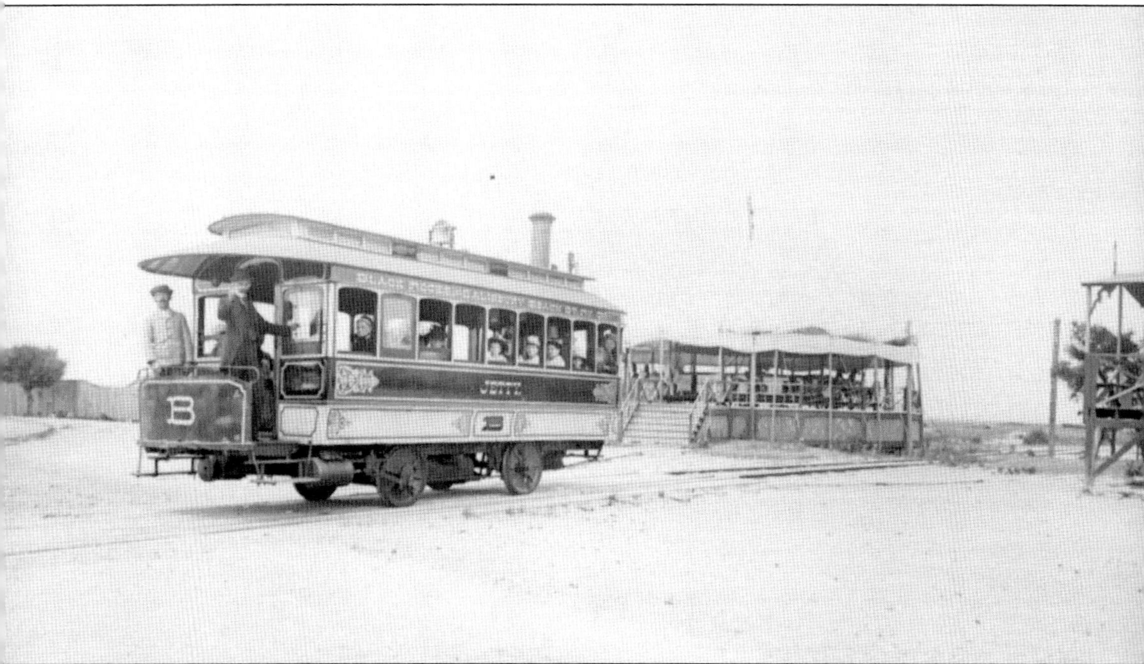

The trolley that ran between Black Rocks and the center of the beach is shown traveling along the tracks. The name of this car is "the Jetty." The rocks for building the jetties were pulled by this car. This dummy engine was run by steam and replaced the engines pulled by horses in 1890. The horses were plagued by the greenhead flies and the increasing traffic in the area. They also had trouble pulling a well-filled car through the sand. In 1902, the line was electrified. (Courtesy Joseph Callahan.)

Someone pasted the title "American Lady" below this picture of a lovely young woman waiting on the dock for the steamer. She is wearing a jaunty nautical outfit from 1907. Sailor-type outfits were often made of pique and were perfect for a day at the seashore.

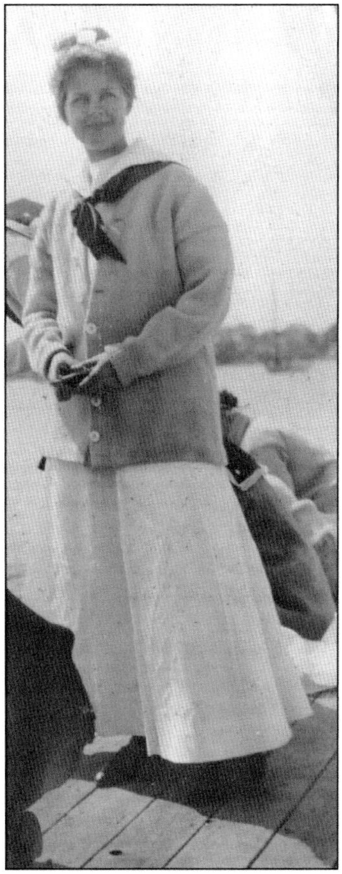

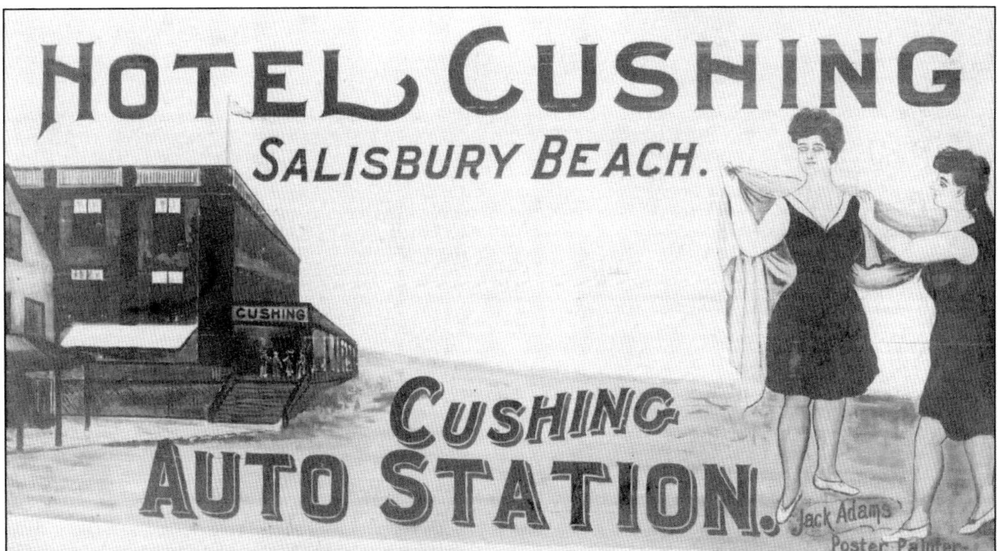

This comical postcard sent from the Hotel Cushing was designed by Jack Adams, a poster painter. The Hotel Cushing was located on Cushing Avenue, which was later renamed Broadway. (Courtesy Arnold Marookian.)

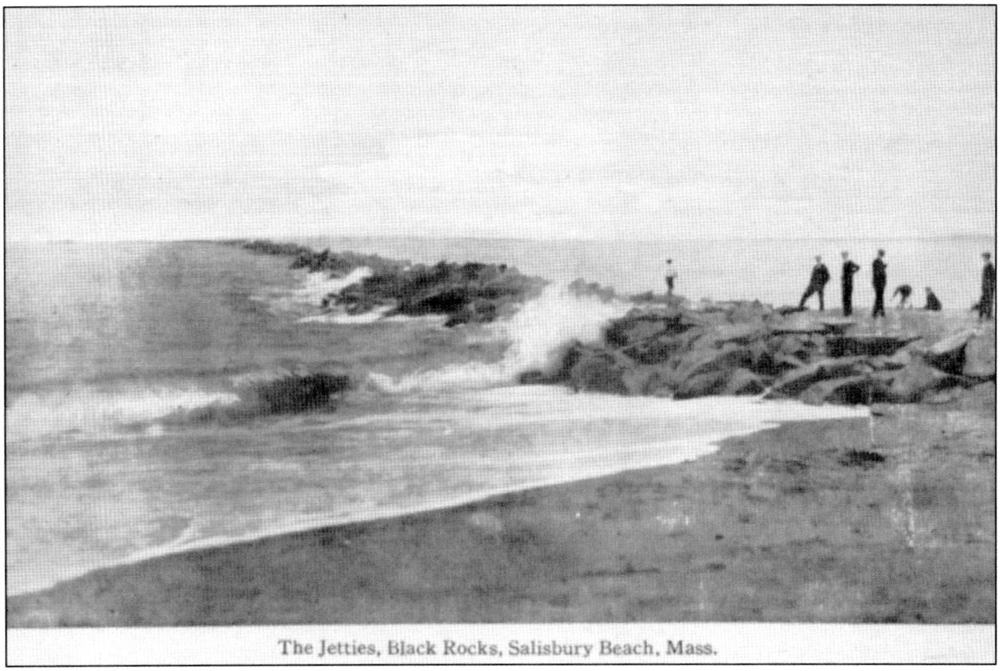

A group of people stands on the jetties by Black Rocks. The jetties extend into the Atlantic Ocean at the mouth of the Merrimack River. Over the years, many people have had to be rescued, as the tide would trap them on the rocks. (Courtesy Arnold Marookian.)

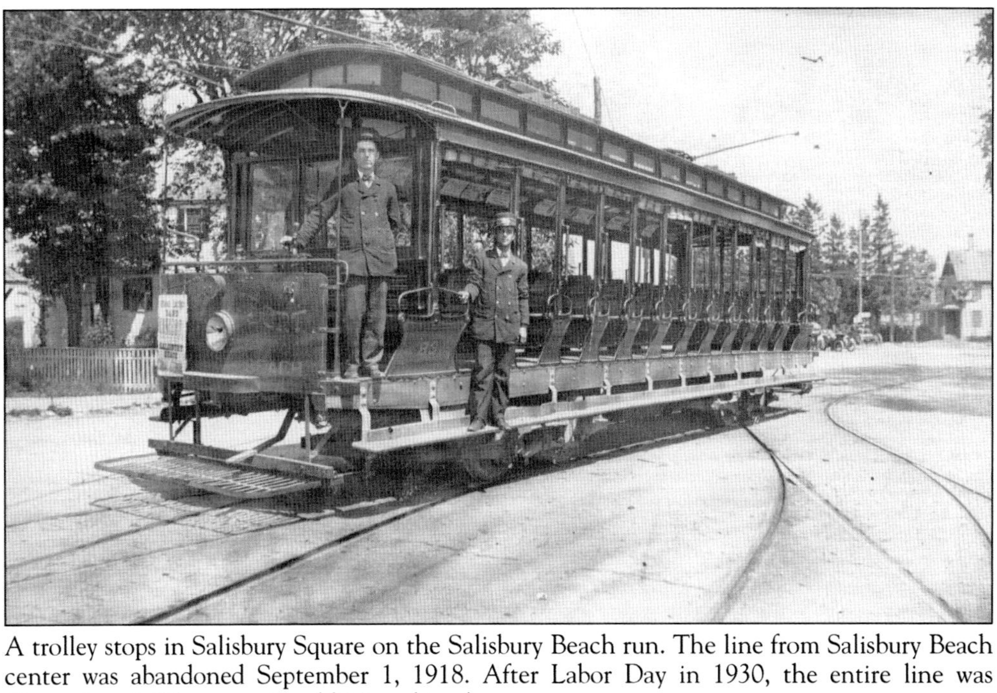

A trolley stops in Salisbury Square on the Salisbury Beach run. The line from Salisbury Beach center was abandoned September 1, 1918. After Labor Day in 1930, the entire line was discontinued. (Courtesy Arnold Marookian.)

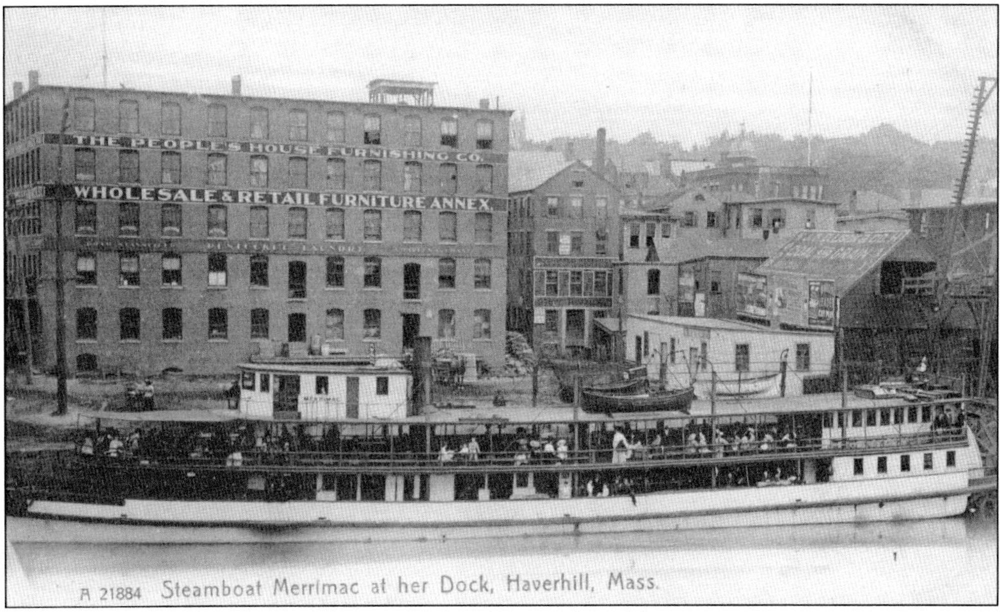

The steamboat *Merrimac*, which was 168 feet long and could carry 1,100 passengers, is waiting at the dock in Haverhill, Massachusetts, for the trip to Salisbury Beach. It normally completed two round trips a day between Haverhill and Black Rocks. (Courtesy Arnold Marookian.)

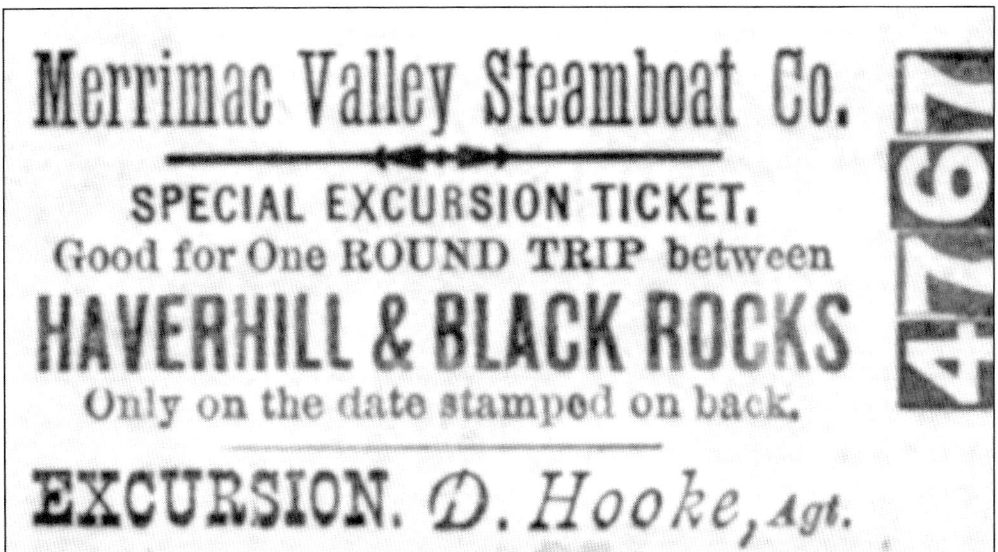

A round-trip ticket to ride from Haverhill to Black Rocks. The fare looks like it was 25¢ at the time this ticket was printed. Because the mills closed for the last ten days before Labor Day, the final fling of the summer, when many families shared rented cottages, was referred to as "the Last Ten Days." (Courtesy Joseph Callahan.)

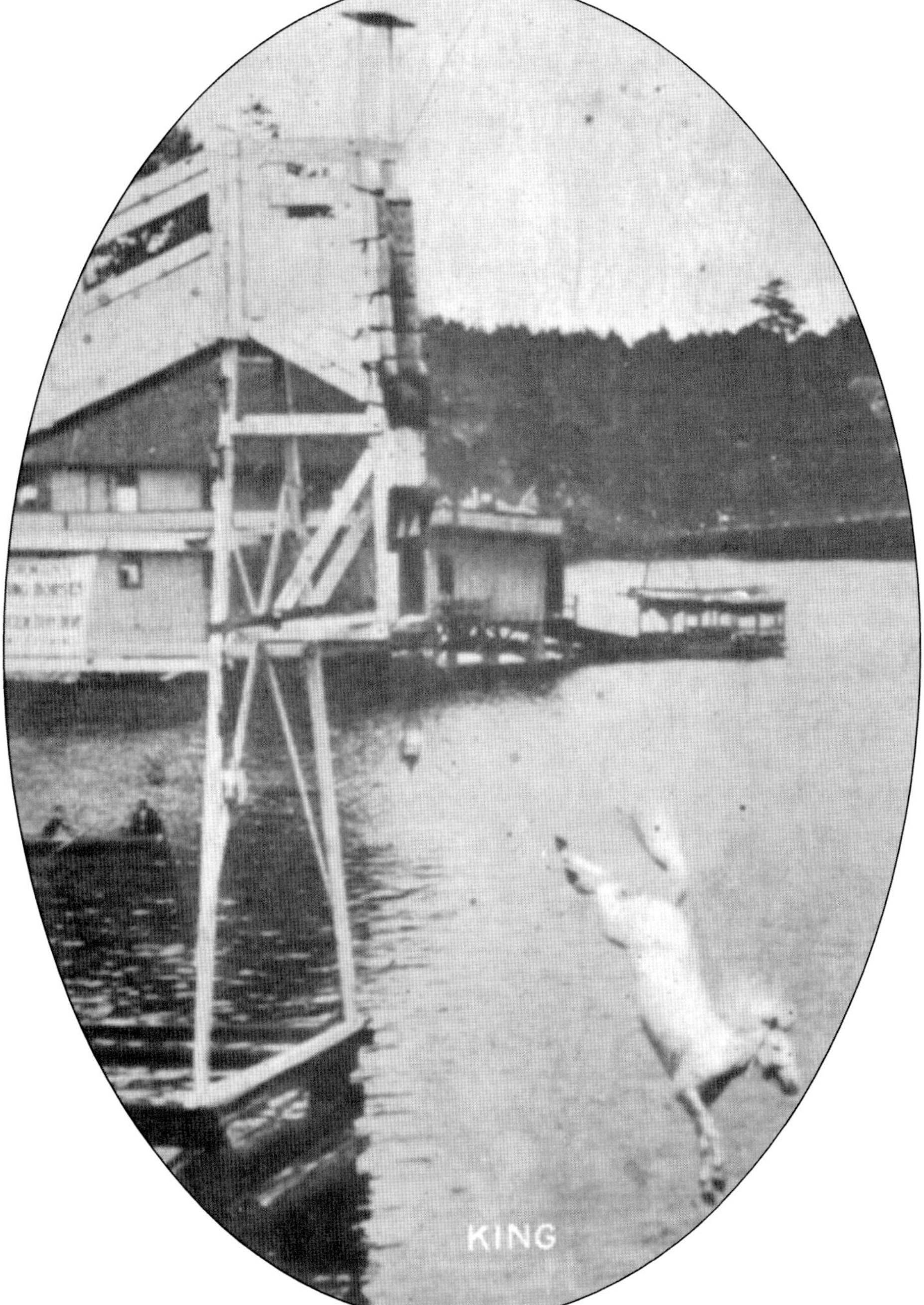

This horse, named King, performs a high-dive into a tank of water on August 6, 1906. Although this picture was not taken at Salisbury Beach, it was used as an advertisement for his appearance there. King was part of J.W. Gorman's Diving Horses. The Society for the Prevention of Cruelty to Animals would probably not let this event take place today.

Three

All the Old Familiar Places

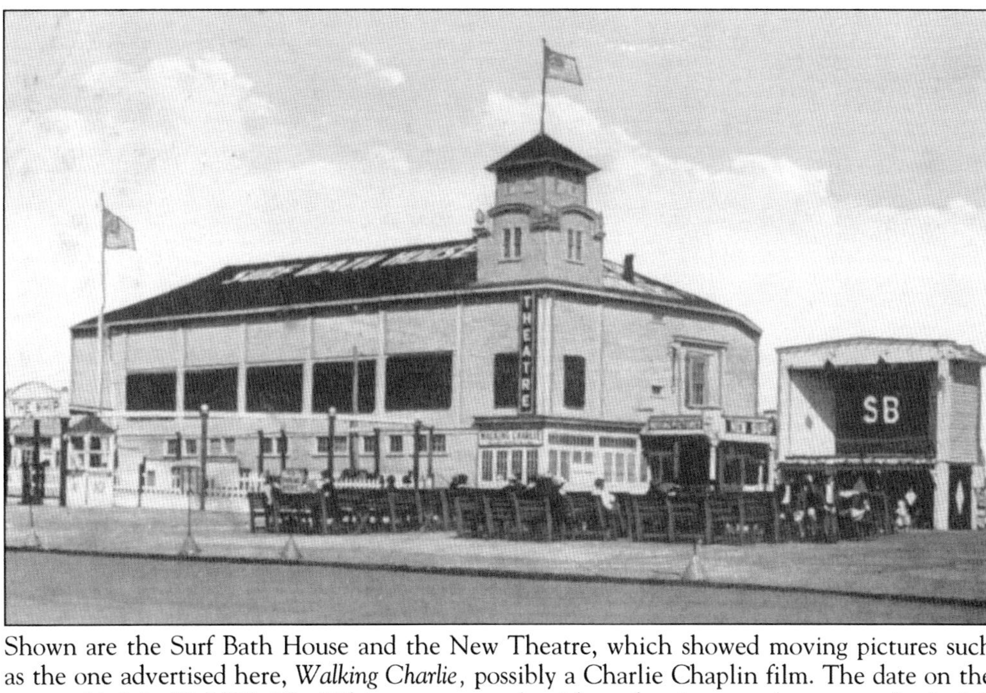

Shown are the Surf Bath House and the New Theatre, which showed moving pictures such as the one advertised here, *Walking Charlie*, possibly a Charlie Chaplin film. The date on the postcard is July 18, 1928. The Whip, a very popular ride at the time, can be seen at the far left of the picture. (Courtesy Joseph Callahan.)

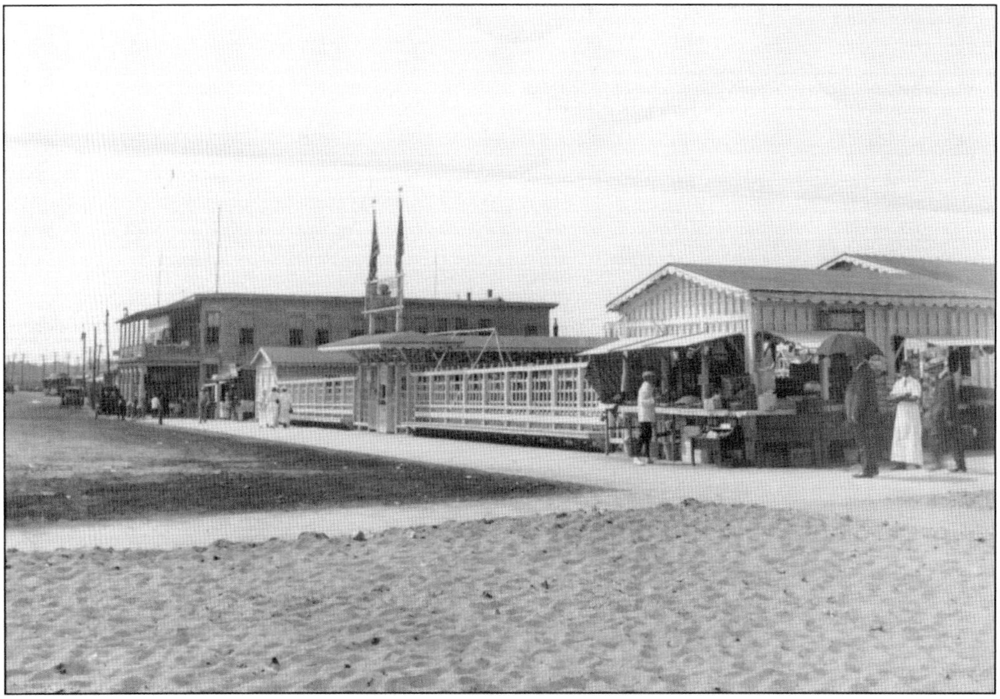

The Salisbury Beach Association, a realty trust, was formed in 1911 by Walter Colson, James E. Simpson, and Portal M. Black. This association purchased all the land on the beach from the Merrimack River to Hampton Beach. After the fire of 1913, they built the Newark Hotel (far left), the first cement building on Salisbury Beach and the headquarters of Battery B of the U.S. Coast Guard Artillery during World War II.

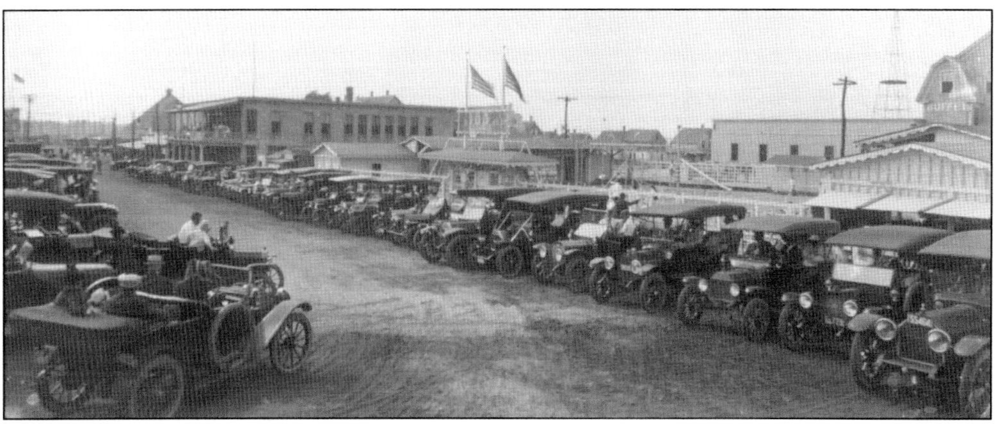

Many cars are parked outside the Newark Hotel for a busy day at the beach. The hotel had a dining room that seated 125 people. The price of room and board for two in a room was $2 a day. The first proprietors, Philip and Louisa Helfrich, came from New Jersey, explaining the name of the hotel. (Courtesy Roger Shaheen.)

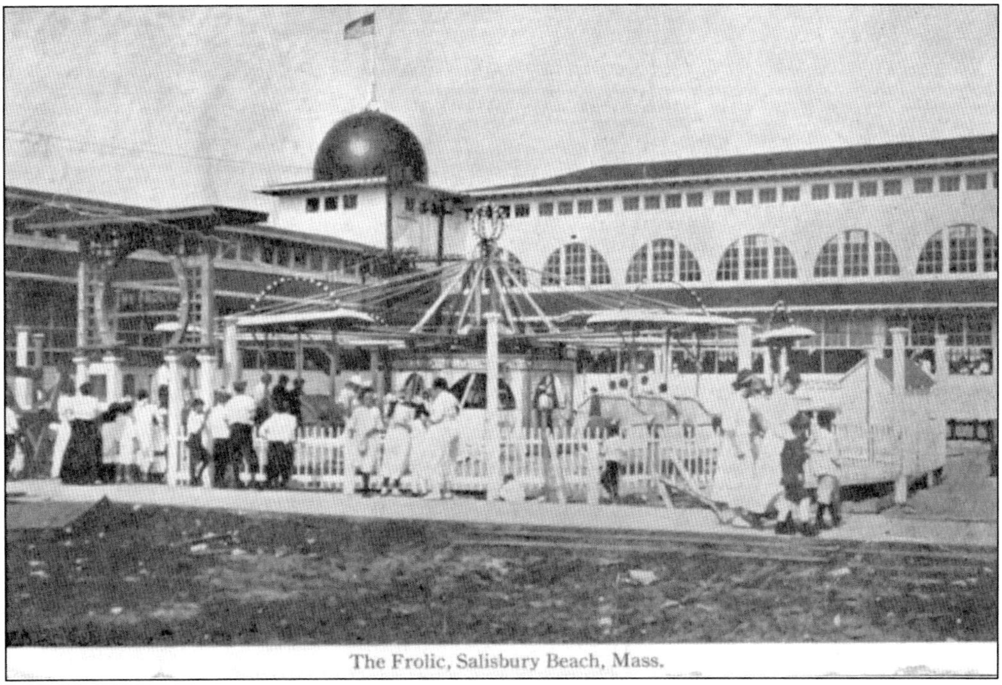

In this photograph taken between 1916 and 1920, people are waiting in line for a ride called the Frolic in front of the original Ocean Echo. This ride might have been the inspiration for the name of the Frolics nightclub, which is what the second Ocean Echo became after it was renovated in 1937. (Courtesy Arnold Marookian.)

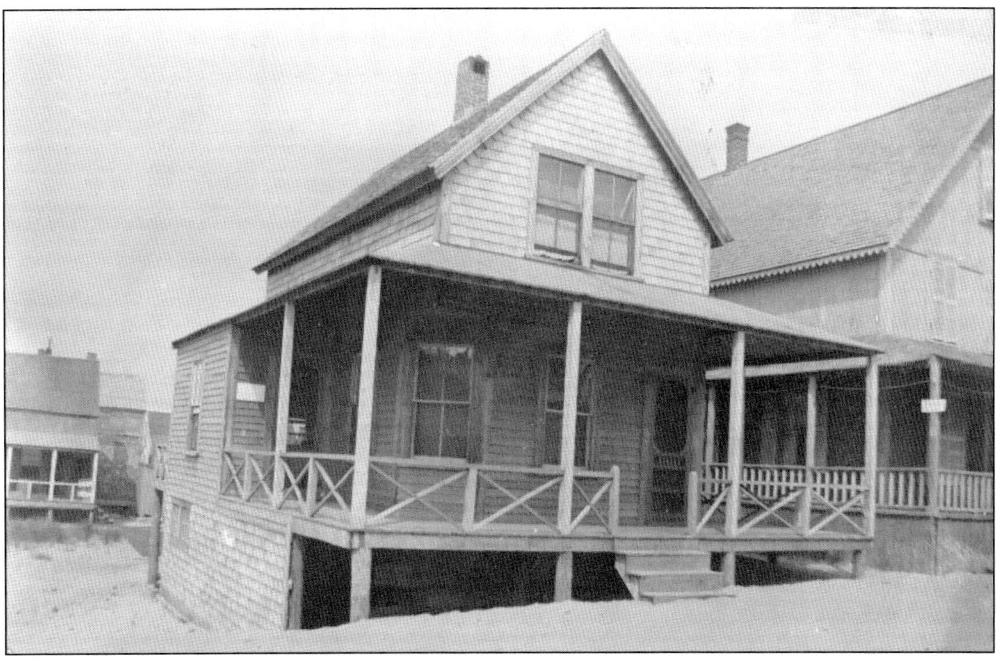

This typical cottage at Salisbury Beach was owned in 1907 by a woman named Alice. Probably weary of all the summer demands, Alice claims that in August she has no time to herself until Labor Day because the rooms are always full. (Courtesy Arnold Marookian.)

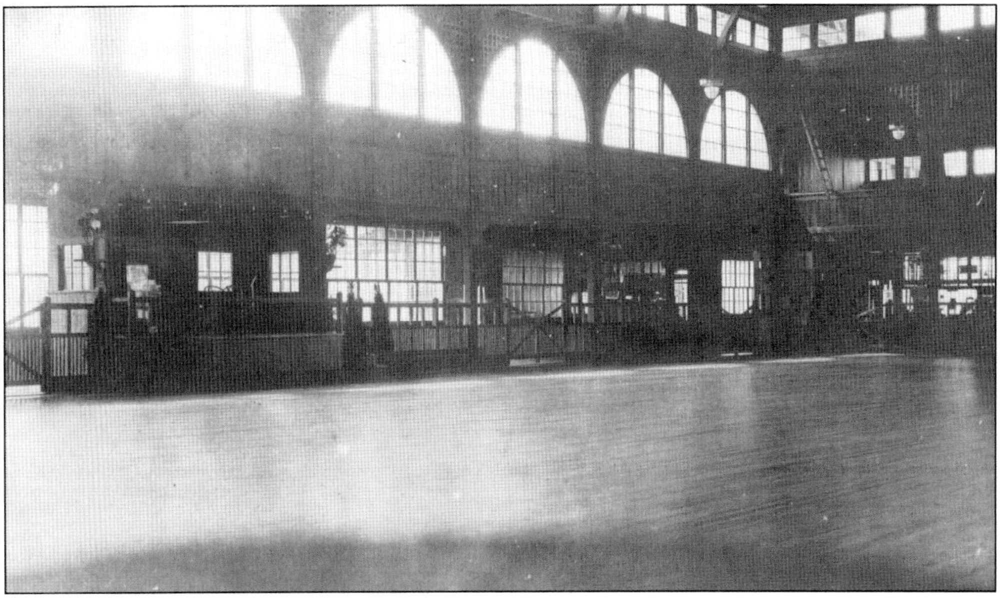

Inside the empty ballroom at the Ocean Echo, ghosts of performers linger in the shadows as sunlight filters through the many windows. Numerous big bands played in this room, including those of Glenn Miller and Lionel Hampton. (Courtesy Arnold Marookian.)

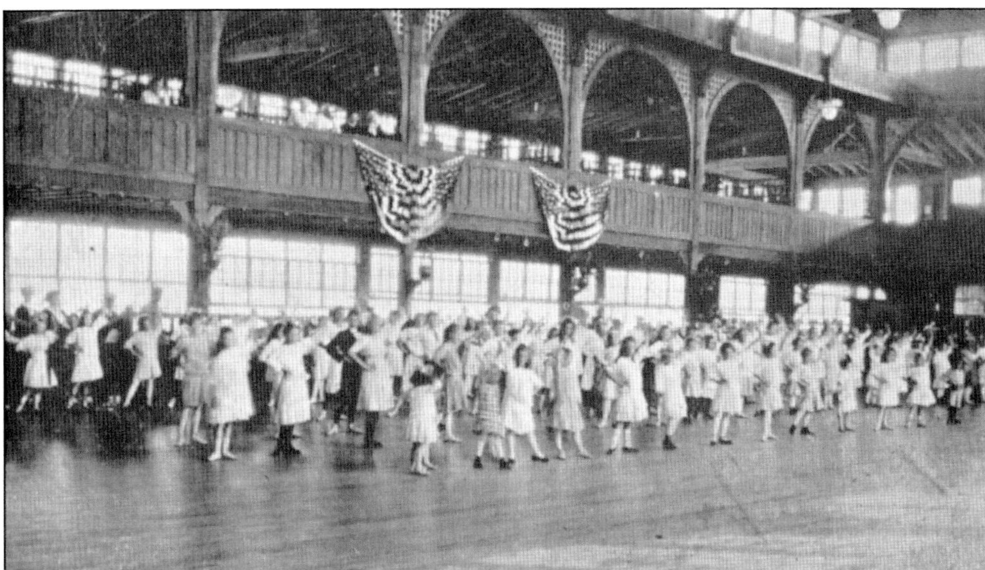

Children of all ages raise their arms as they participate in the free dance lessons offered at the Ocean Echo ballroom. The room is decorated with flag banners for the Fourth of July. (Courtesy Joseph Callahan.)

The Hope Chapel at Salisbury Beach was dedicated in 1889, but burned in 1901. This picture of the second Hope Chapel was taken in 1905. The second chapel, dedicated in July 1902, burned in October 1908. It was rebuilt and rededicated in July 1909 only to burn yet again in May 1967. The people of Salisbury Beach have always been determined not to let their "Hope" be defeated by any disaster.

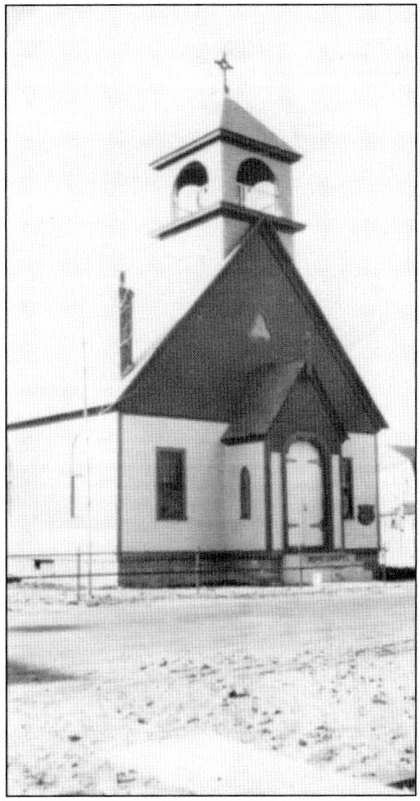

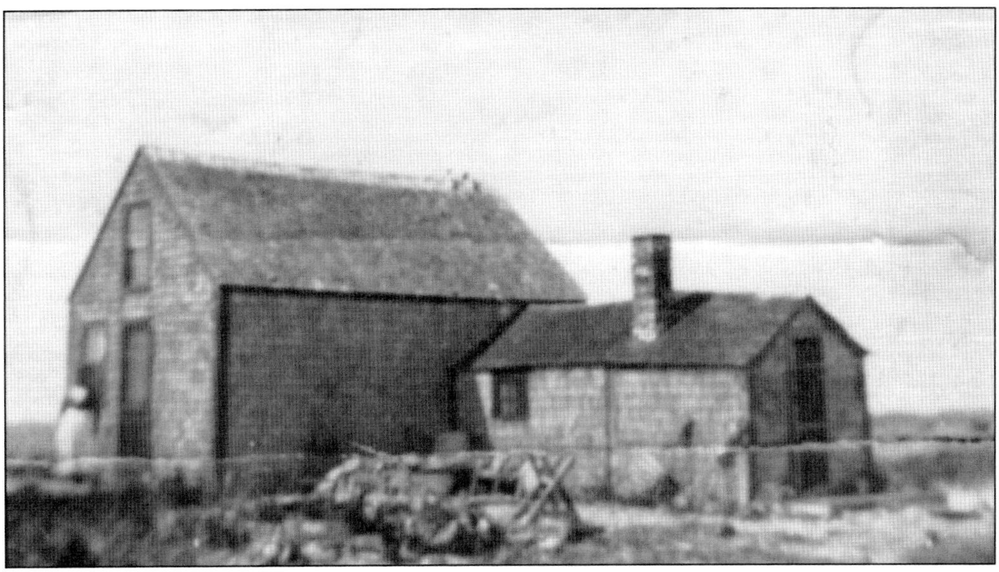

Shown is the original homestead at Black Rocks owned by the Pierce family. Daniel and Bessie Pierce were the first children to be born at Black Rocks. Bessie claimed when the river froze between Black Rocks and Plum Island, her dad drove horses across to Newburyport. The scrapbooks of Bessie Pierce helped the author piece together and add a personal touch in describing events that took place at the beach.

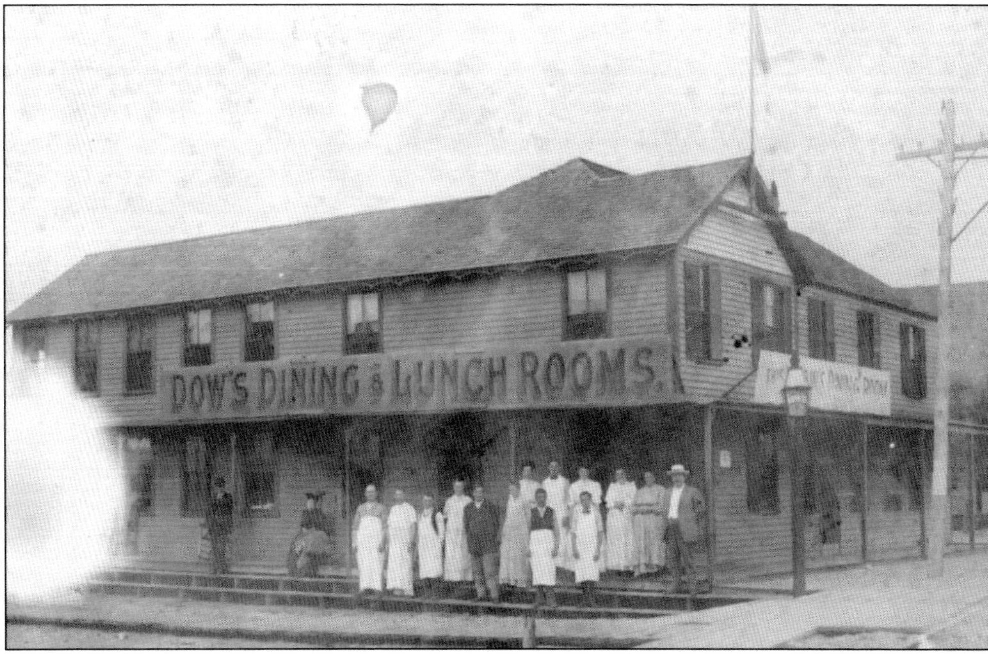

The staff members of Dow's Lunch Room on Railroad Avenue stand on the side porch of the restaurant. Bessie Pierce, the first girl to be born at Black Rocks, appears to be the third person from the right in this picture. Dow's burned in the fire of 1908.

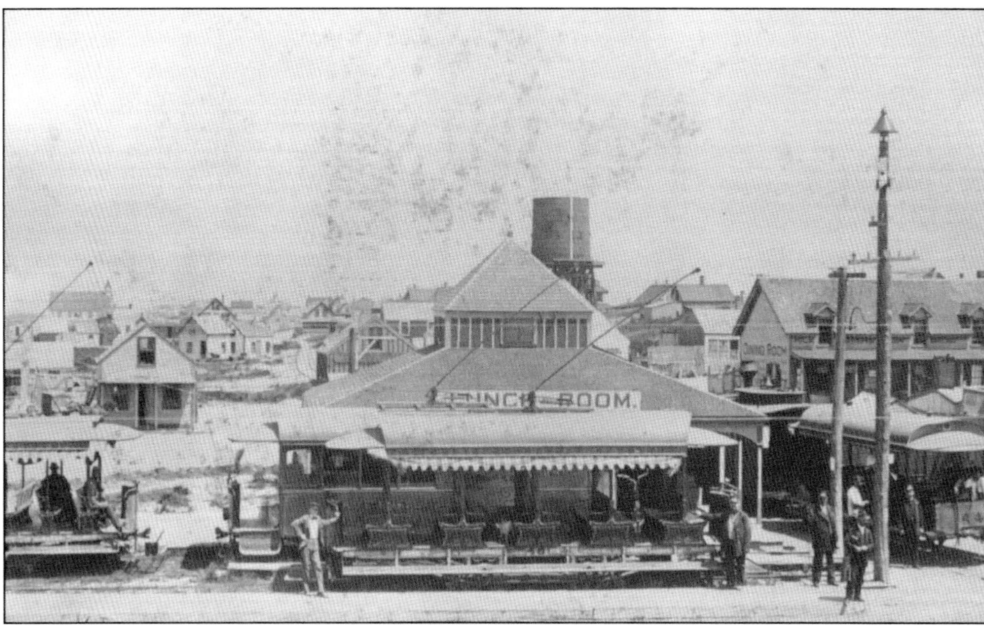

Trolleys line up in the Gay Nineties of Salisbury Beach. When the line was electrified in 1902, many of the old trailer cars were motorized. This picture depicts an open car with back-to-back seats, the combination passenger-baggage car, a steam dummy engine, and a trailer. Two conductors pose on either end of Car No. 48. (Courtesy Roger Shaheen.)

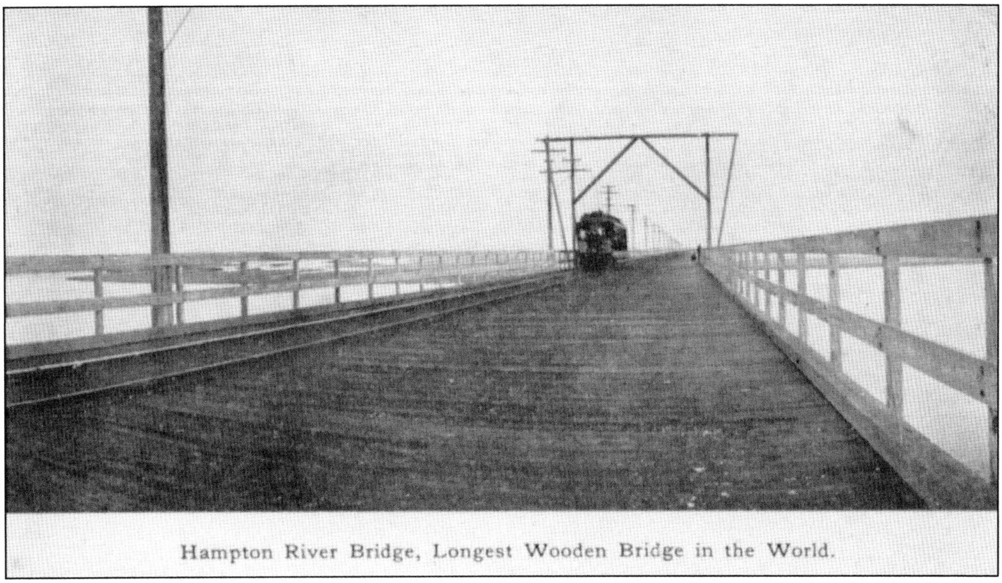

A trolley heads across the Hampton River Bridge, reported on the postcard to be the longest wooden bridge in the world at the time. The 4,623-foot bridge connected Salisbury Beach to the New Hampshire coast. On May 15, 1902, it opened to trolley travel. A pedestrian had to pay 5¢ to cross the bridge. The bridge was damaged extensively by ice in 1918 and in 1920. (Courtesy Arnold Marookian.)

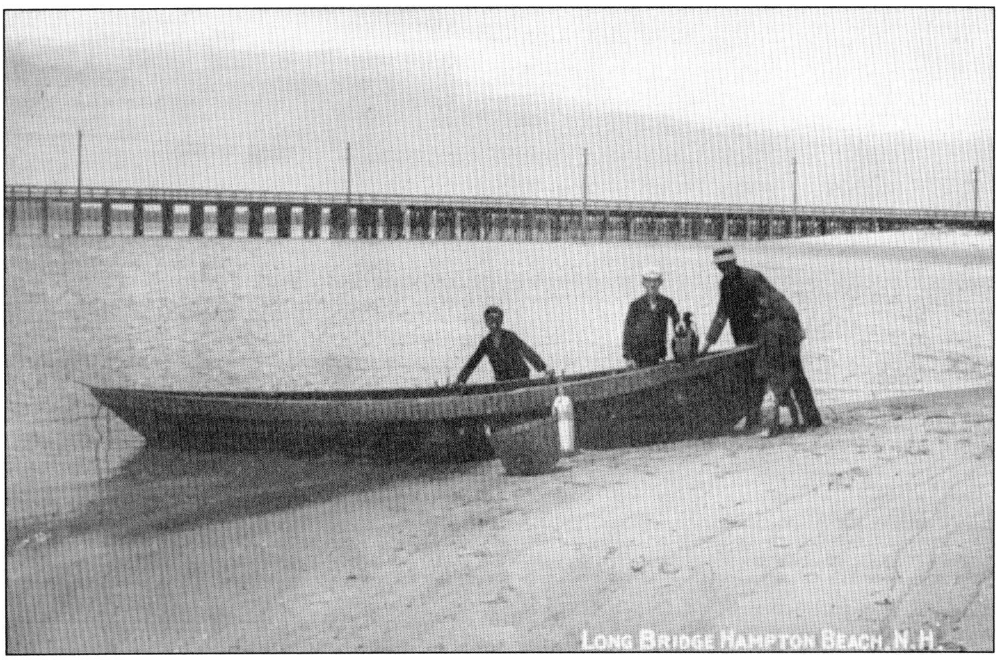

Two boys and their father launch their boat into the Hampton River while the mile-long bridge looms in the background. As trolley ridership declined on the Northeastern line, tolls for automobiles increased sharply on the bridge, also owned by the line. The bridge became a valuable source of income for the line. Tolls were only collected from May 1 to October 1. (Courtesy Arnold Marookian.)

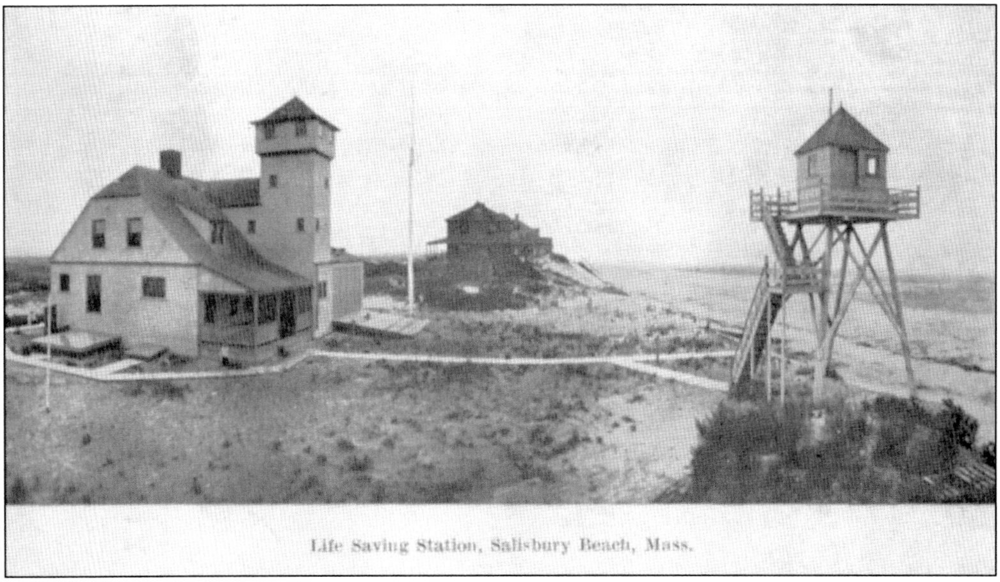

The lifesaving station of Salisbury Beach was located about a mile north of the center of the beach. Pres. Grover Cleveland signed the authorization for the building in June 1896, and construction began in the fall of 1897. Before being transferred to Salisbury in 1903, Willard Charles, one of the early captains of the Salisbury Station, had served at Cuttyhunk Island. He built a cottage named the Cuttyhunk on the beach after he retired.

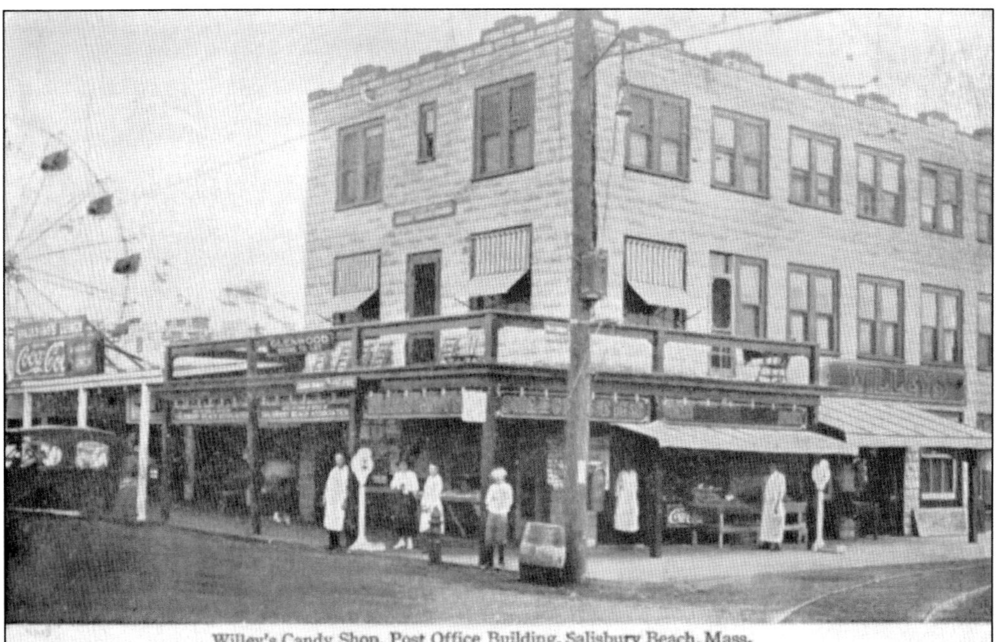

Willey's Candy Shop, located in the post office building, is still famous for making delicious caramel corn and saltwater taffy. The post office building was once the home of the Glenwood Hotel. The candy shop continues to sweeten the beach today with mouth-watering confectioneries. (Courtesy Arnold Marookian.)

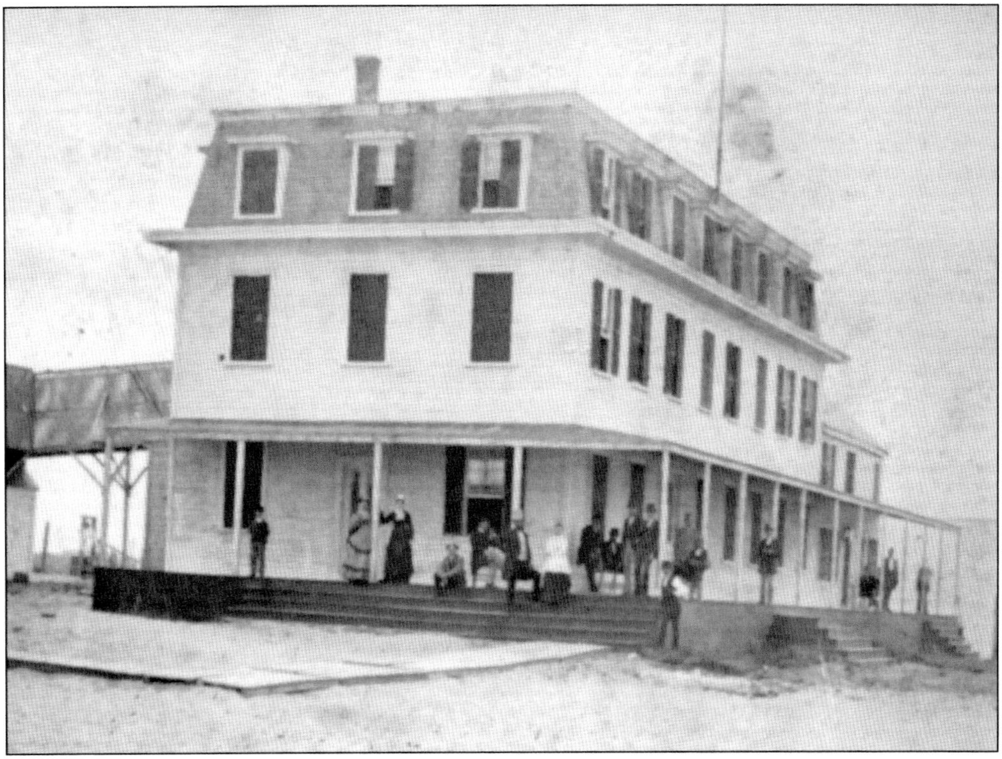

On July 14, 1887, the Seaside House, with 36 sleeping rooms, a barbershop, stable, and a saloon (might have been the problem), was one of the establishments raided by the Salisbury police aided by Amesbury officers for allegedly selling liquor illegally. The establishment had burned in February 1883, but was rebuilt. (Courtesy Scott Nason.)

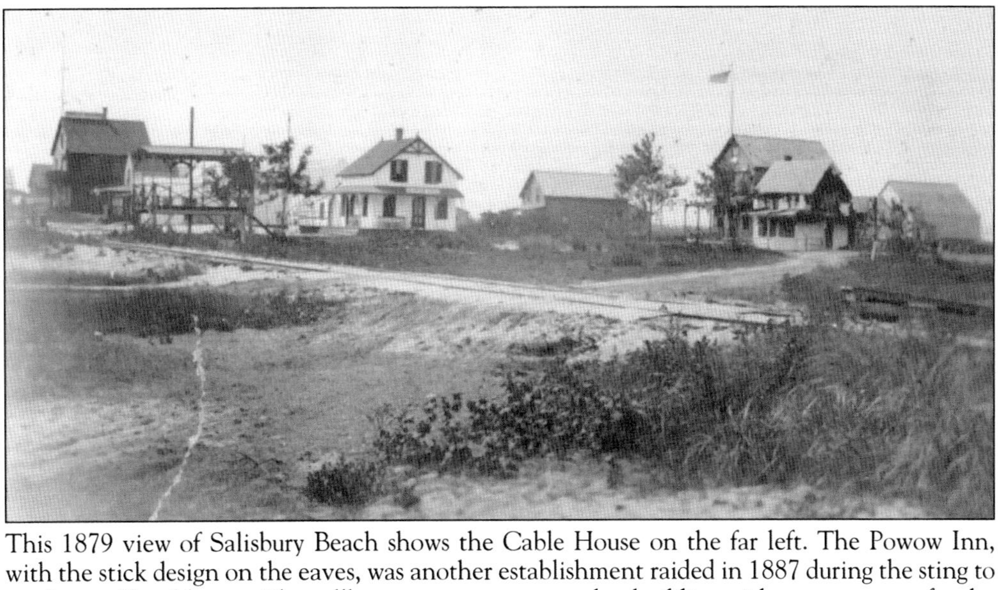

This 1879 view of Salisbury Beach shows the Cable House on the far left. The Powow Inn, with the stick design on the eaves, was another establishment raided in 1887 during the sting to confiscate illegal liquor. The tollhouse, a two-story wooden building with an apartment for the toll keeper, is on the right covered in ivy. The tollhouse burned in September 1900. (Courtesy Arnold Marookian.)

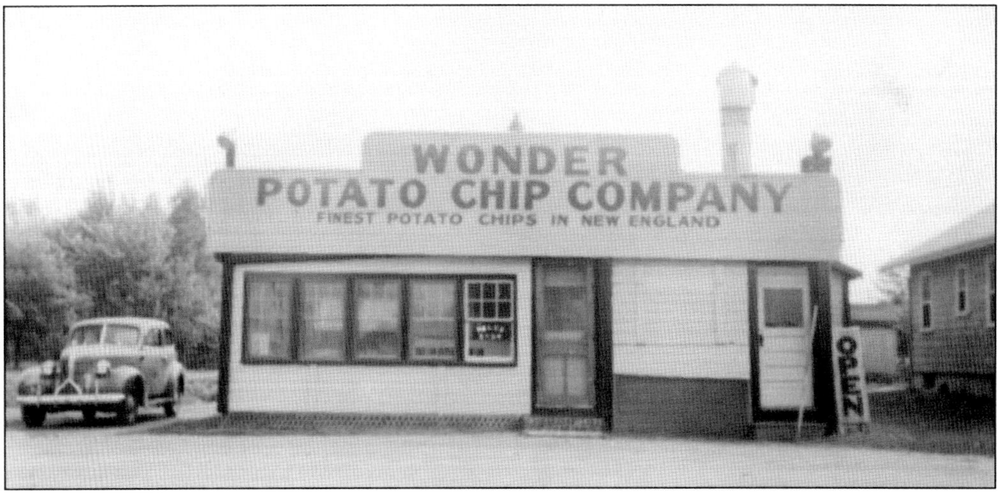

The Wonder Potato Chip Company remained in business for 50 years on Beach Road in Salisbury. The company was run by Ruth and Richard Harden, who sometimes worked in 100-degree temperatures from dawn to dusk. The company weathered the Great Depression, World War II, the debut of television, a gasoline crunch, and soaring inflation.

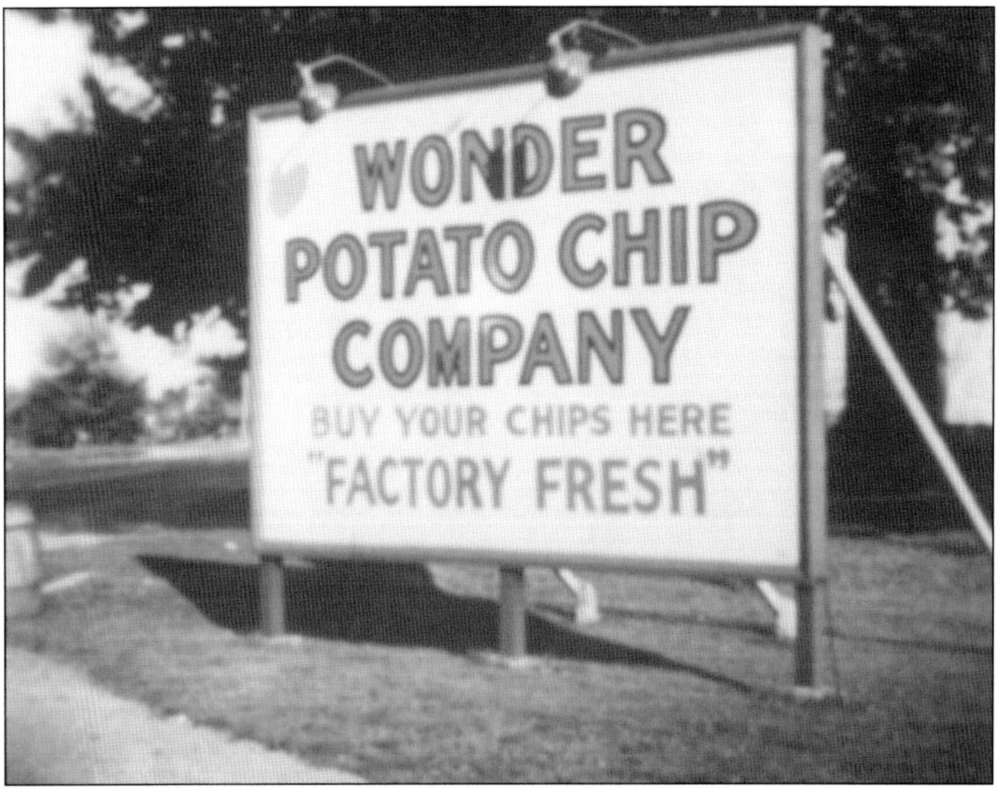

The sign for the Wonder Potato Chip Company was a fixture on Beach Road for years. The chips sold for 25¢ a bag in 1933; the last bag sold for $1.20 in the fall of 1982. The chips were made with only three ingredients: potatoes, cotton seed oil, and salt. Richard Harden often drove 208 miles round-trip to Auburn, Maine, to buy the best quality potatoes. The chips were wonderful, as the author can attest from having eaten many of them over the years.

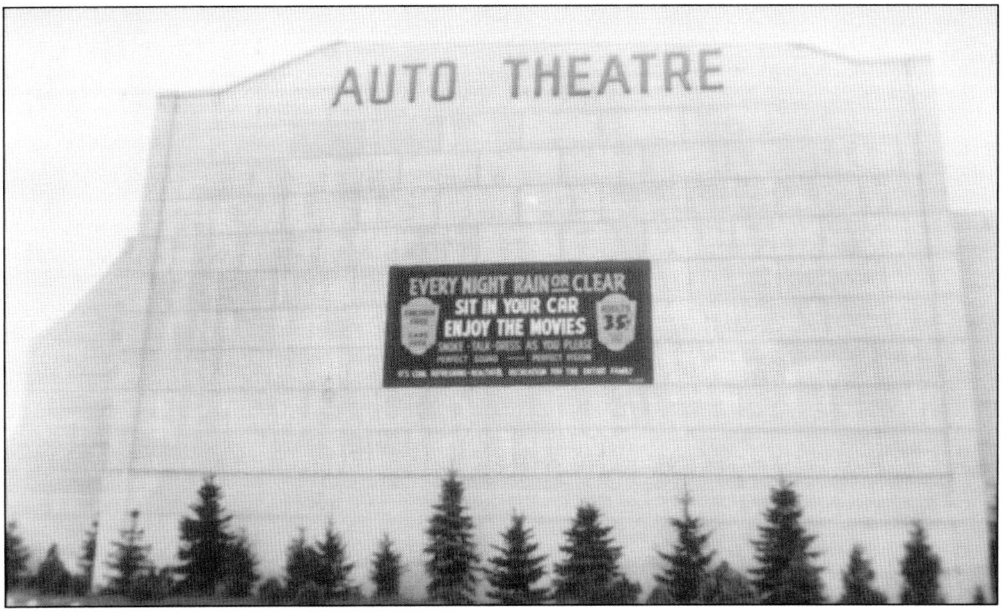

The Auto (drive-in) Theatre, an icon of a passing culture, stood next to the Wonder Potato Chip Company on Beach Road. In 1942, admission was 35¢ for each adult. The sign is wonderful, stating "Smoke-Talk-Dress As You Please."

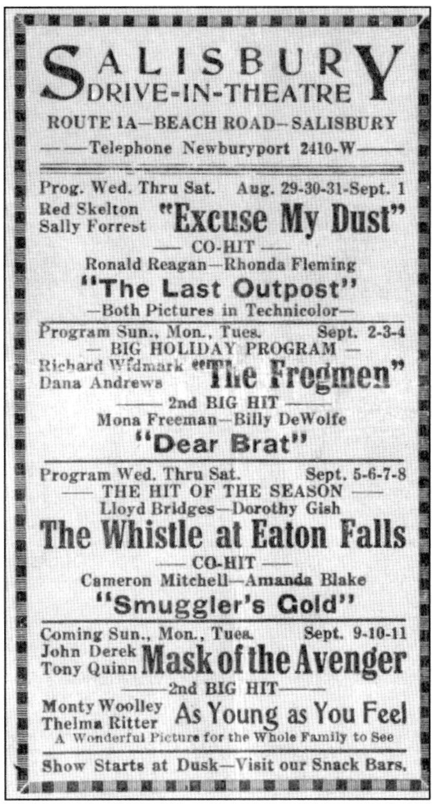

The drive-in theater was later renamed the Salisbury Drive-In-Theatre and remained open into the late 1970s. This flyer announces what is playing on a sultry summer eve in the early 1950s. (Courtesy Arnold Marookian.)

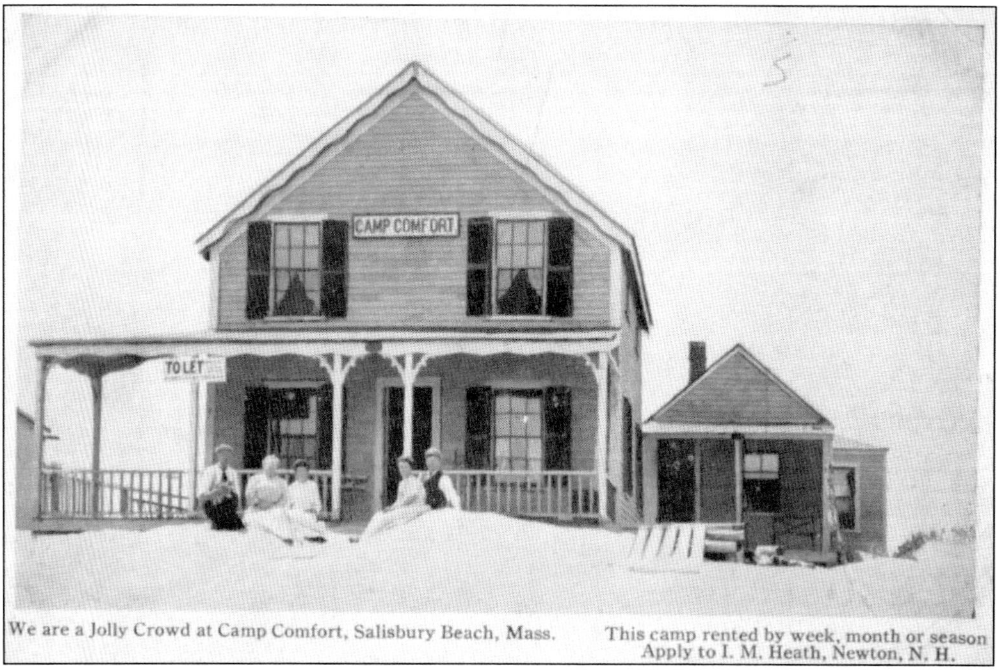

The name of Camp Comfort says it all, but some of the guests are sitting in the sand and not more comfortably enjoying the porch. The postcard claims, "We are a Jolly Crowd at Camp Comfort, Salisbury Beach, Mass." The camp, typical to most beach cottages, rented by the week, month, or the season. (Courtesy Arnold Marookian.)

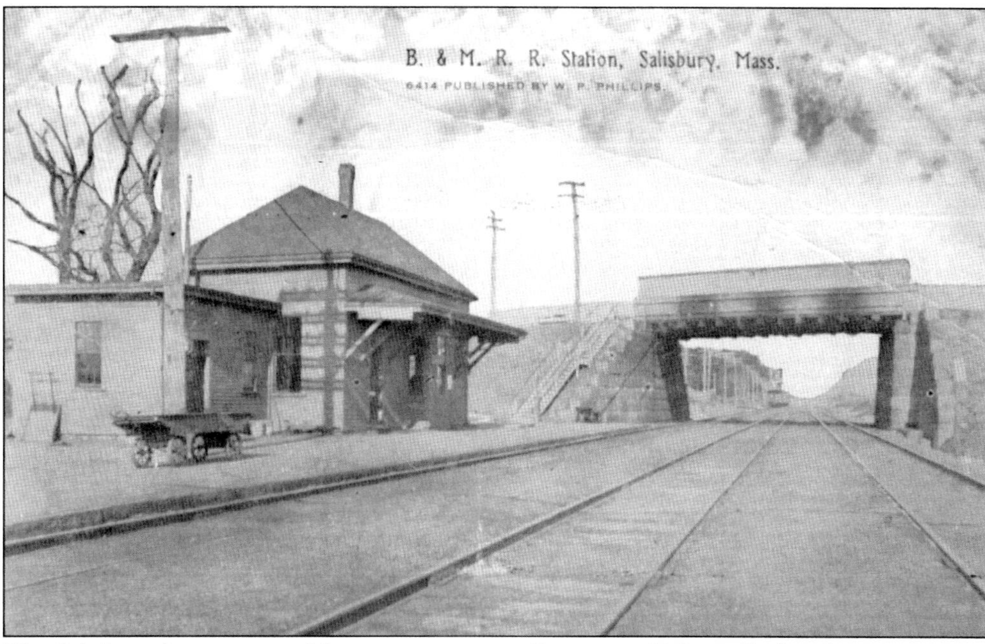

The Salisbury depot operated for many years as a Boston and Maine Railroad station. Steam trains stopped here in 1902, when the station was in its prime. Many of the amusement parks were originally established by the municipal railway companies to attract passengers to ride the trains on weekends. (Courtesy Arnold Marookian.)

Four

IT'S SO QUIET IN THE RUINS

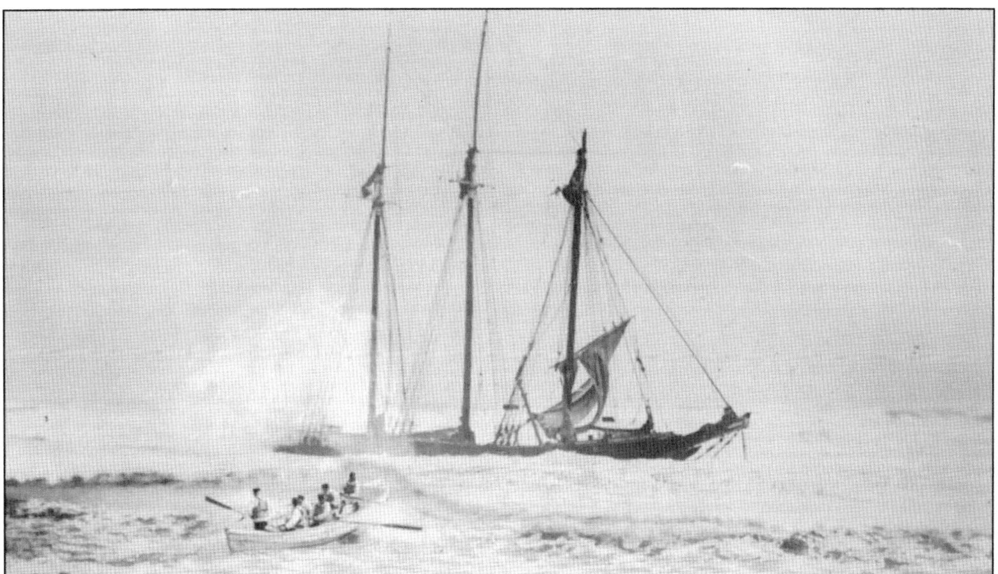

A lifeboat is being rowed over rough waves on April 13, 1894, to investigate the *Jennie M. Carter*. The boat was loaded with paving stones. The back of the ship was smashed and the stove in the captain's cabin was still burning, but a black cat was the only living creature aboard. The body of Capt. Wesley T. Ober later washed ashore at Plum Island.

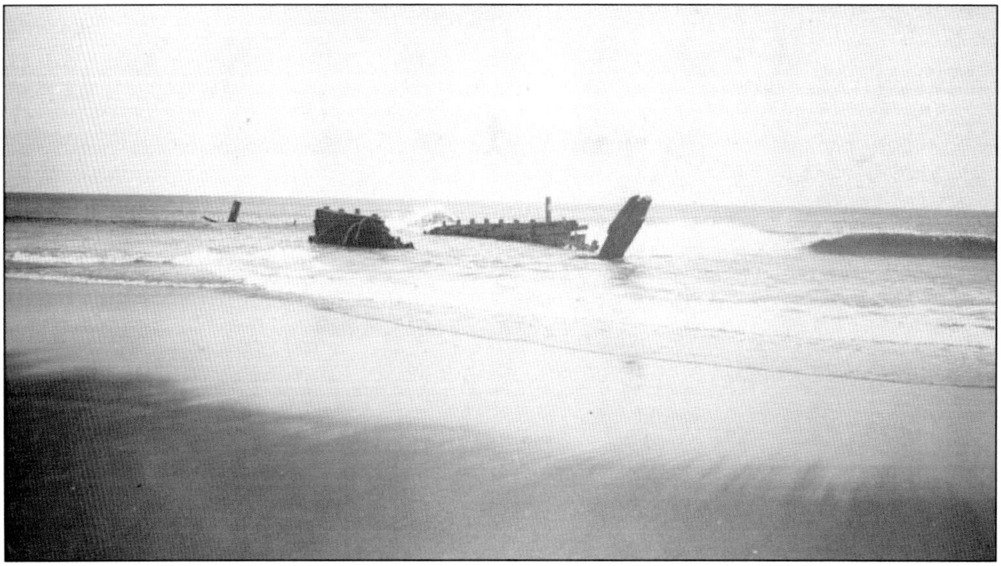

The wreck of the *Jennie M. Carter*, photographed in 1914, could be seen for many years on the shore of Salisbury Beach. The ship was 130.3 feet in length and drew 9.8 feet of water. It was built in Newton, Maryland, in 1874 and was registered at 296 tons. It is believed if the crew had stayed on the ship, they would have survived. (Courtesy Joseph Callahan.)

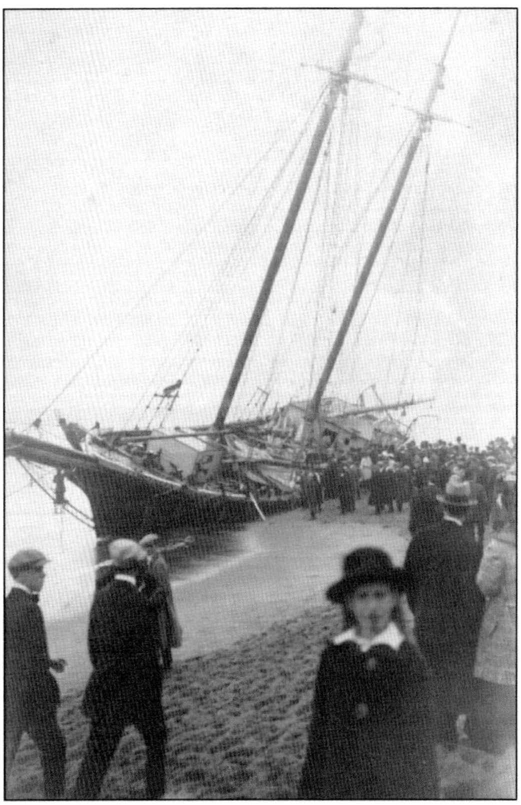

A crowd has gathered at the wreck of the *Virginian*, which sank on June 9, 1916, while loaded with cordwood. When a wreck such as this one washed up on the shore, extra cars had to be added to the trolley run to transport spectators and souvenir hunters to the site. (Courtesy Joseph Callahan.)

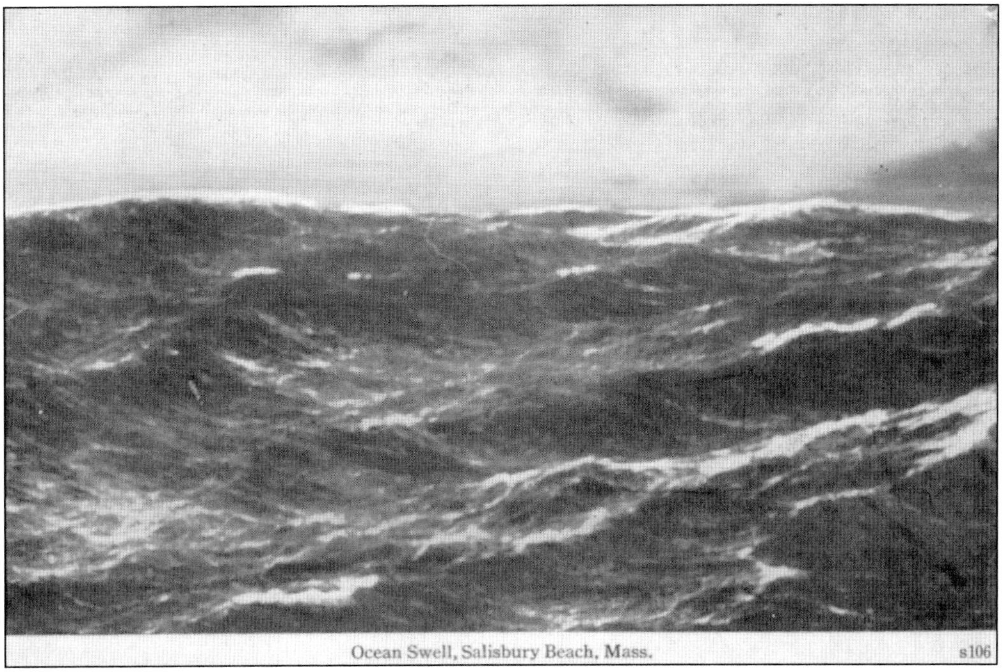

An ocean swell illustrates the danger and unpredictability of the sea. Among the many shipwrecks off the shore of Salisbury were the *Virginian*, the *Jenny M. Carter*, the *Florida*, the *Sir Francis*, and the *Marble Bird*. (Courtesy Arnold Marookian.)

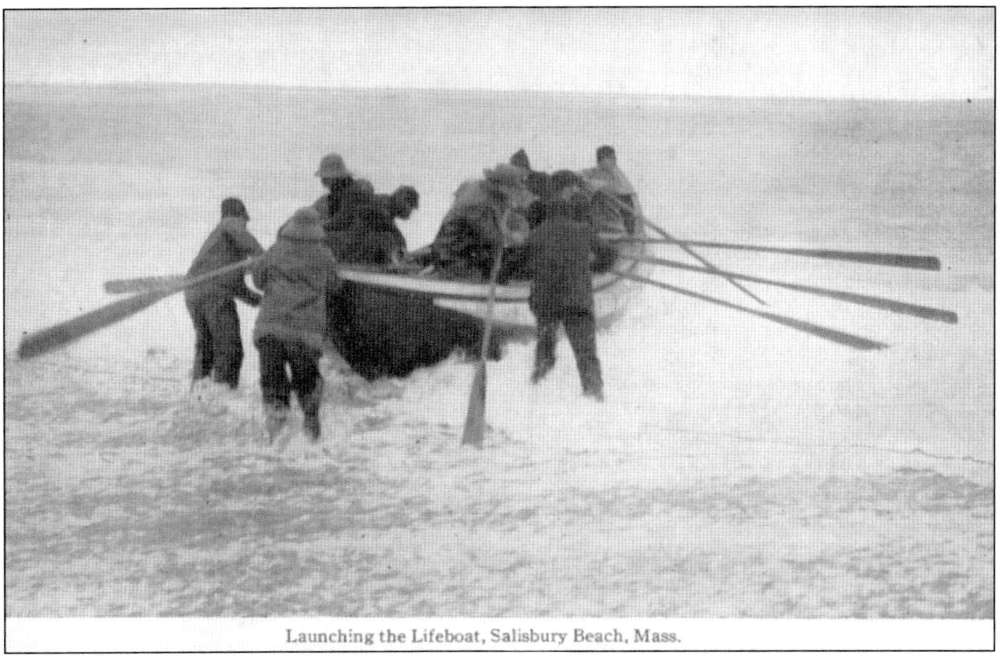

A crew launches a lifeboat at Salisbury Beach. The bravery of the men who are rescuers at sea, fighting the oceans unforgiving wrath, is unmatched. Ever since Salisbury Beach hired lifeguards to patrol the beach, no drownings have occurred while the guards have been on duty. (Courtesy Arnold Marookian.)

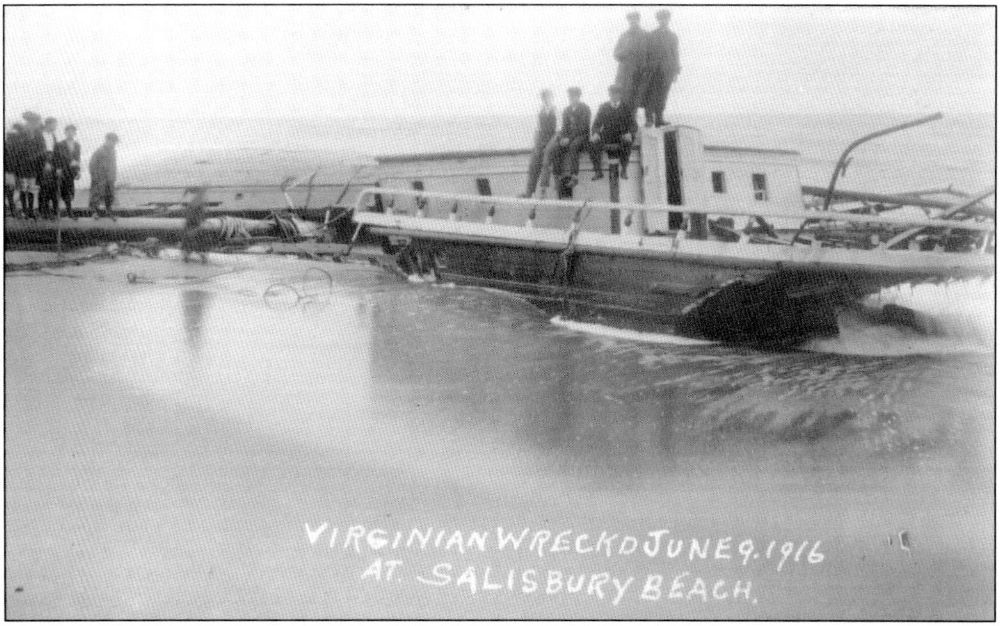

This group of people poses on the wreck of the *Virginian*. The popularity of movies like *Titanic* and *The Perfect Storm* shows the public's endless fascination with shipwrecks and the myths and legends surrounding them. The allure of disasters is a significant part of our culture. (Courtesy Arnold Marookian.)

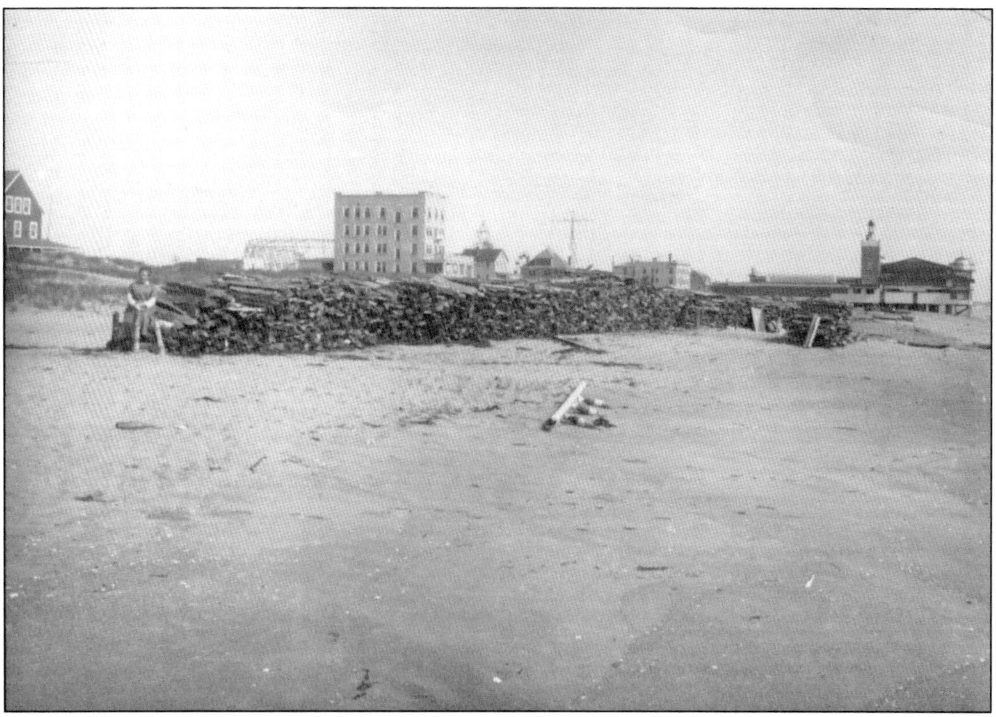

The Edwards Hotel is a backdrop for the pile of cordwood that was the cargo of the shipwrecked *Virginian*. The Ocean Echo can be seen on the far right of the photograph.

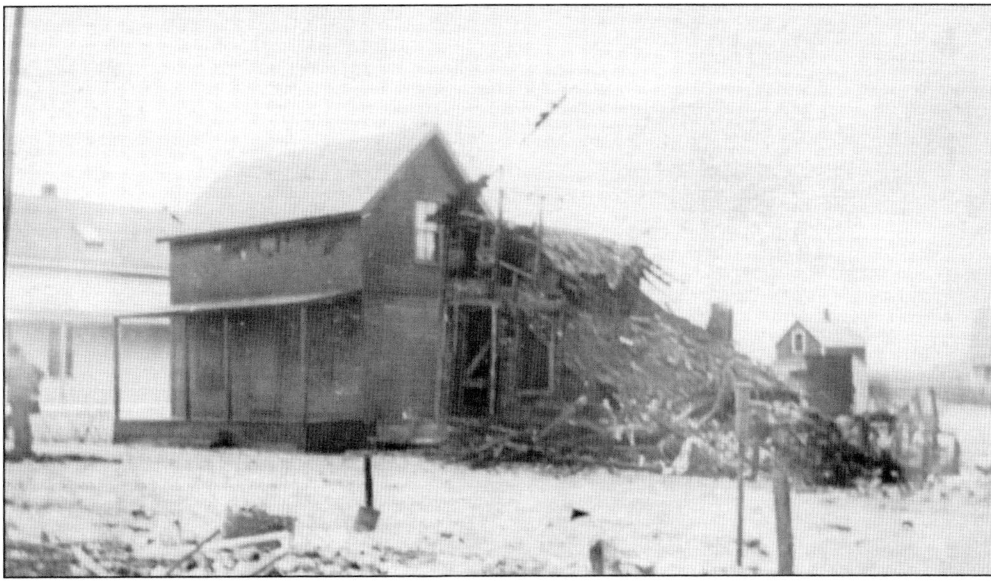

This picture shows the aftermath of the fire on October 26, 1908, which consumed 64 buildings. Before towns had fire departments, every household was expected to own fire buckets and a large linen bag for removing valuables from a burning building. The Wakefield House, Berlin Hotel, Magnolia Meat Market, Hope Chapel, and Pepperell Hotel were just a few of the establishments lost in this fire.

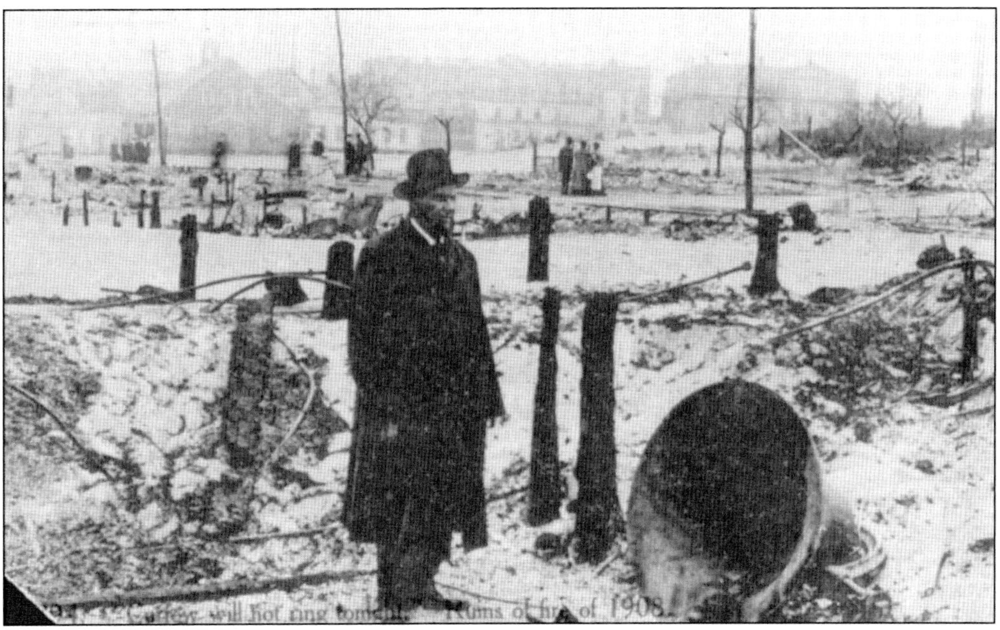

Dr. Spaulding assesses the damage of the fire of 1908. The fire was started in the "Quartette" cottage, south of the Seaside Hotel. The center was saved because the wind was blowing from the northeast. Two Amesbury men suspected of arson were arrested. This postcard states that curfew will not ring tonight as the damaged chapel bell lies on its side. The irony is that this church bell would have rung twice to announce the fire that destroyed it.

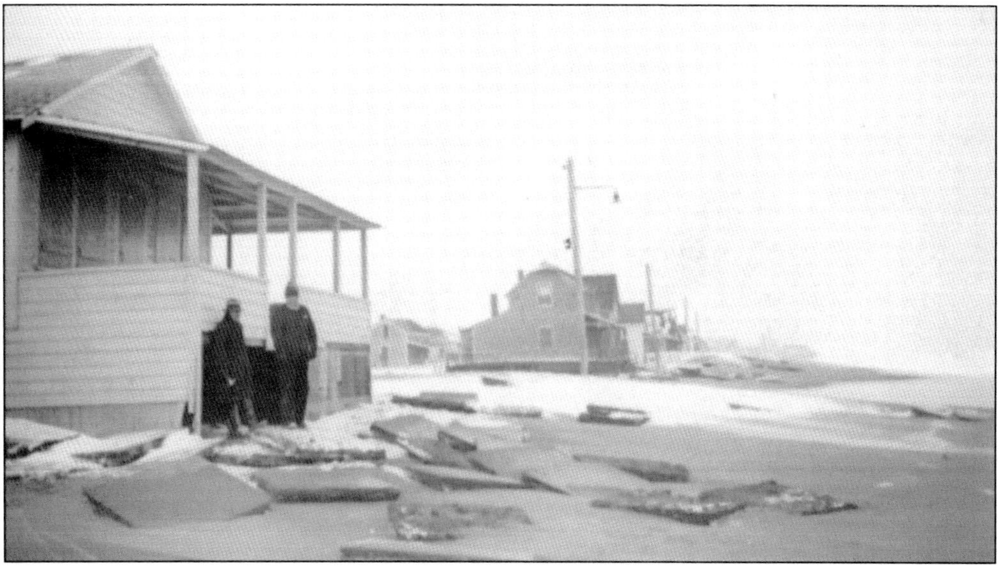

A storm in December 1932 broke up cement slabs from the sidewalk and tossed them all over the beach. According to Ruth Harden, the state had recently done some work flattening the sand dunes to create a "Coney Island" type of beach. This action caused more devastation to certain areas of the shore.

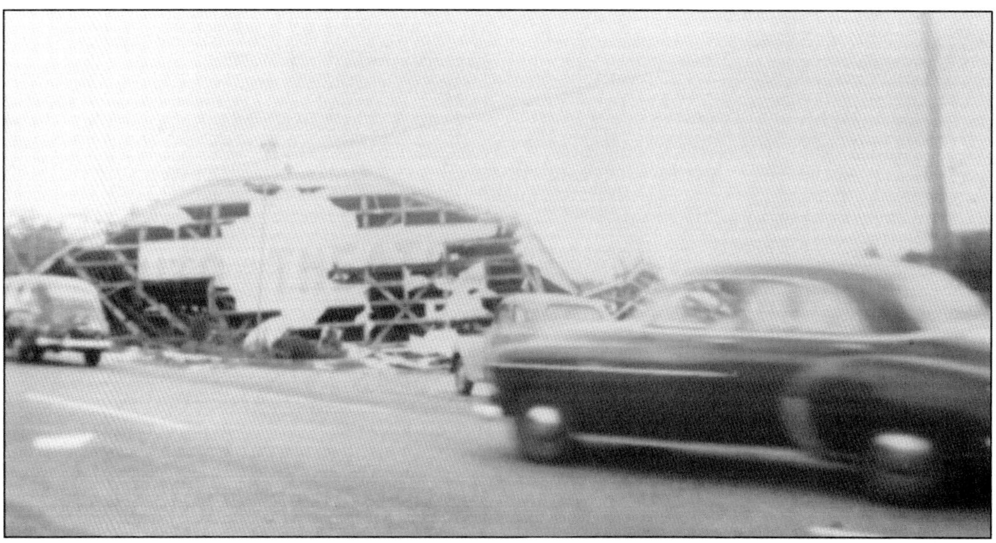

The Salisbury Drive-In is in shambles from the devastating winds of the Hurricane Carol of 1954. Carol hit the New England coast on the morning of August 31, with winds gusting to 125 mph. The drive-in was rebuilt and operated for many years, later showing some racy pictures with X ratings.

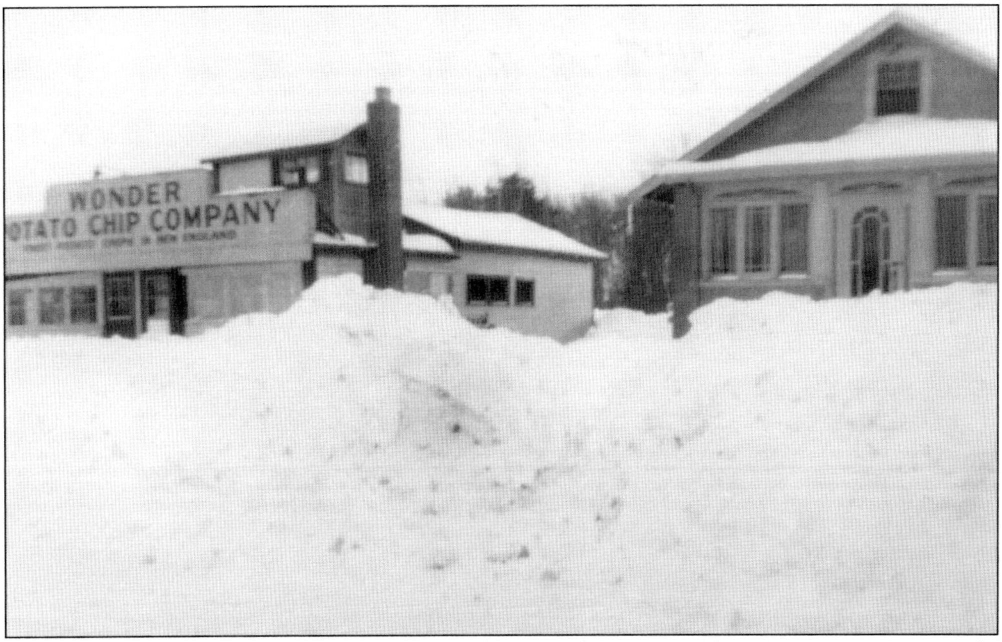

After a major northeaster in January 1948, the Wonder Potato Chip Company was partially buried in snow drifts. A typical northeaster lasts for three days and can deposit an enormous amount of snow.

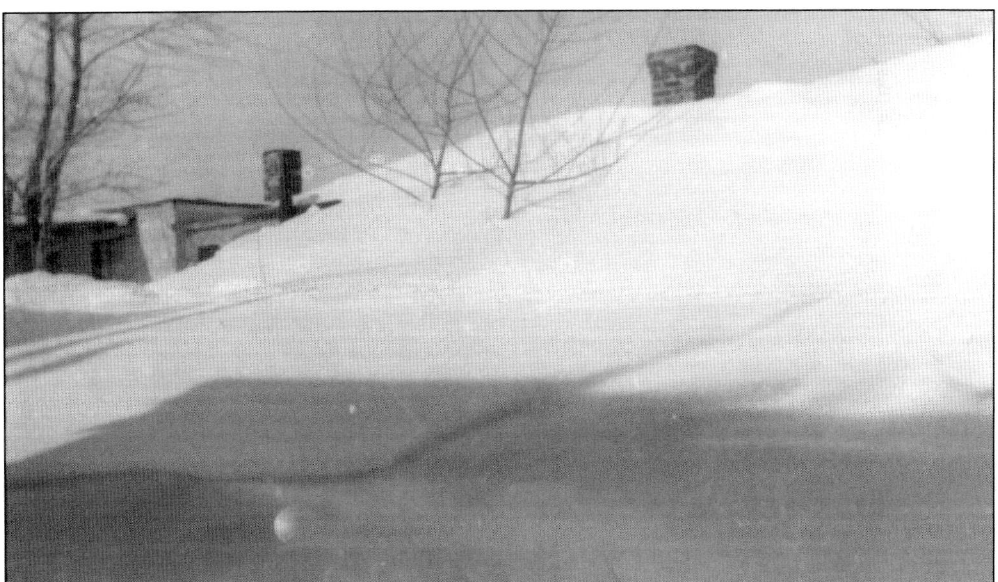
The winter of 1948 must have blasted the coast with much snow. The chimney of Bessie Pierce's house is the only thing visible through the snow drifts.

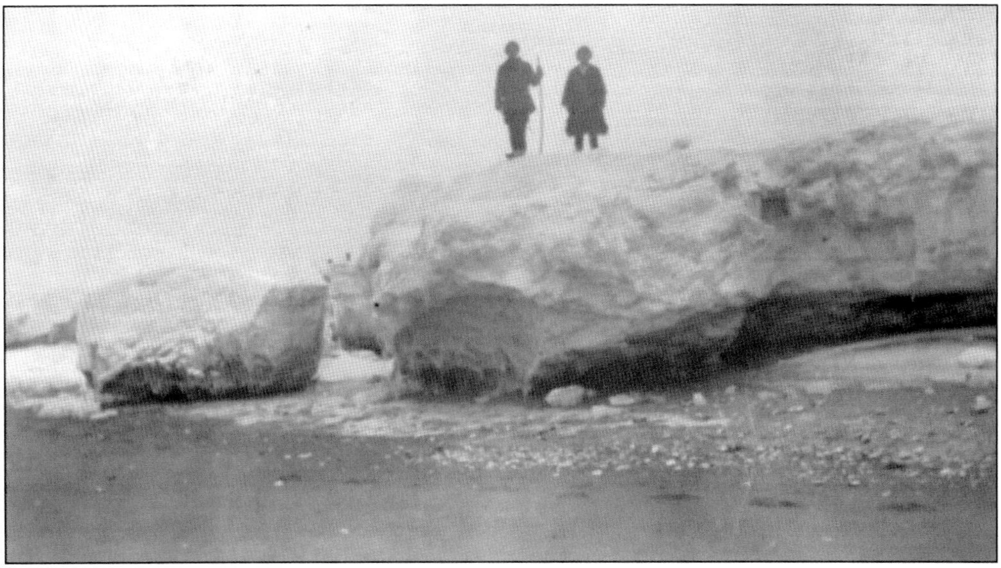

This iceberg washed up next to Black Rocks in the winter of 1919. Franklin and Walter Merrill stand on top of the unusually big piece of ice. Franklin was killed at the age of 27 on the Wildcat roller coaster at the beach.

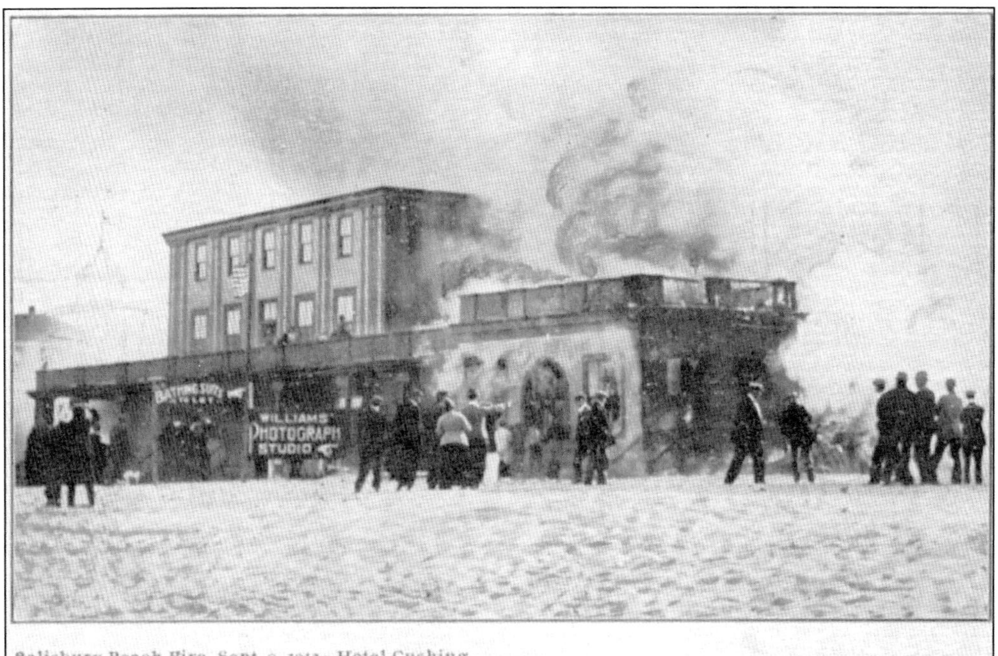

The most devastating fire to hit Salisbury Beach occurred on September 9, 1913. The fire broke out when chemicals exploded in a photographic studio owned by Arthur Williams at the rear of the Hotel Cushing. High winds spread the fire to the hotel and destroyed the beach center. In all, 125 buildings were destroyed. (Courtesy Arnold Marookian.)

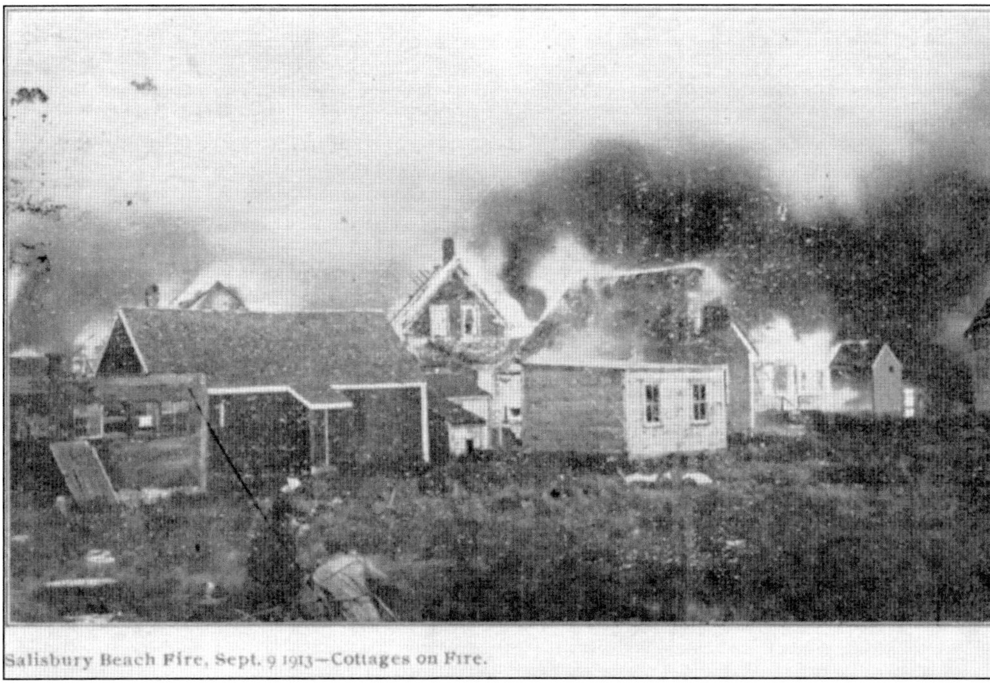

Cottages light up the night with flames leaping 100 feet as the blaze of 1913 spreads rapidly through the center of the beach. When the wooden clackers were sounded as a fire alarm, every able-bodied person was expected to form a bucket line from the nearest source of water. (Courtesy Arnold Marookian.)

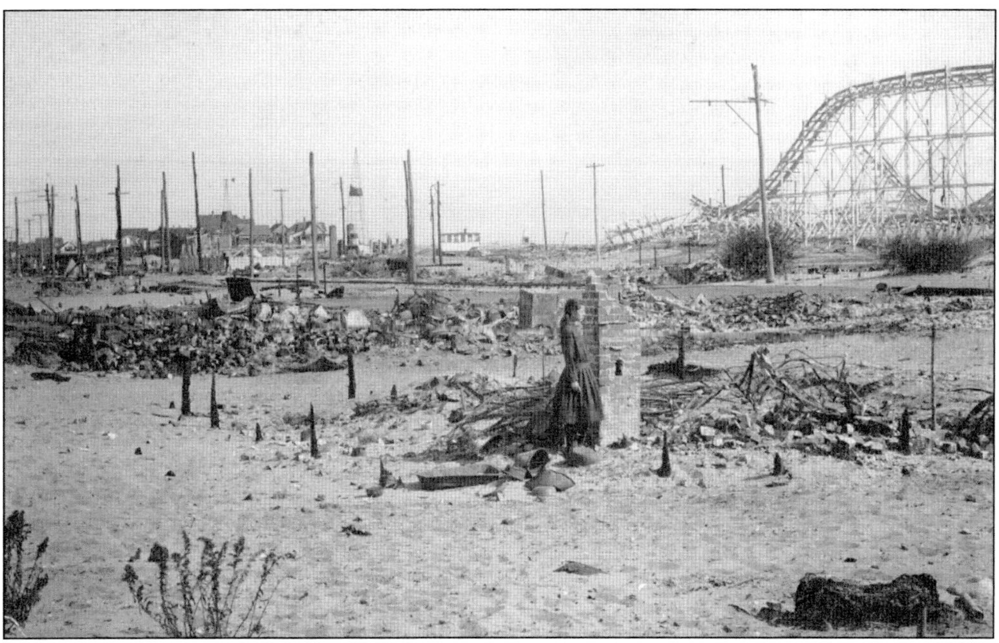

Several of the rides, including the Giant Thriller roller coaster, the Spiral Thriller, and Culver's Flying Horses were destroyed in the fire of 1913. (Courtesy Arnold Marookian.)

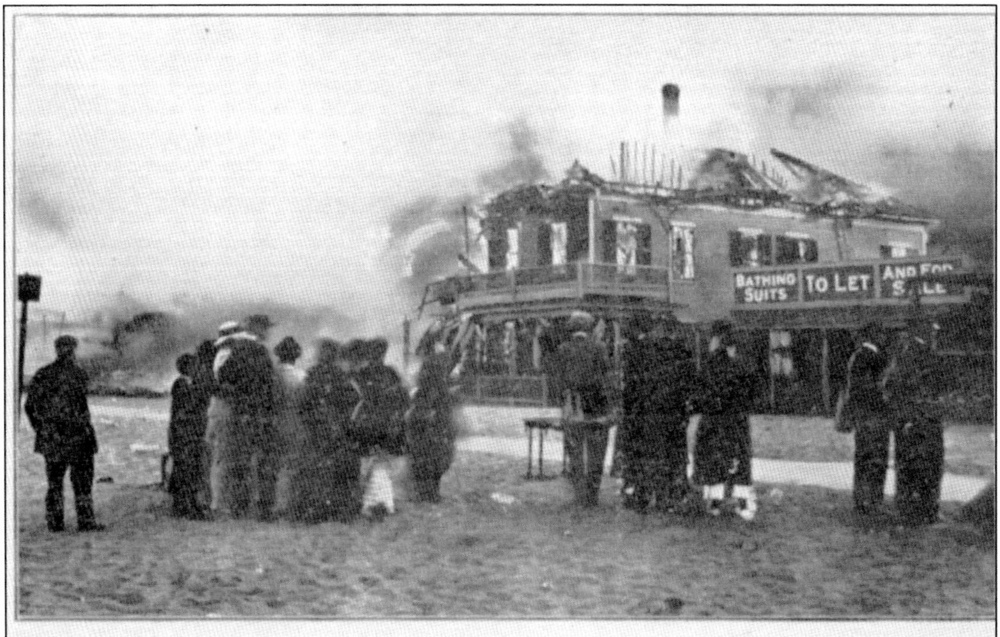

Salisbury Beach Fire, Sept. 9, 1913—Ocean View House.

The Ocean View is engulfed in flames in the fire of 1913. Embers were carried all the way to Black Rocks from the center by the high winds. The beach never entirely recovered from this fire. The genteel atmosphere of another era seemed to disappear along with the heart of the beach. (Courtesy Arnold Marookian.)

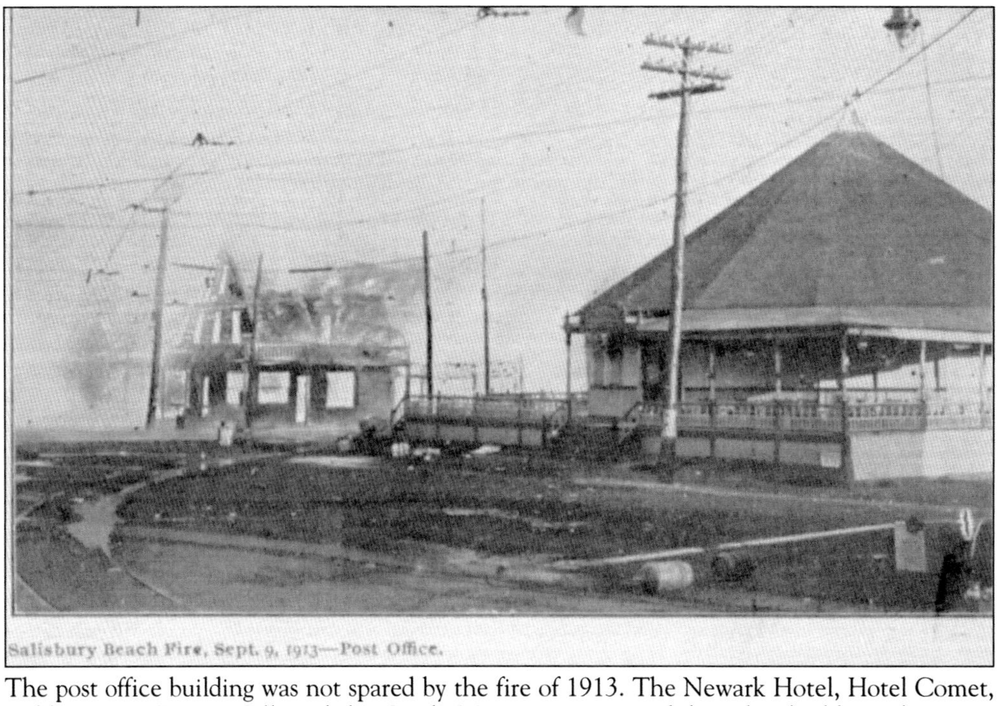

Salisbury Beach Fire, Sept. 9, 1913—Post Office.

The post office building was not spared by the fire of 1913. The Newark Hotel, Hotel Comet, Cable House, Dance Hall, and the Castle Mona were some of the other buildings that were destroyed in this fire. (Courtesy Arnold Marookian.)

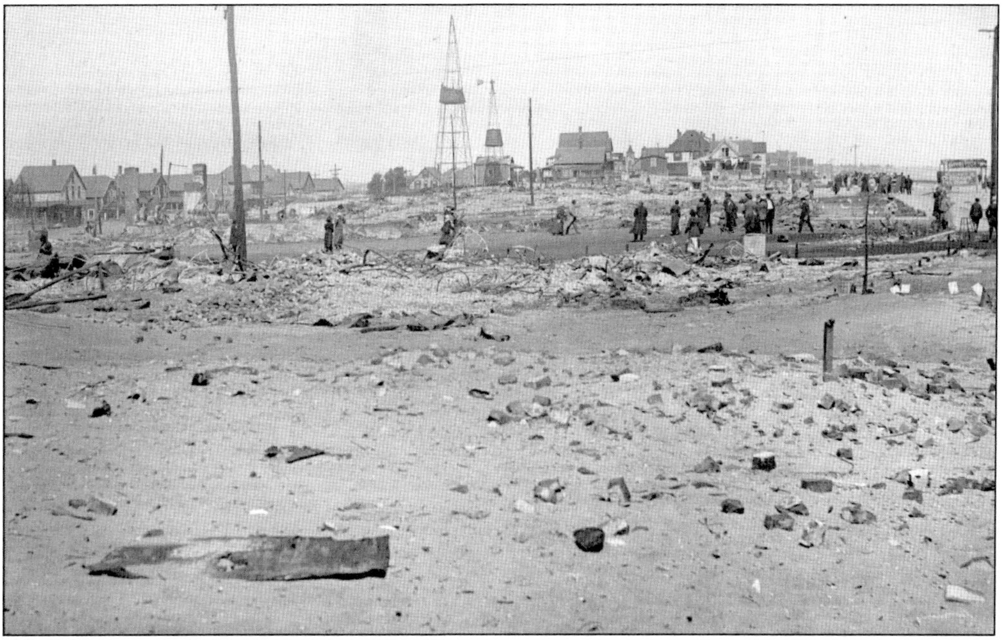

The devastation to the entire center of the beach is apparent in this picture as dazed people wander the area reviewing the ruins. Fire would hit the beach many times in the coming years. The fire of 1948 destroyed 35 buildings. (Courtesy Arnold Marookian.)

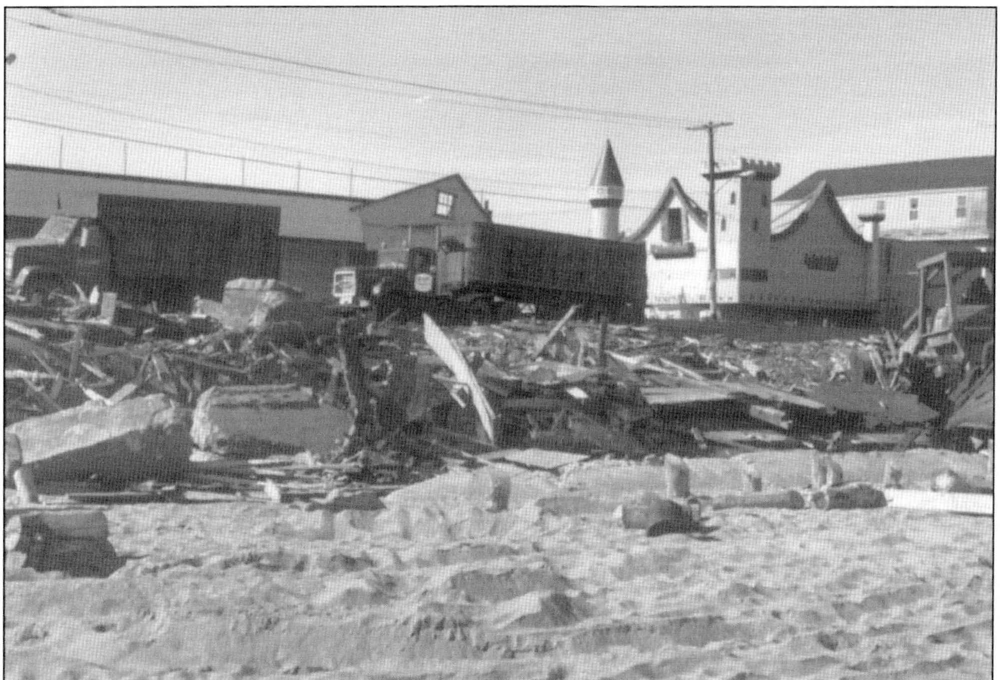

One of the worst northeasters to hit the New England coast in the 20th century was the Blizzard of 1978. This view shows the devastation caused by the hurricane winds to the North End of Salisbury Beach. The Witch's Castle, a very popular and spooky amusement, can be seen on the far right.

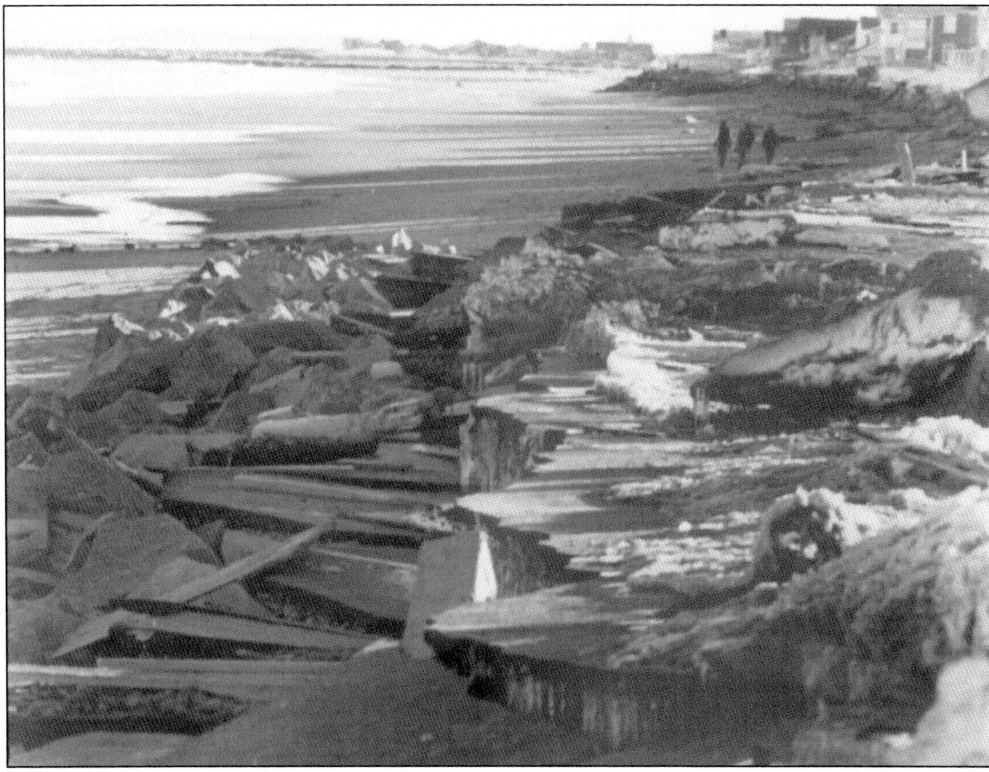

The erosion to the shoreline is overwhelming from the enormous high tides during the Blizzard of 1978. At a town meeting in 1981, Dr. Fred Clark of the State Department of Environmental Management predicted that because the beach was becoming narrower and steeper, waves would be rolling through Salisbury Beach center by the year 2000.

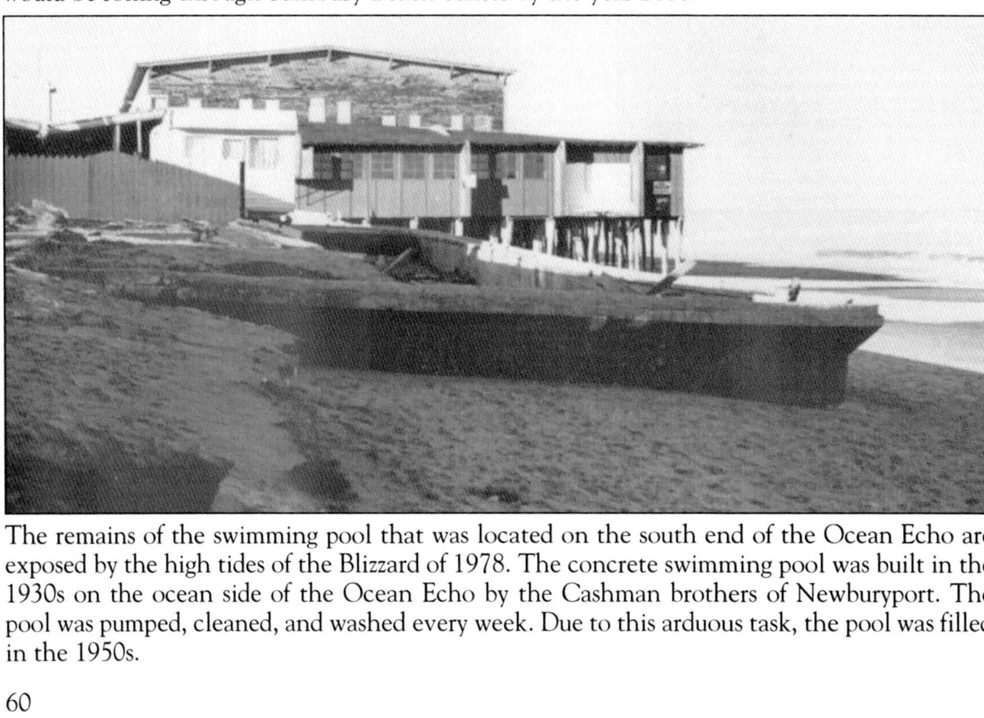

The remains of the swimming pool that was located on the south end of the Ocean Echo are exposed by the high tides of the Blizzard of 1978. The concrete swimming pool was built in the 1930s on the ocean side of the Ocean Echo by the Cashman brothers of Newburyport. The pool was pumped, cleaned, and washed every week. Due to this arduous task, the pool was filled in the 1950s.

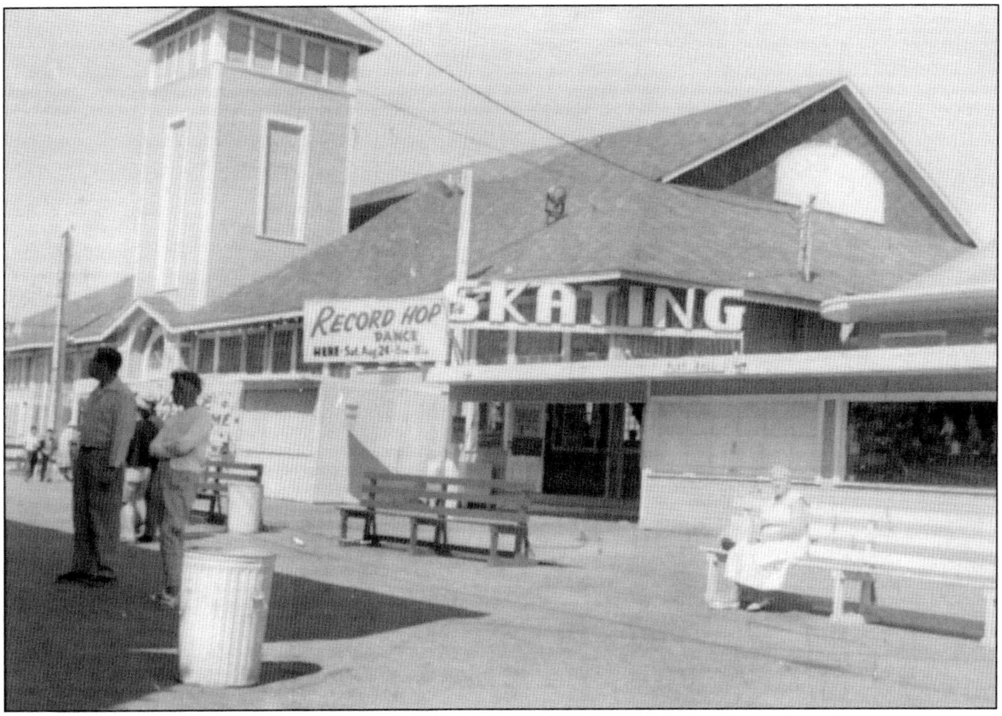

The skating rink, as it appeared in 1957, was gutted in a storm with high tides occurring in April 1958. Salisbury Beach was the hardest hit area on the shoreline during that storm, which caused an estimated $100,000 of damage and destroyed concessions and roadways. The kitchen of the Frolics nightclub was almost completely shorn off.

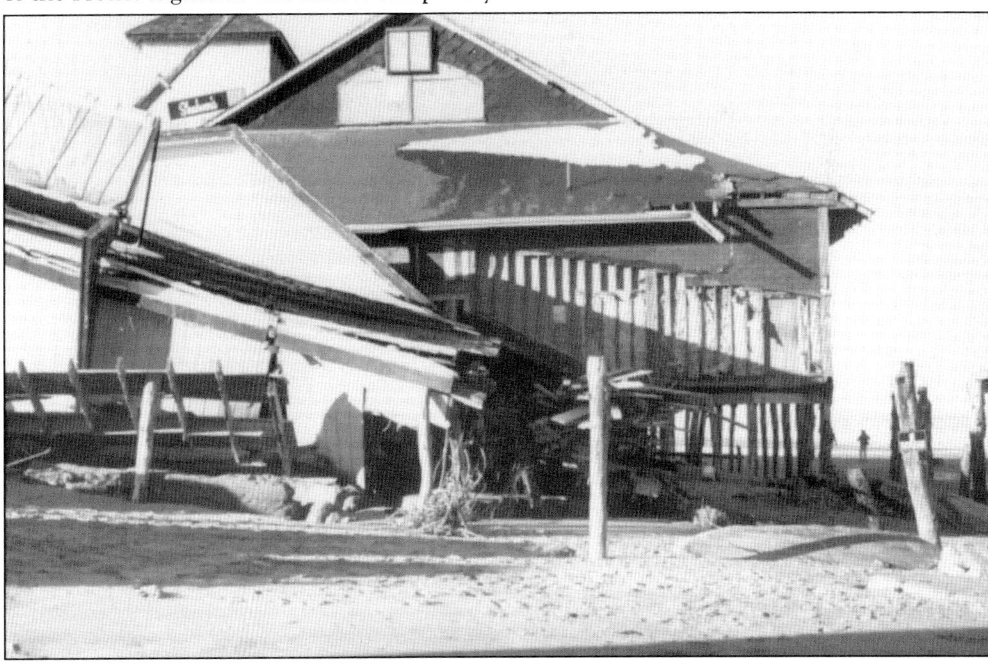

Although the skating rink was still standing after having been damaged in an earlier storm, it was no match to the waves and high winds of the Blizzard of 1978.

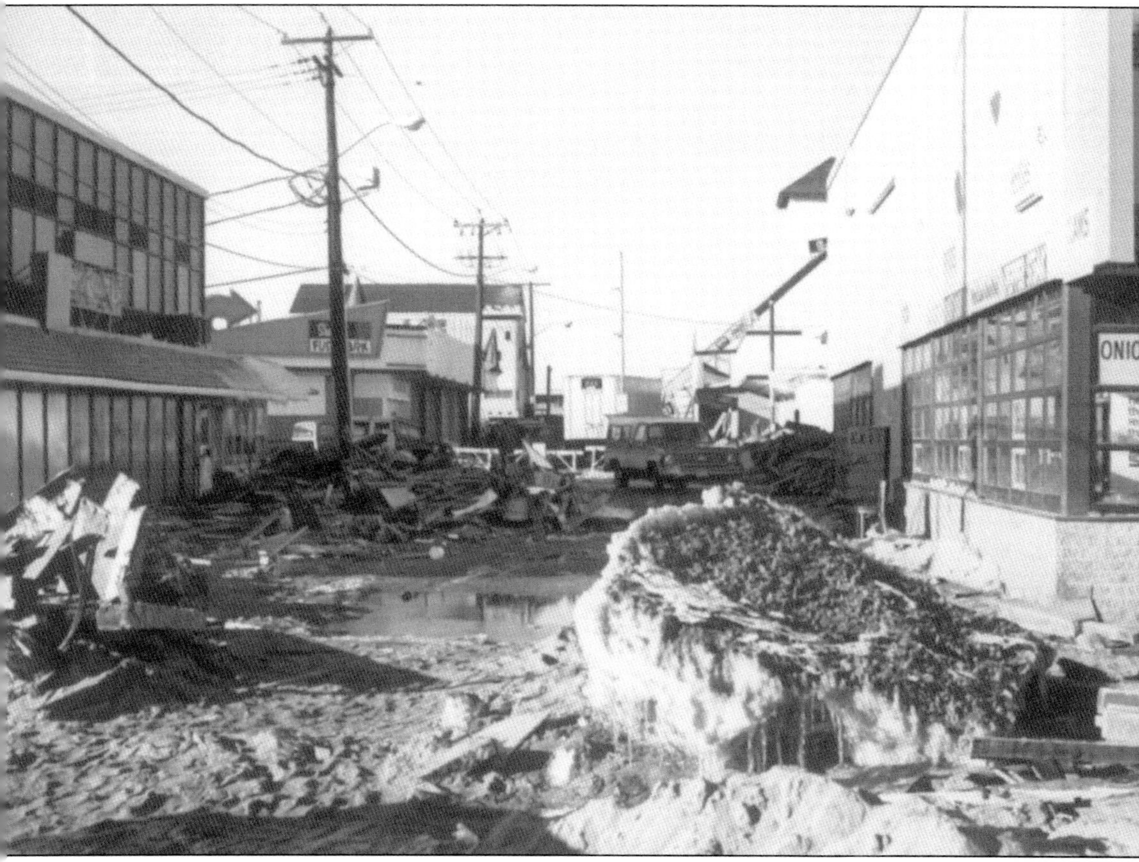

The center is layered with debris washed up by the Blizzard of 1978. It was often claimed that Salisbury Beach never recovered from the fire of 1913, but this blizzard was a final blow to the foundation of the old beach.

Five

If I Could Have a Talking Picture of You

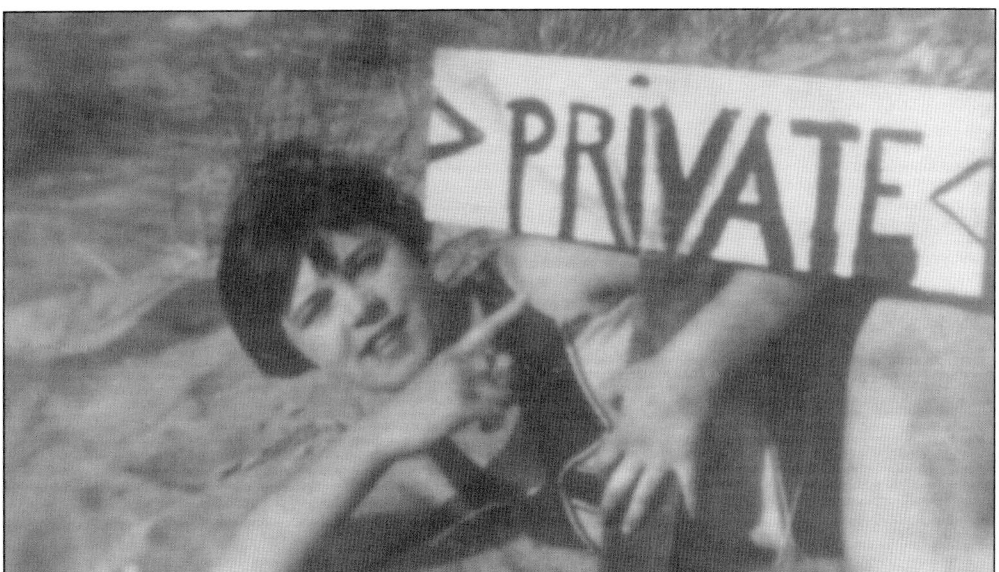

Ethel Brabbing, at the south end of the beach, points to her sign with an amused expression. The year is 1928, and she is 15 years old. Her family, from Amesbury, owned one of the cottages that were moved from the south end to the north end of the beach when the state took over the land. After marrying, her name became Ethel Bourque. She was famous for her editorials over the years to the *Newburyport Daily News*.

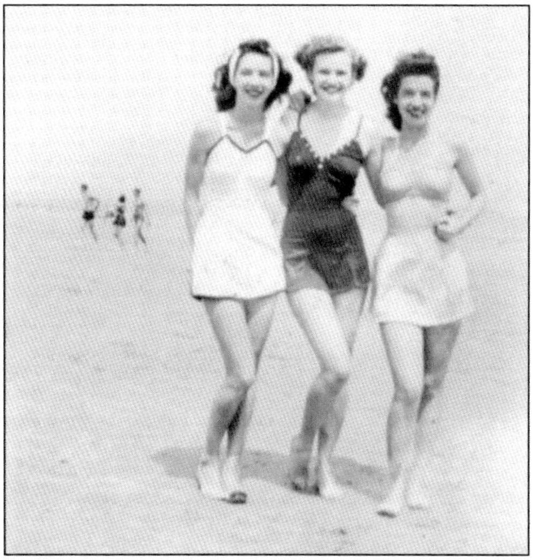

Kay O'Connell, Mary McWilliams, and Ann O'Connell from Malden, Massachusetts, pose at Salisbury Beach in 1943. Movie stars, such as Esther Williams and Dorothy Lamour, played an important role in setting the trends in swimwear in the 1940s. The bare midriff was not seen at the beach until the 1930s. One-piece bathing suits at this time were designed like corsets and were often as uncomfortable with stays, zippers, and shirred elastic.

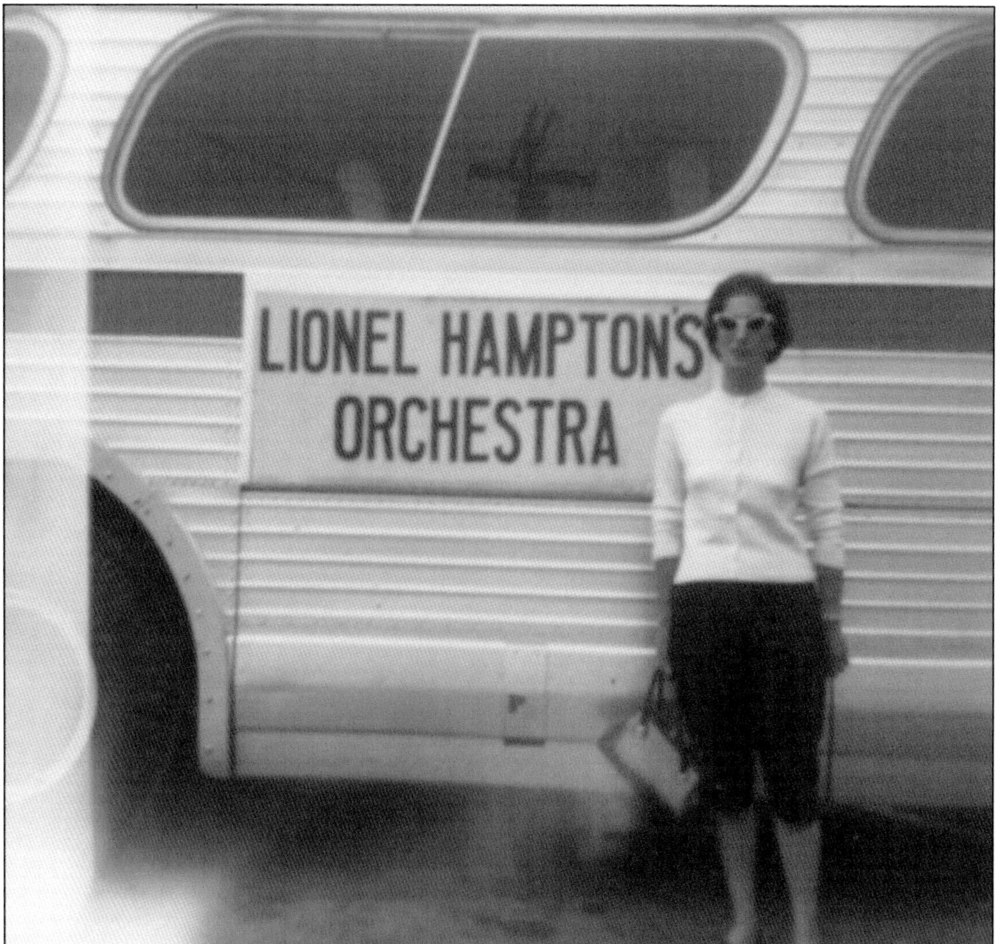

In August 1963, Flora Grassi (Thomas) waits outside the Frolics, dressed in her capri pants to get the autograph of the famous Lionel Hampton to bring to her home in Bradford.

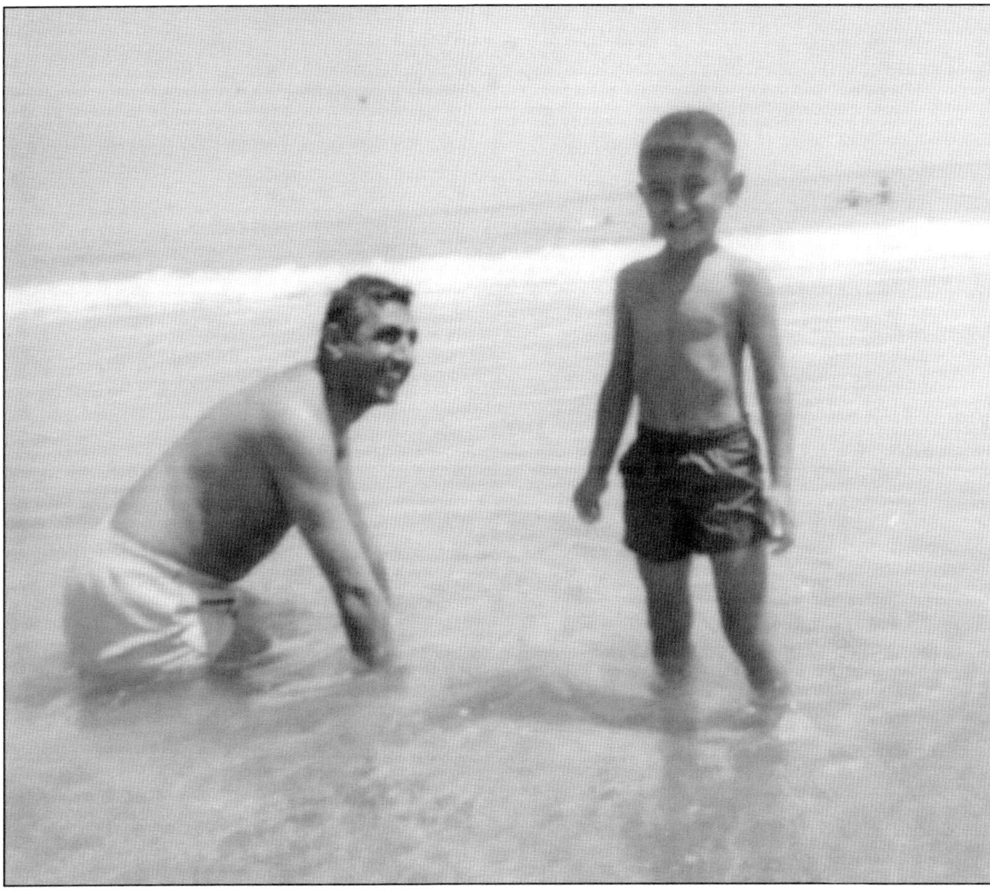

Salem Thomas from Bradford enjoys the happy face of his son, John, at Salisbury Beach in the summer of 1959. The laughter of children is as much a part of the beach as the sand and surf.

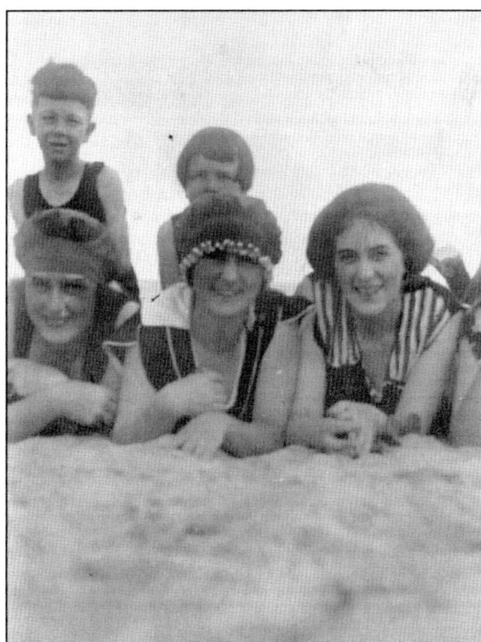

The second woman from the left in this group from Haverhill is Margaret Noonan, who later became an undertaker in Haverhill. The woman on the far left is Marion Donovan, chosen the first Miss Haverhill in 1917.

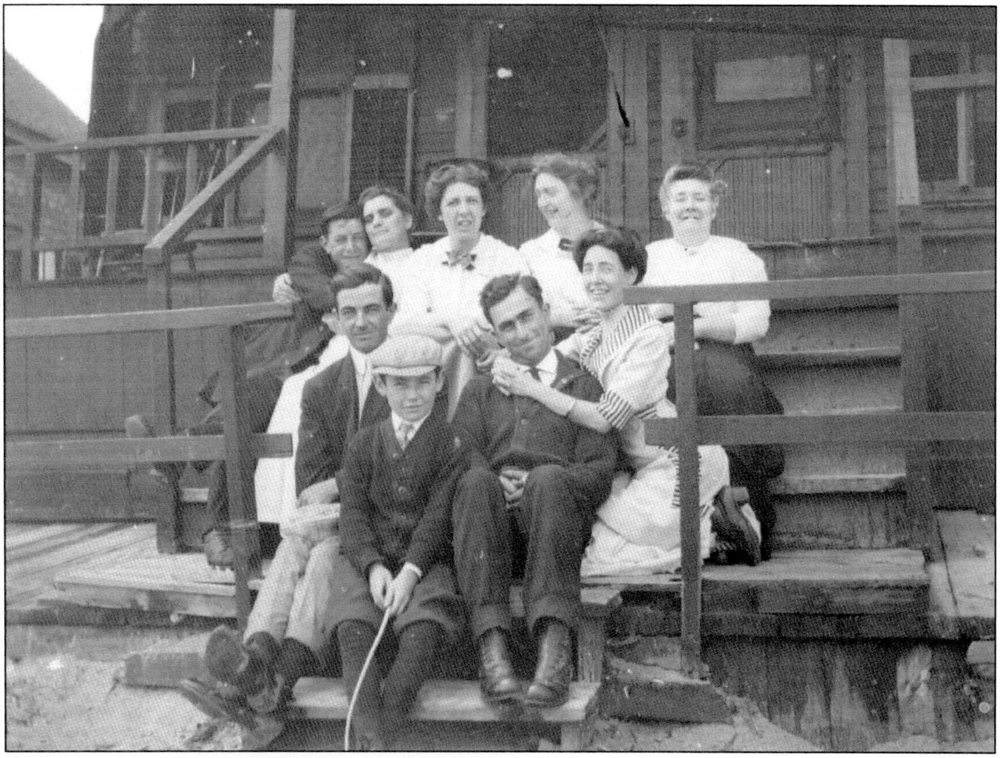

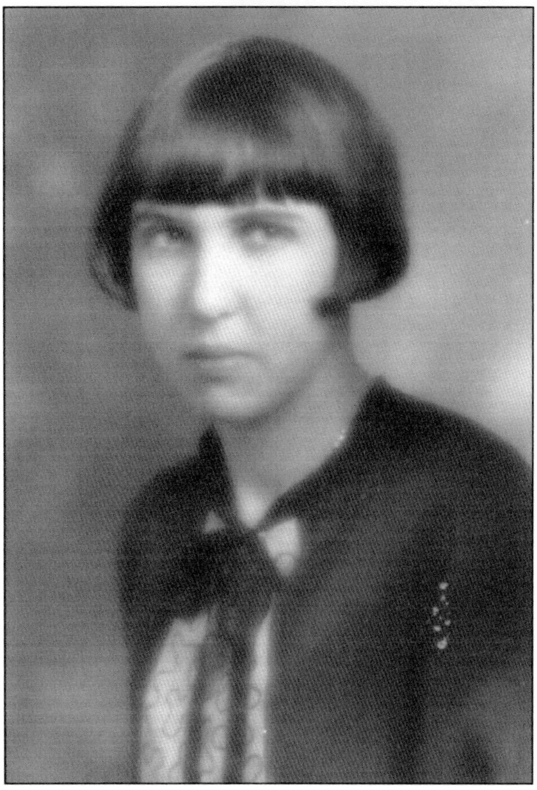

On the steps of a cottage at Salisbury Beach, Nonie Donovan of Lawrence protectively enfolds her husband, Jack Donovan, in her arms. Agnes Donovan is the third woman from the left in the top row. The others are Nonie's relatives from Lawrence. Jack Donovan died only three years later of tuberculosis.

Hazel Lamprey looks demurely into the camera, with her bobbed hair style of the 1920s. Hazel graduated from high school in 1927. At that time, Salisbury did not have a high school, and most students attended school in either Amesbury or Newburyport after the eighth grade.

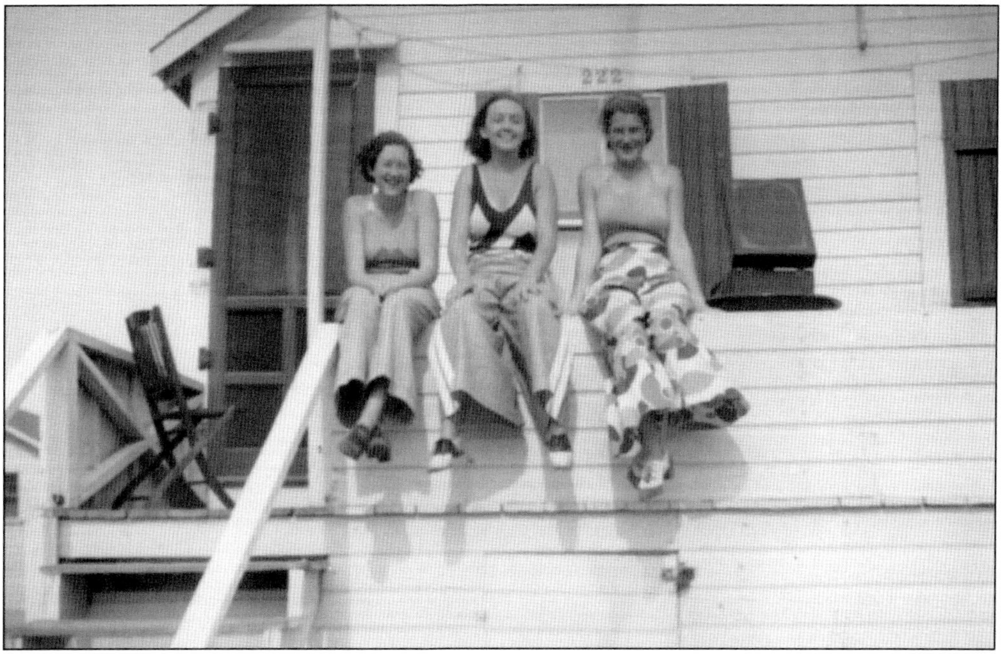

Known as "the Three Musketeers of Salisbury Beach," Ruth Naylor (Harden) from Metheun, Edna Barraclough, and Dot Naylor sit on the porch of Ruth's family home at Salisbury Beach in the summer of 1933. The girls are wearing bell-bottom, flowered pants, a style that became popular again in the late 1960s. It appears they may be listening to records.

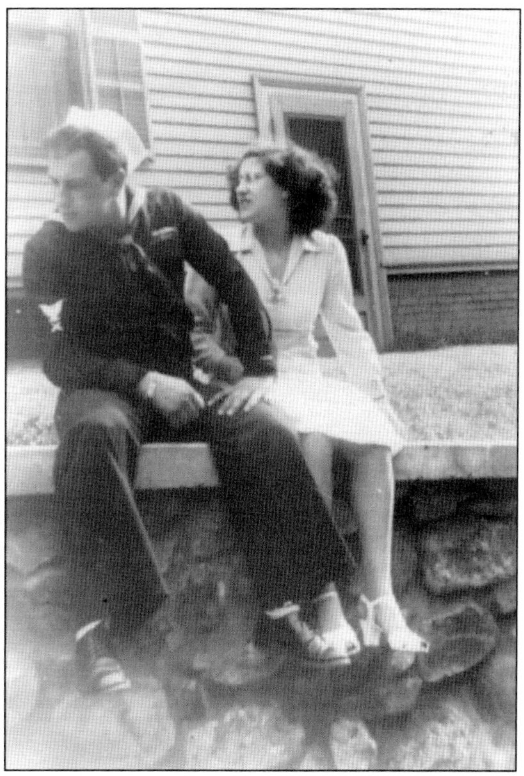

Sam Grassi is on leave from the navy on July 5, 1944. He and his sister, Flora, wait in Haverhill for a ride to the Frolics in Salisbury Beach to celebrate his homecoming. In 1918, Salisbury Beach was declared off-limits to sailors by the navy because of the accessibility of liquor.

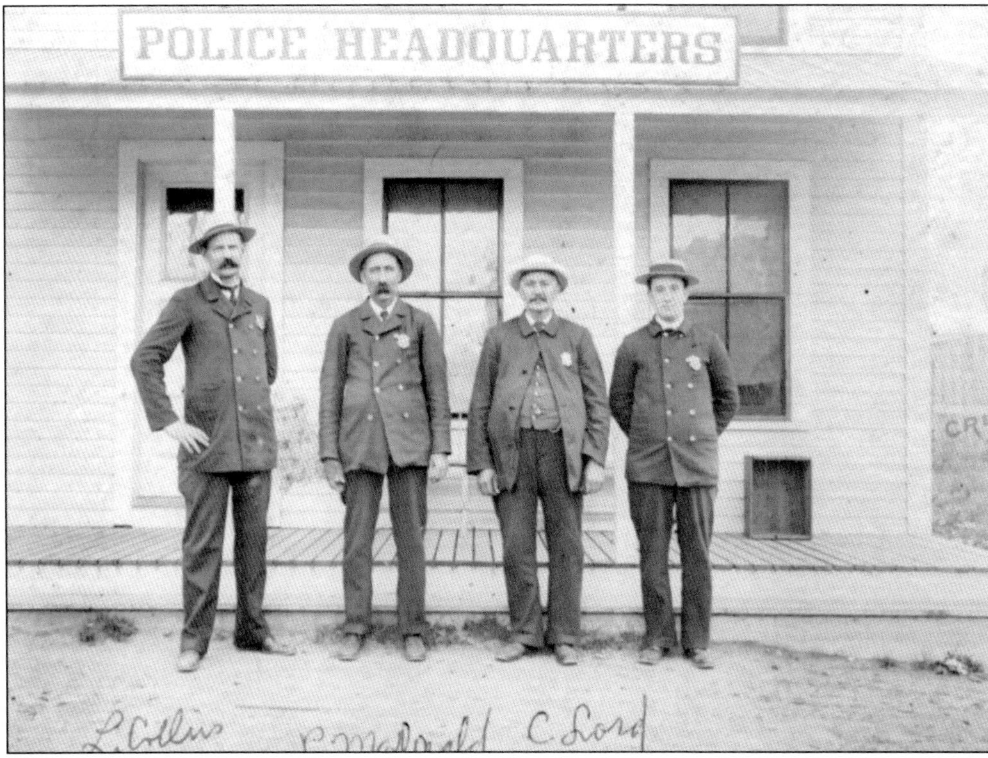

A former Salisbury police force stands outside police headquarters at the beach. They are, from left to right, Off. Levi Collins, Off. P. MacDonald, Off. C. Lord, and Off. D. Hirt.

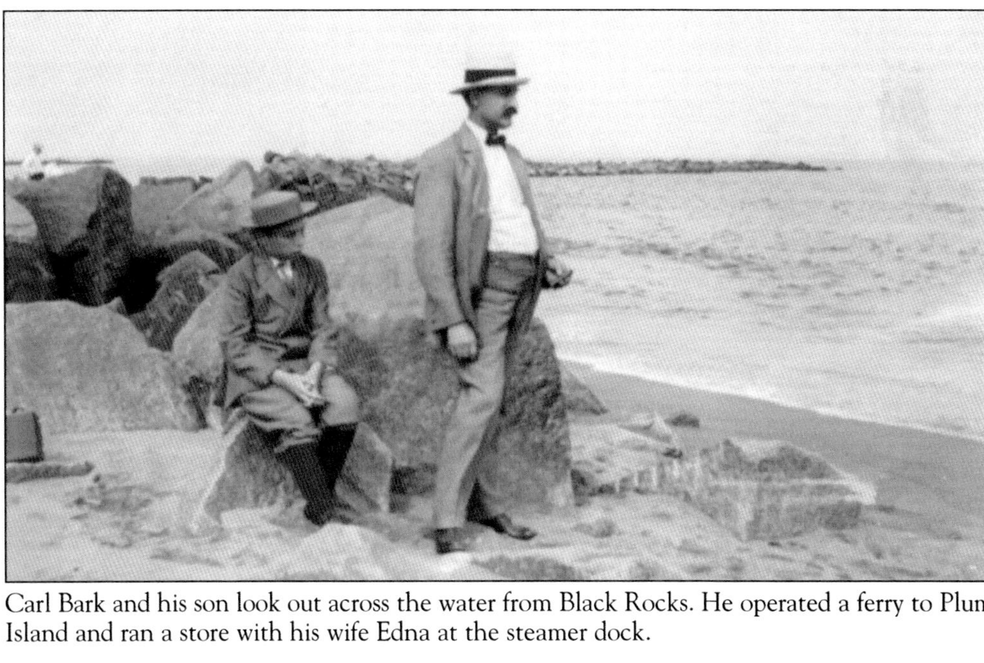

Carl Bark and his son look out across the water from Black Rocks. He operated a ferry to Plum Island and ran a store with his wife Edna at the steamer dock.

John Thomas, from Bradford, in July 1959 looks anxious to dive in to the ultimate Salisbury Beach food a hot dog with all the works. The man sitting in the car is visiting from Utica, New York.

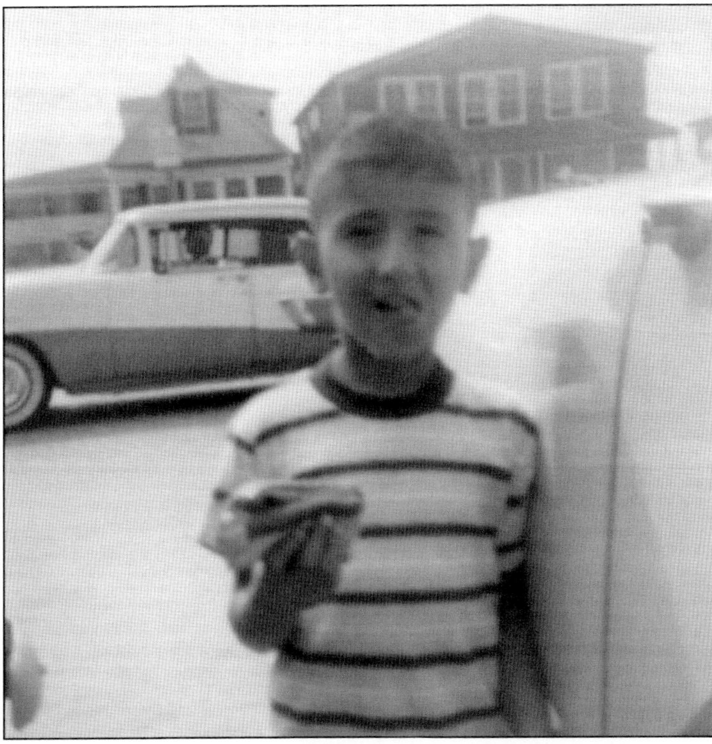

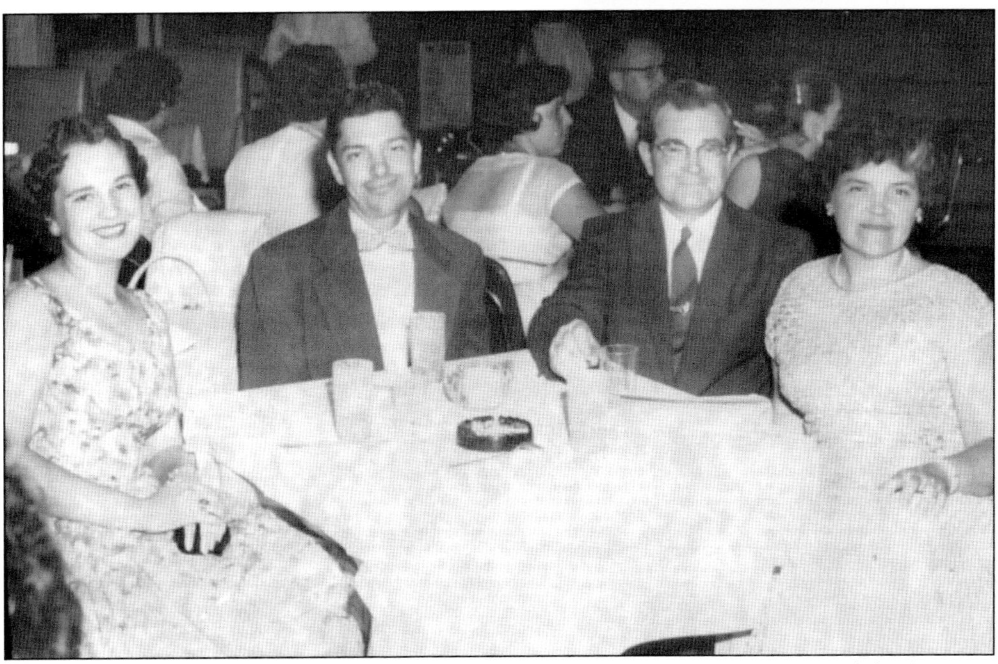

Florence (Burwinkel) Sherman (now of River Park, Florida), John Bevelacqua, Ralph Sherman, and Mary Sherman enjoy cocktails at the Frolics nightclub while waiting to see Liberace perform in the summer of 1960. In 1937, a 75-foot cocktail bar was installed in this building. The *Boston Post* referred to the new Frolics as "an architectural triumph which set an enviable pace for high grade night life entertainment."

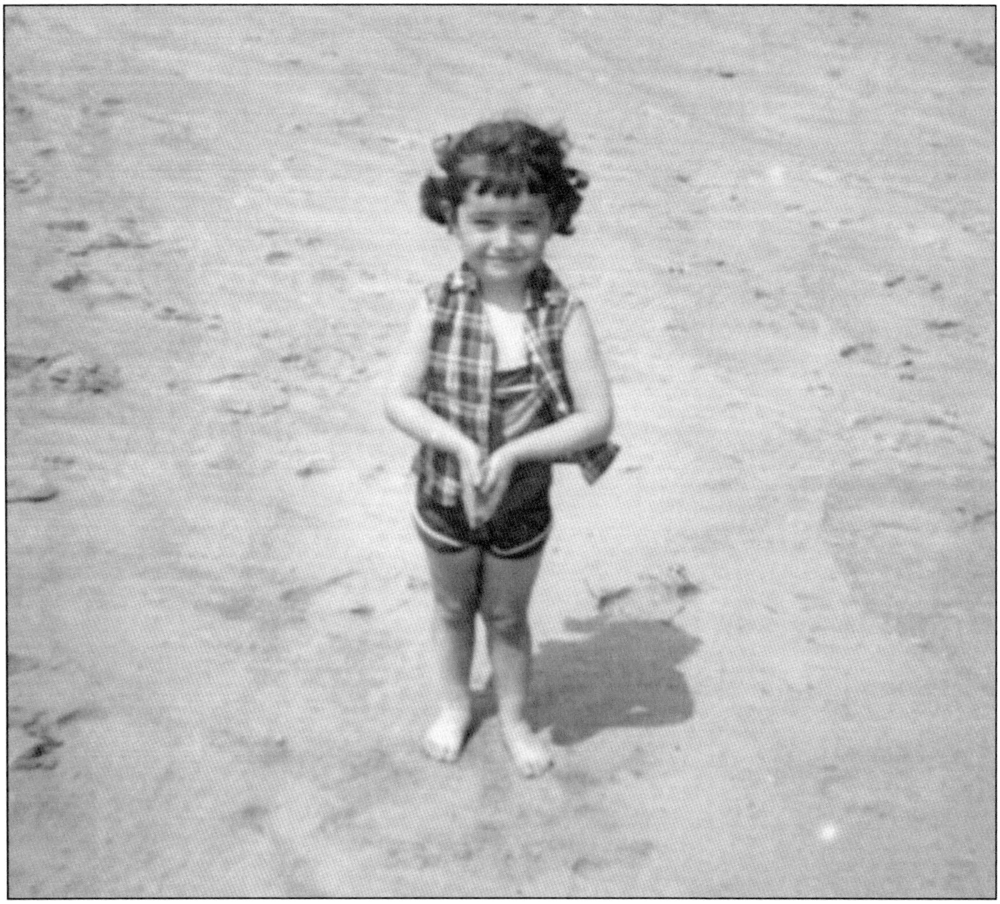

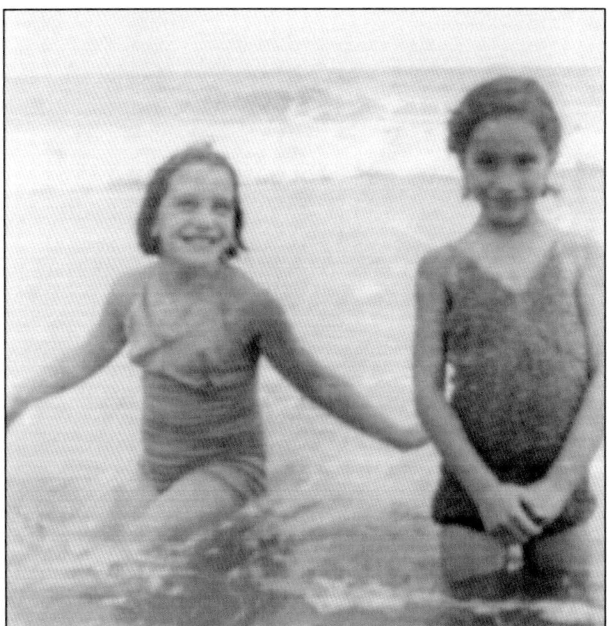

In the summer of 1958, Jamie Lekas, looking adorable in her little beach ensemble, stands on the sands of Salisbury Beach, where her family often visited from Bradford.

Jean Mattenson and Elaine Debrosky, from Haverhill, brave the chilly waters of Salisbury in 1941.

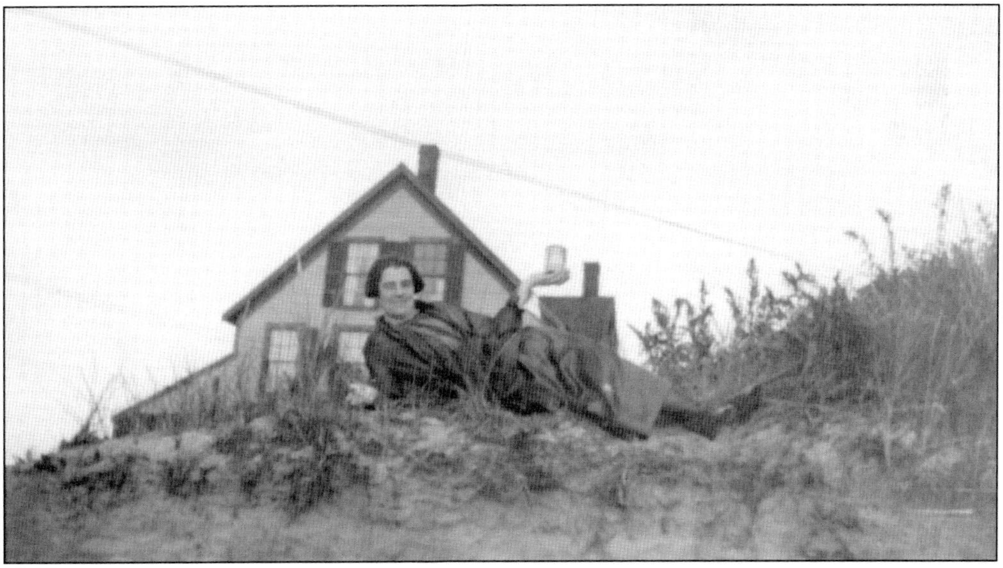

Bessie Pierce holds up a can of an unidentified substance. She is in front of the second house built by the government for her father, William Pierce, the range light keeper, so he could be closer to the range light pole on Black Rocks. Bessie was the first girl to be born at Black Rocks.

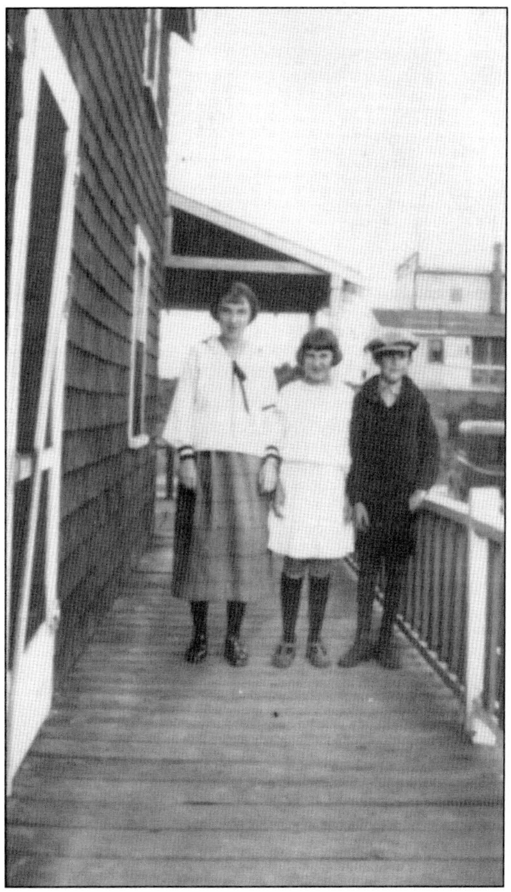

On the morning of Memorial Day 1922, Elsie, Hazel (arrayed in a light blue voile dress made especially for the celebration), and Charlie Lamprey are standing on the porch of their cottage, the Cayuga. Their cottage was moved from the south end to the north end of the beach.

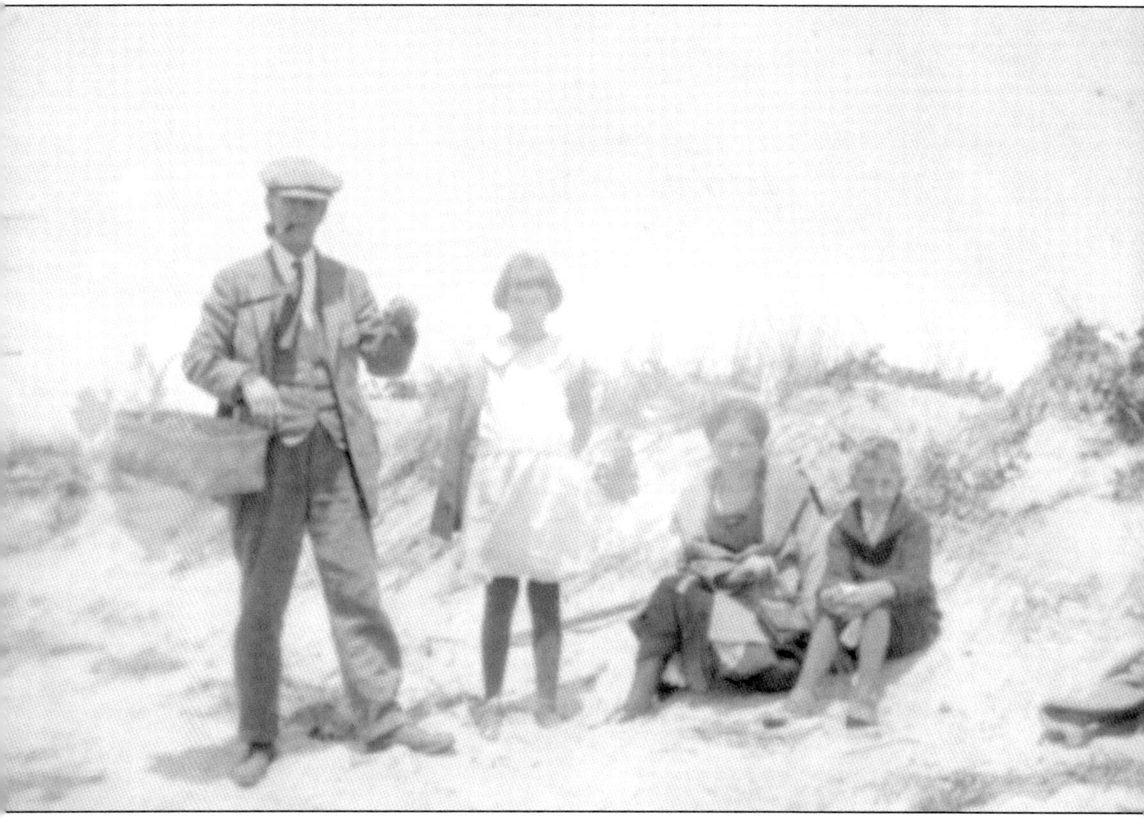

Charles Lamprey, Hazel Lamprey, stepmother Ella Lee, and Charlie Lamprey are crabbing at Butler's Toothpick at the Black Rocks. Sand dunes appear as the backdrop in the snapshot as "Pa" holds up his catch.

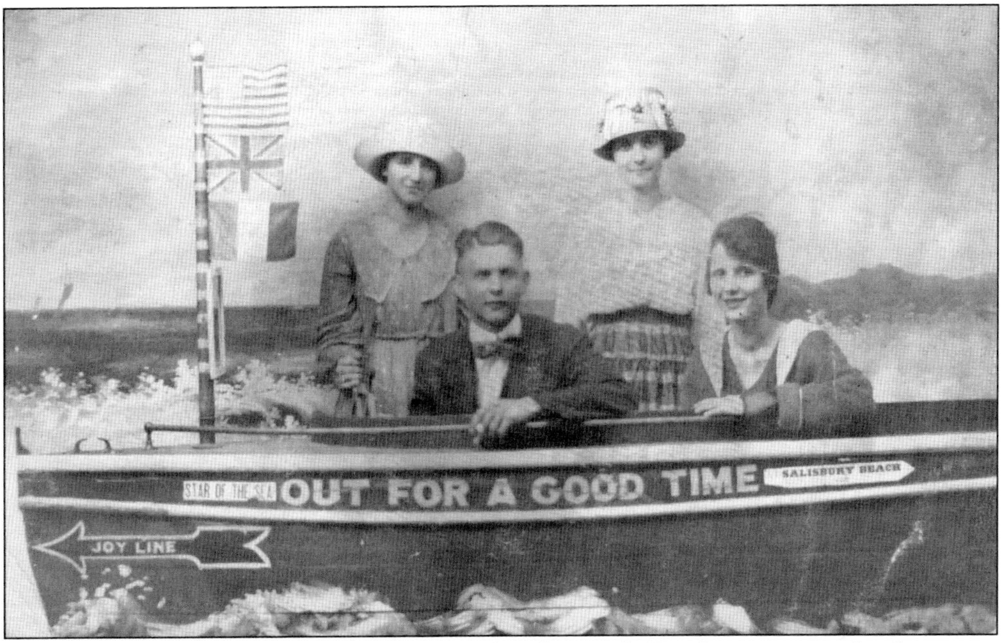

Chase's, a photography shop at Salisbury Beach, advertised, "Purchase a personalized souvenir to remember your time at the beach." This photograph may have been taken at Chase's.

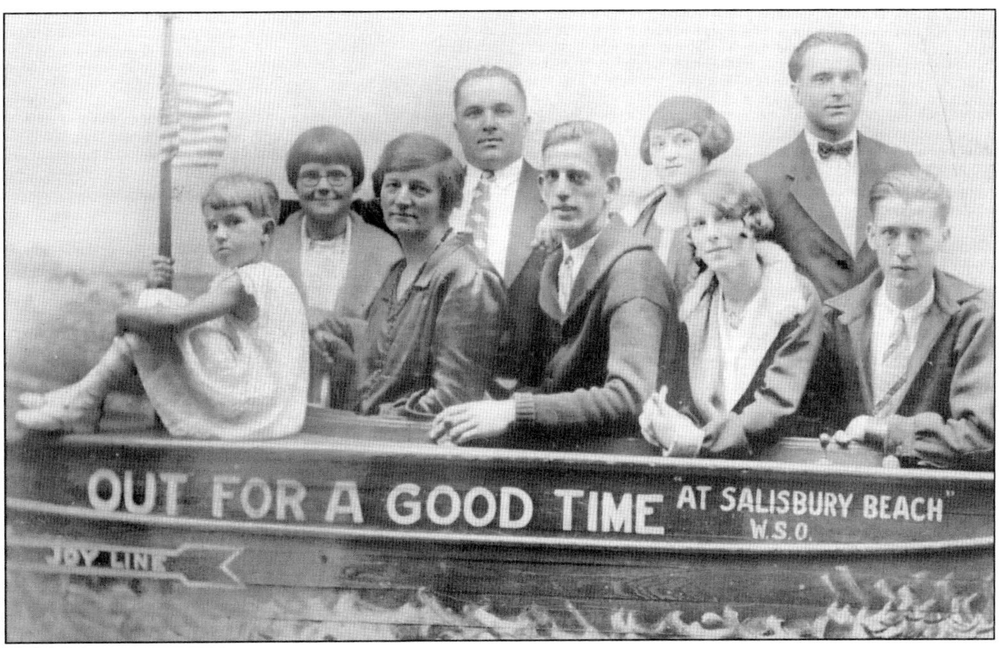

A souvenir photograph is similar to the above novelty, with a notation on the back: "Ralph Sweeney's Old Time Photographs." It is not clear whether Chase's and Sweeney's were competing stores or the pictures were taken at different times.

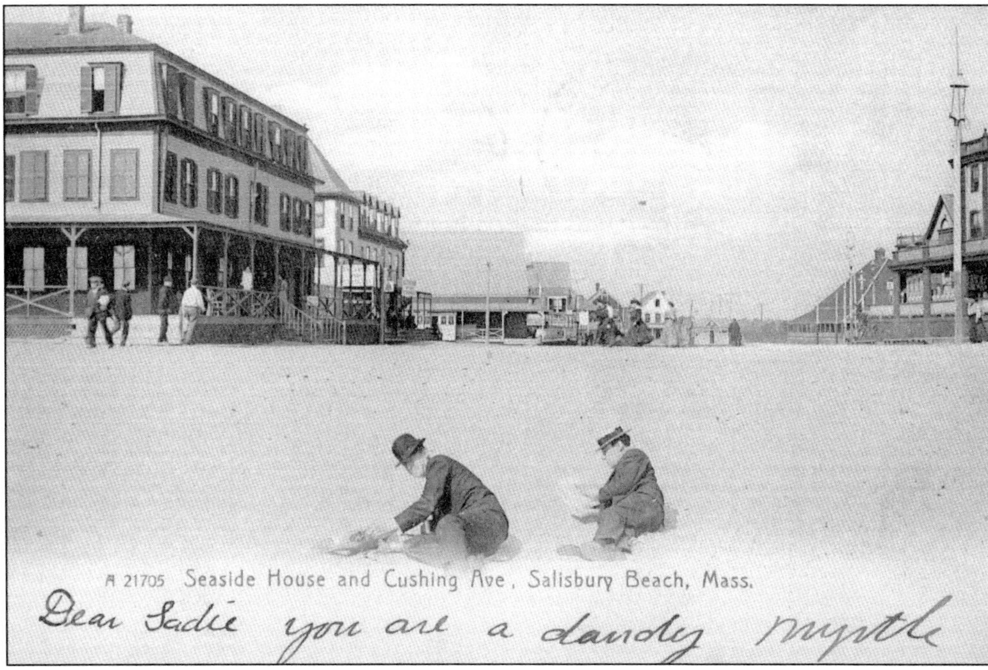

These two gentlemen appear on many earlier Salisbury Beach postcards. In this scene, the models are dressed in their Sunday best and are relaxing at the center of the beach. This picture was taken before the fire of 1913, when Victorian elegance was still prominent.

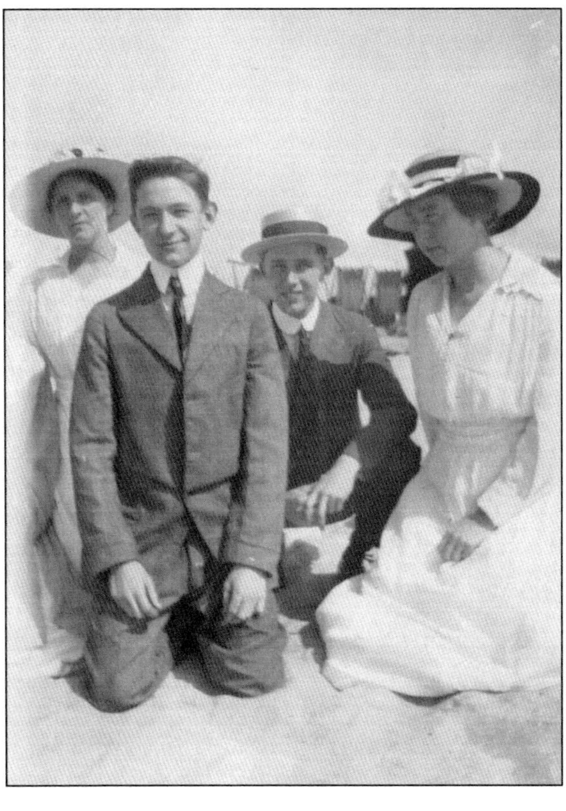

Frank Hayes of South Boston is surrounded by some of his friends. His future wife, Marion Donovan from Haverhill, is seated on the right. An outing to Salisbury Beach was often a way for people to enjoy getting together with friends on Sunday afternoon.

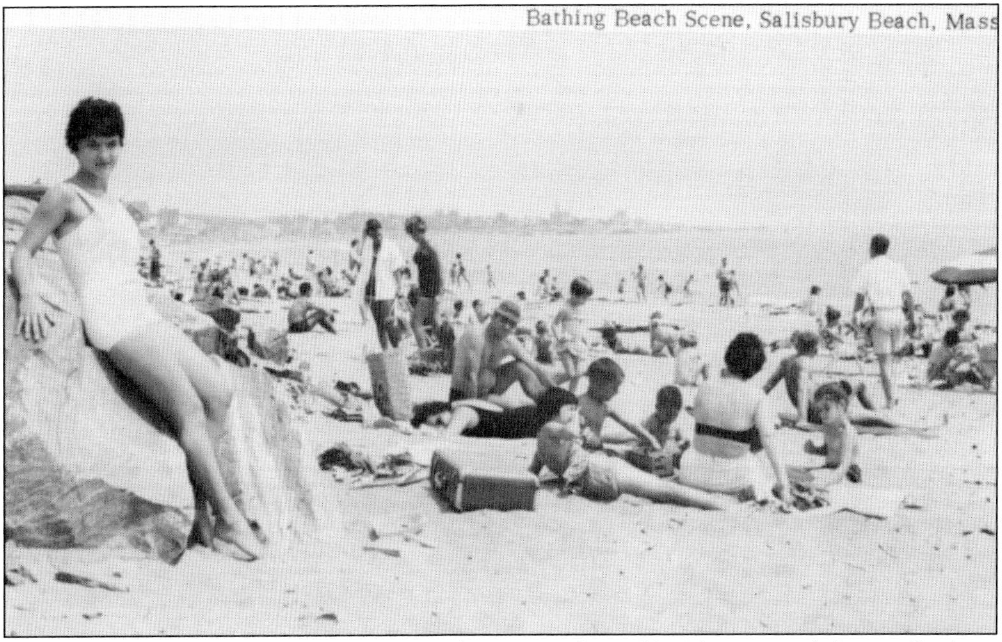

The beach appears to be filled with sun worshippers in the 1950s. The postcard shows a "bathing beach scene," but actually shows many families picnicking and enjoying the ocean together. Sandwiches could be picked up at Mickey's delicatessen at the corner of Driftway if a family forgot to pack food. Packy's Diner in the center offered a great turkey sandwich for only 75¢.

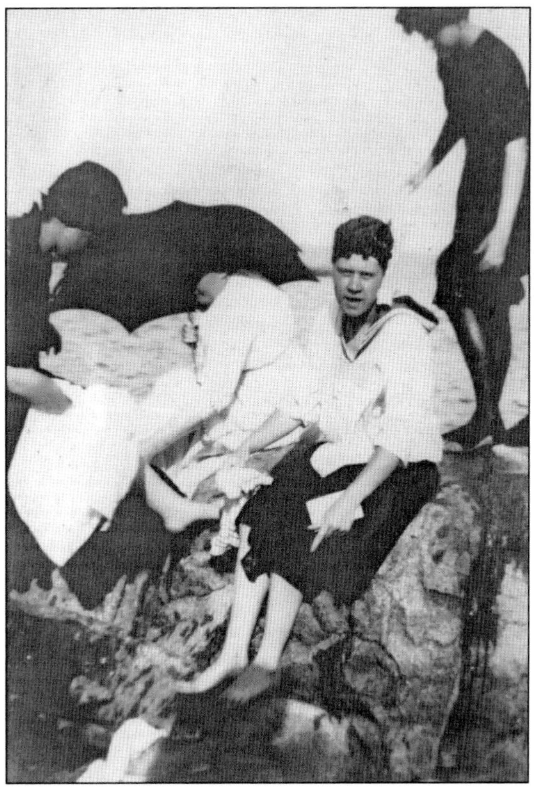

A group of students from Bradford perches on the a jetty with friends in 1911. Sand is removed from the feet and shoes are hastily put back on before the arrival of the steamer to return them to Bradford after a fun-filled day at Salisbury Beach.

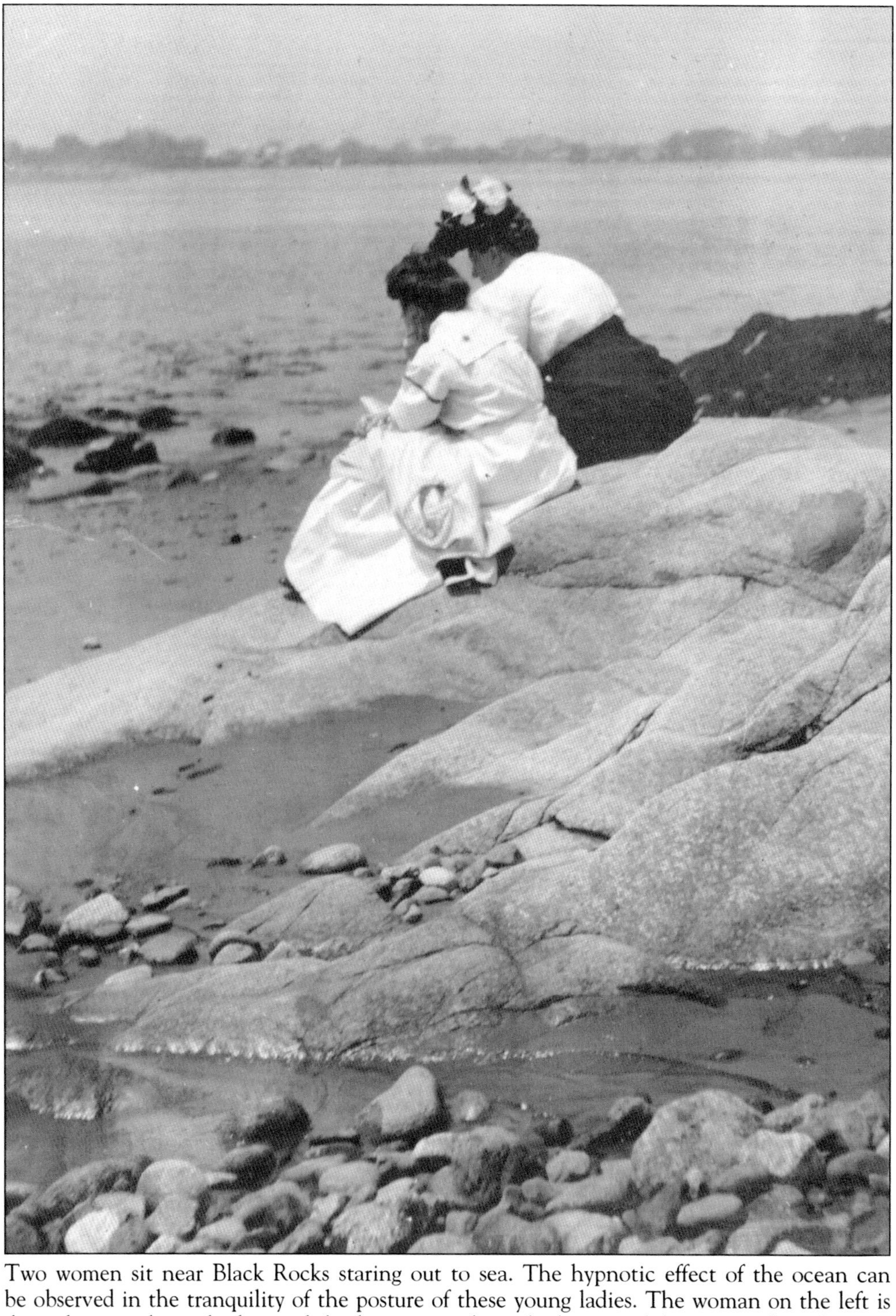

Two women sit near Black Rocks staring out to sea. The hypnotic effect of the ocean can be observed in the tranquility of the posture of these young ladies. The woman on the left is dressed in a sailor-style dress, while the one on the right has opted for a more formal attire, including a bonnet adorned with flowers. This photograph was taken in 1912, when white was a very popular color for summer attire.

A young child from Lawrence sits on the sand in 1925. He looks very happy to be at Salisbury Beach in his black romper outfit. Today, a Children's Day is still held at Salisbury Beach in August. Salisbury Beach has long been a paradise for children of all ages.

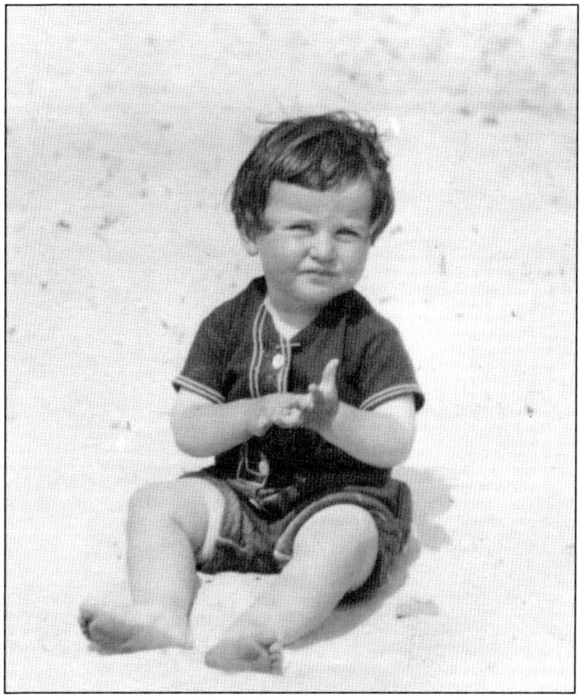

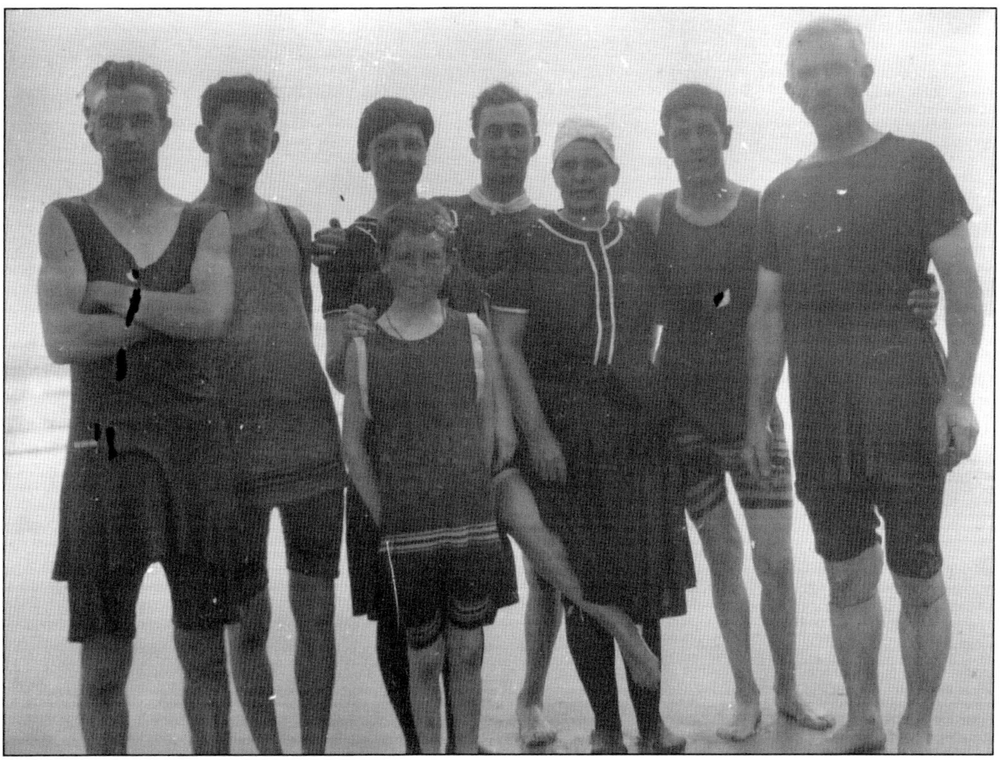

The third person from the left is Nonie Murphy from Lawrence. Fourth from the left is Michael John "Jack" Donovan from Bradford. The man at the far right is Dan Donovan. The rest of the people are Nonie's relatives from Lawrence.

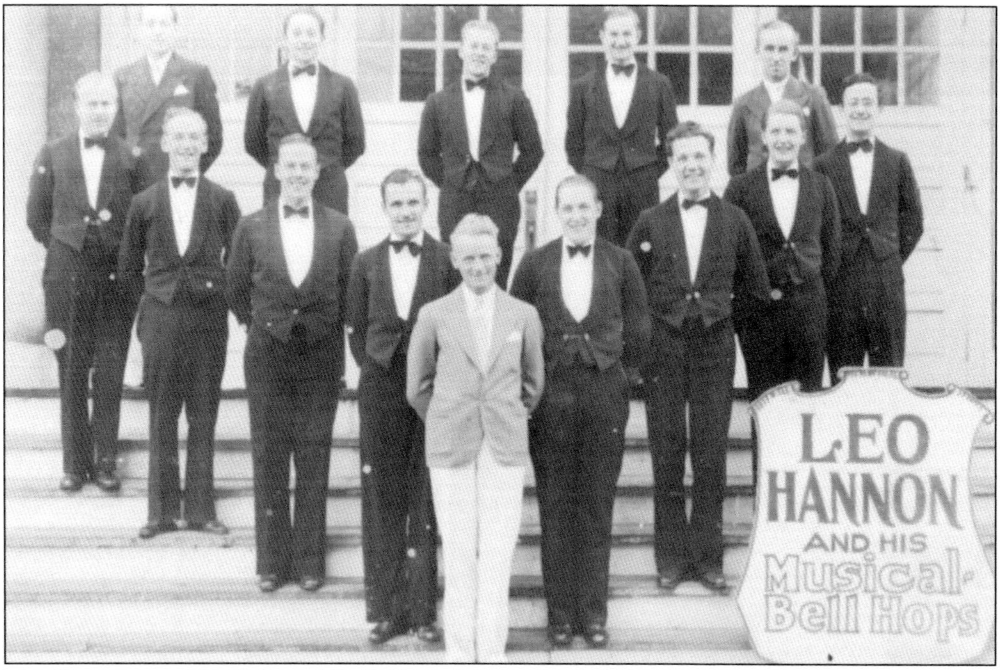

Leo Hannon and his Musical Bell Hops from Lake Whalom in Lunenburg, Massachusetts, played the Ocean Echo and later performed at the Frolics nightclub. The Ocean Echo often held midnight dances. In 1933, when this picture was taken, admission to the dance cost 50¢. The billboard advertised eight hours of dancing so guests "could have danced all night."

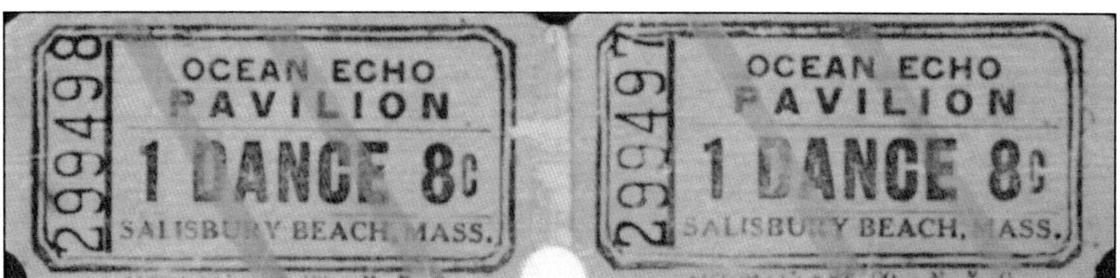

These tickets from the Ocean Echo dance pavilion date to when couples paid for each dance separately. At this time, the cost was 8¢ a dance. A disclaimer on the back of the ticket says, "The management reserves the right to revoke the license granted by this ticket by refunding the purchase price."

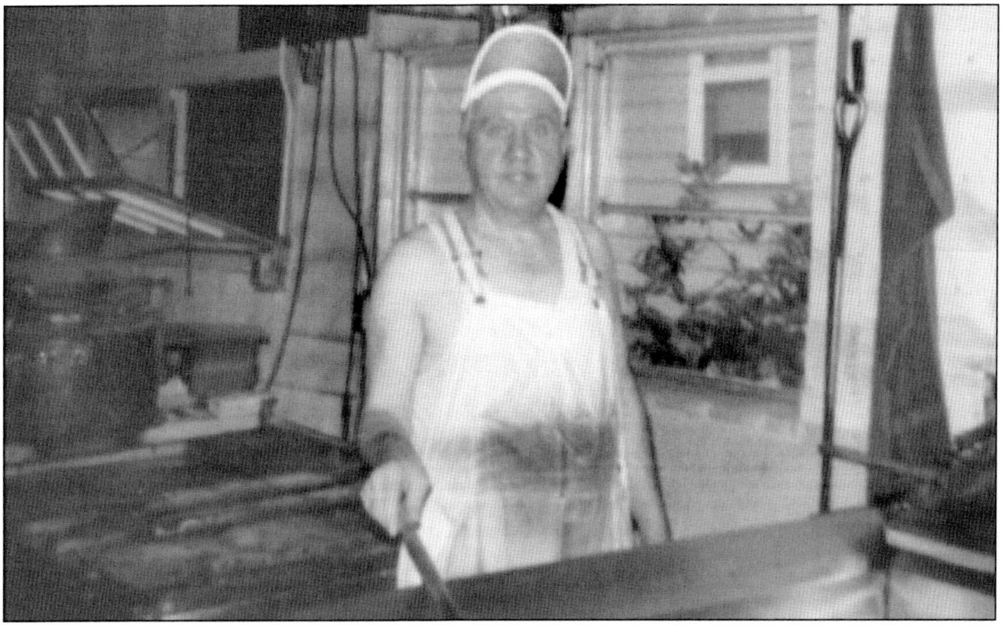

Richard Harden is shown frying the potato chips for the Wonder Potato Chip Company. At the time of this picture, the company had been in operation for 43 years. His parents founded the business and he took it over full time in 1940. He and his wife, Ruth, who bagged and sold the chips, operated the company until 1982.

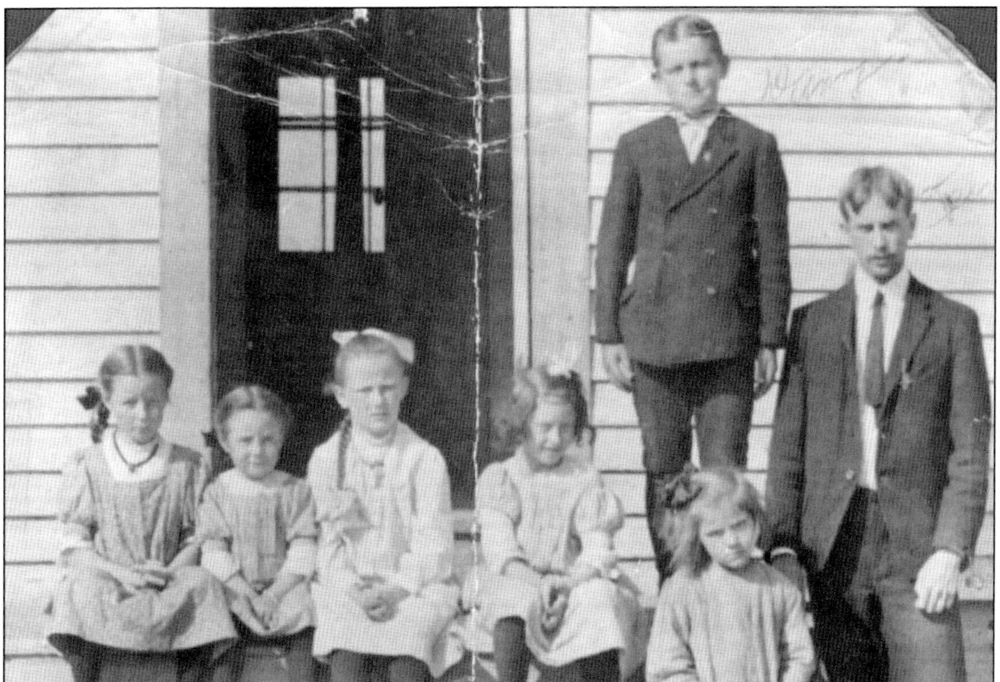

Poised on the stairs of the first school at Salisbury Beach in the 1900s are, from left to right, Gertrude Pierce, Bessie Pierce, Christine Souther, one unidentified student, Danny Pierce (standing), Matilda Pierce, and the teacher. This was a one-room schoolhouse.

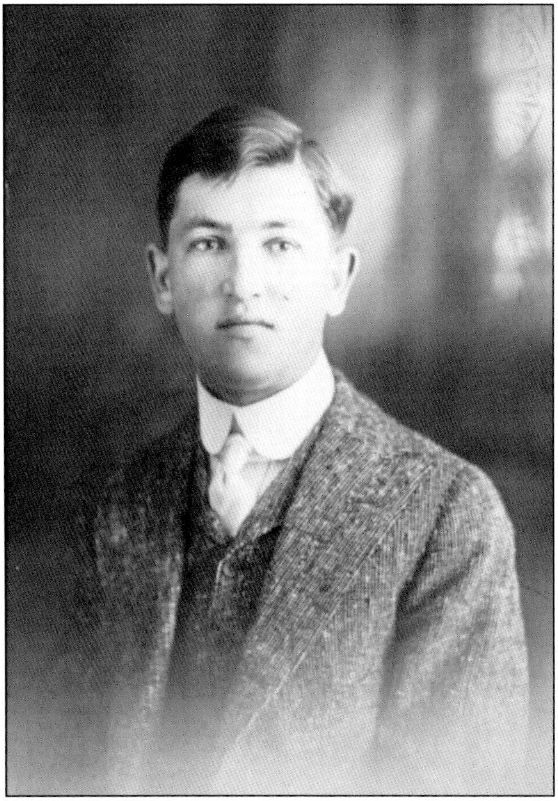

Twenty-one-year-old Maurice Lamprey sent this postcard home to his mother in 1915 from Washington, D.C., Maurice, who grew up at the beach, went to Washington to work for the U.S. Customs Service.

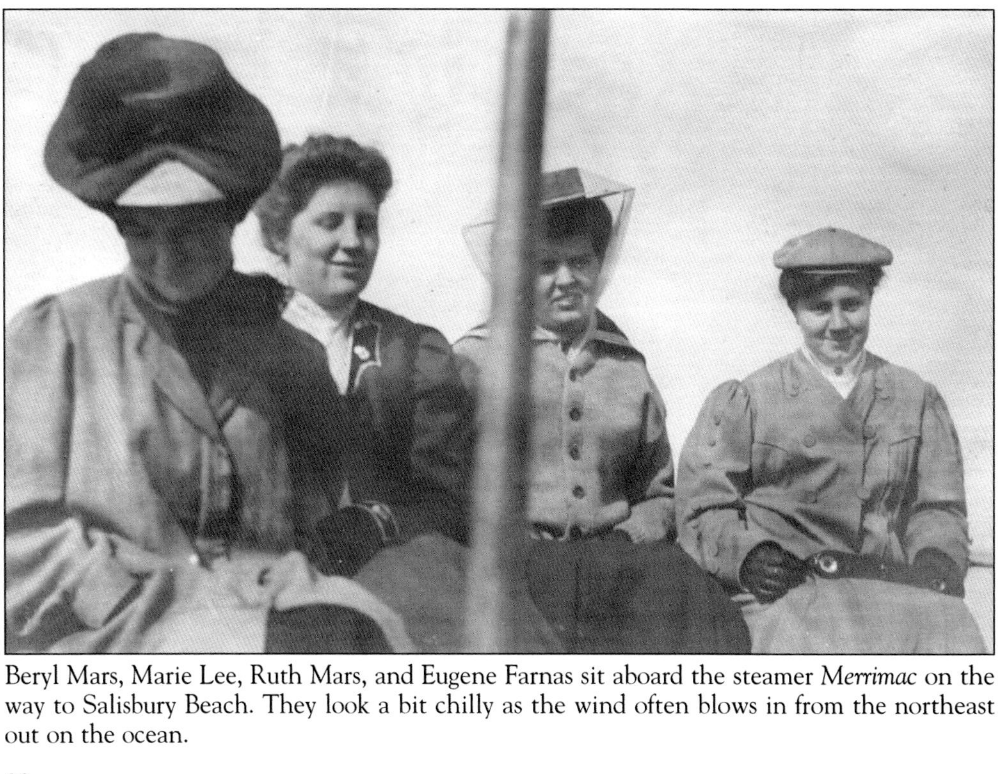

Beryl Mars, Marie Lee, Ruth Mars, and Eugene Farnas sit aboard the steamer *Merrimac* on the way to Salisbury Beach. They look a bit chilly as the wind often blows in from the northeast out on the ocean.

Marion Donovan and Margaret Noonan (wearing their fancy beach hats to protect their bobbed hair) and their friend in stripes illustrate the festive atmosphere of Salisbury Beach with their dress and smiles.

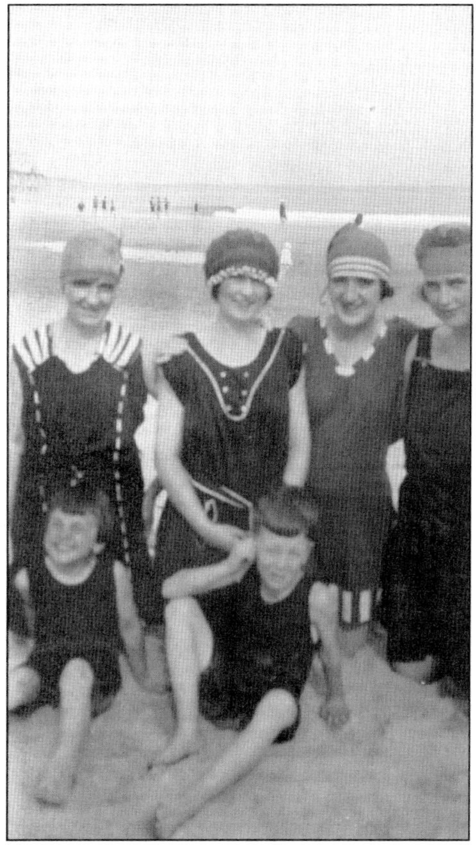

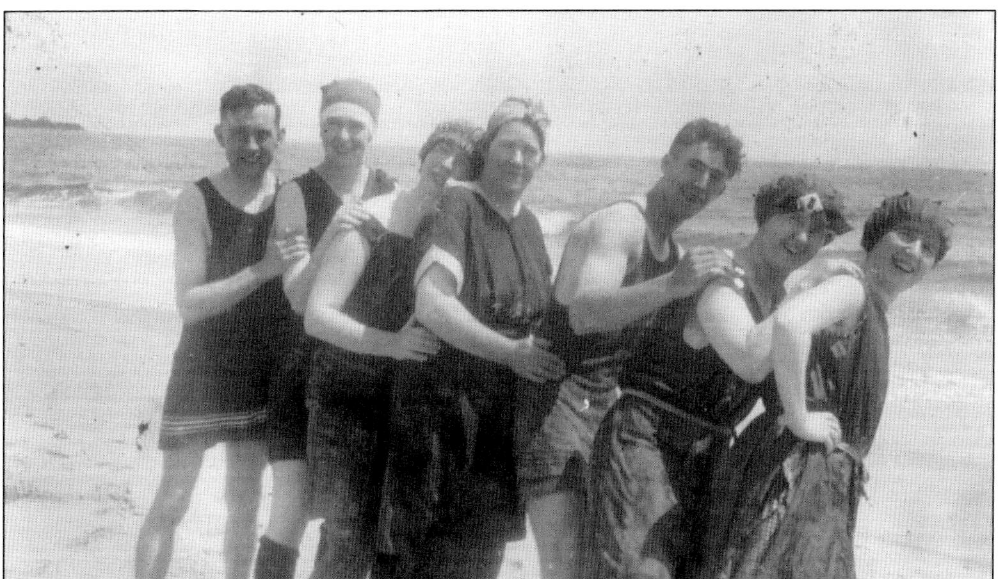

Frank Noyes, Marie Donovan, Marion Donovan, Nora Donovan (in an old-style suit), Harold Donovan, Margaret McCarthy, and Nellie McCarthy form a line at the beach. The McCarthys from Pennsylvania were visiting their Haverhill Donovan cousins.

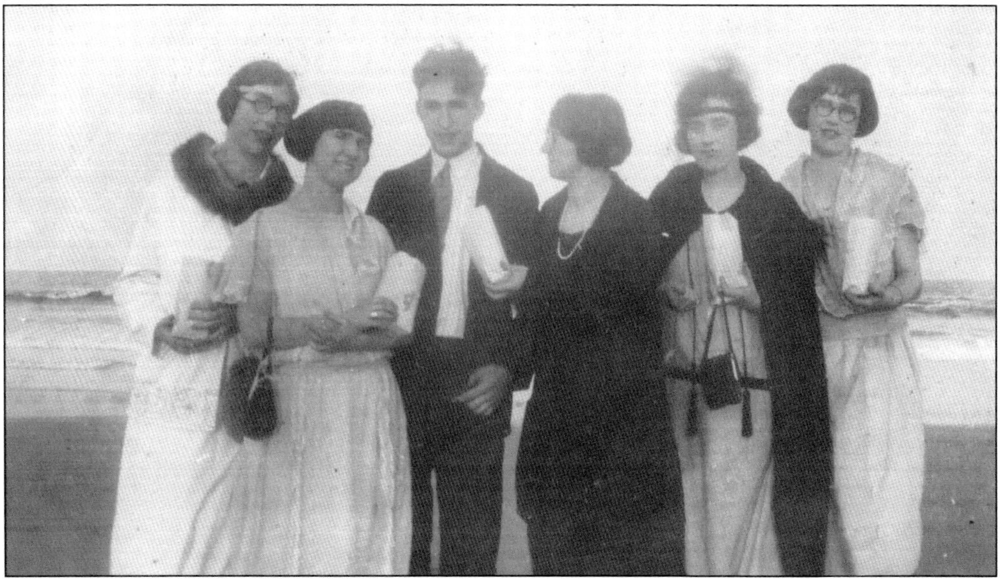

Agnes Donovan, Nellie McCarthy, Harold Donovan, Marzares McCarthy, Marion Donovan, and Marie Donovan stand elegantly dressed for a night at Salisbury Beach—possibly the midnight dance at the Ocean Echo.

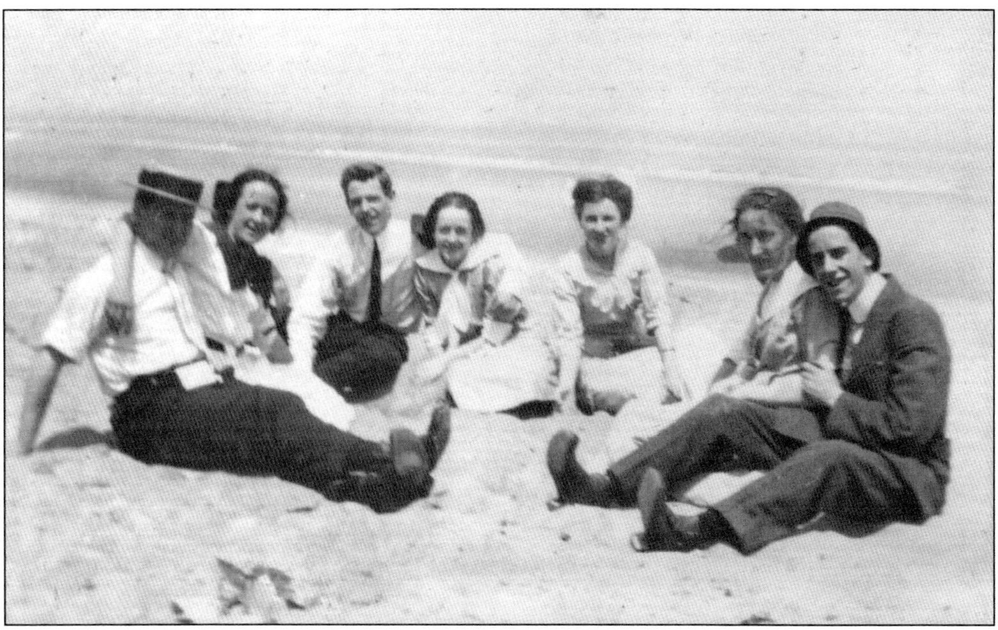

These seniors from St. James High School of Haverhill sit in a circle on the sand oblivious to their fine clothes. It looks like it might have been a chilly day at the beach.

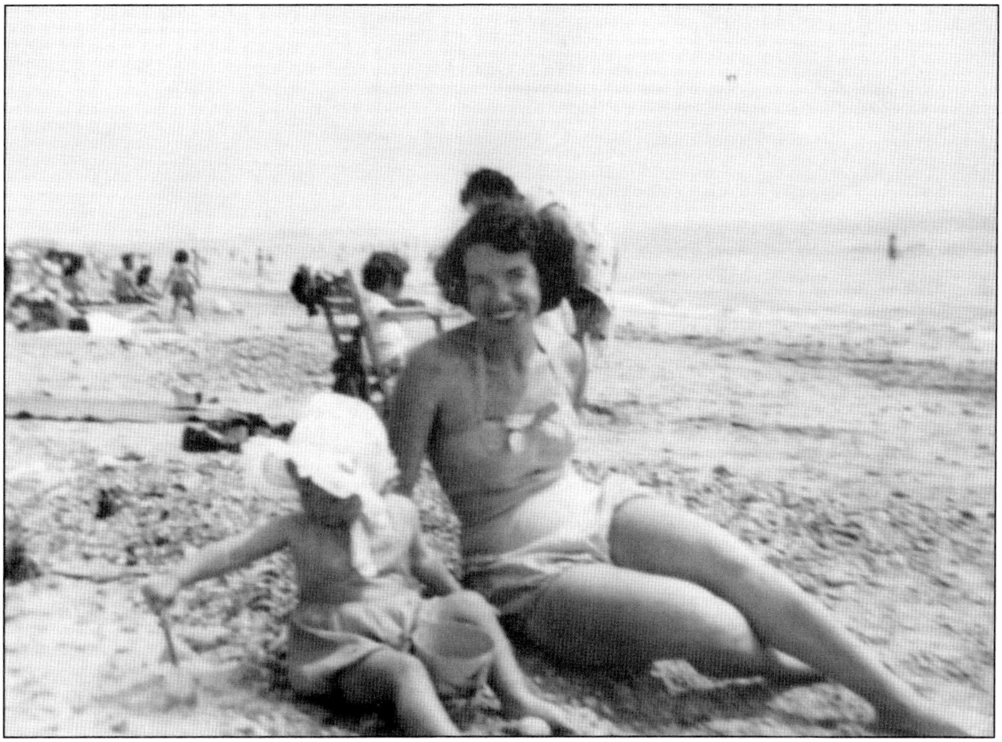

Pamela Mutch (18 months old) digs in the sand with her mom, Ann Mutch, sporting a fashionable bathing suit with romper-style legs from the summer of 1951. They came up from Malden to enjoy a day at the beach. The bikini, although popular in Europe, did not appear on the American shores until the 1960s.

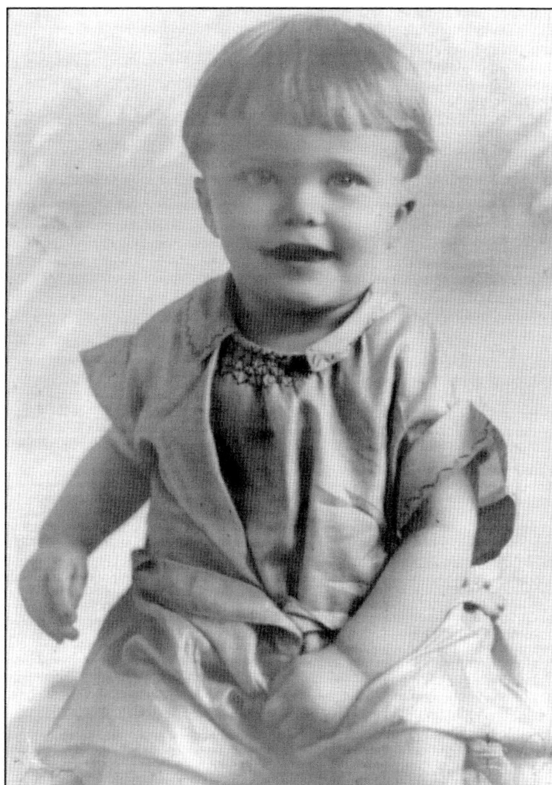

Robert E. Mutch from Melrose, Massachusetts, poses in his swimsuit at Salisbury Beach in 1927. His outfit is the typical batiste swimming clothes of a toddler in the 1920s. He grew up to join the air force and was the recruiting officer in Newburyport and Salisbury in the mid-1950s.

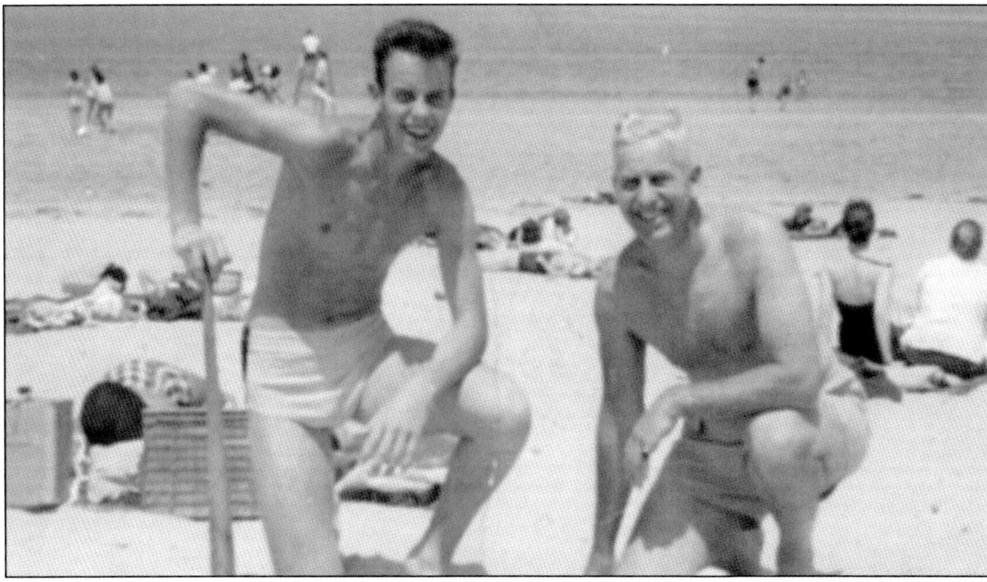

John C. Stevens III and his father, John C. Stevens Jr., from Lunenburg get ready for a game of baseball at Salisbury Beach. Salisbury has been a place for family gatherings since the original Great Gathering.

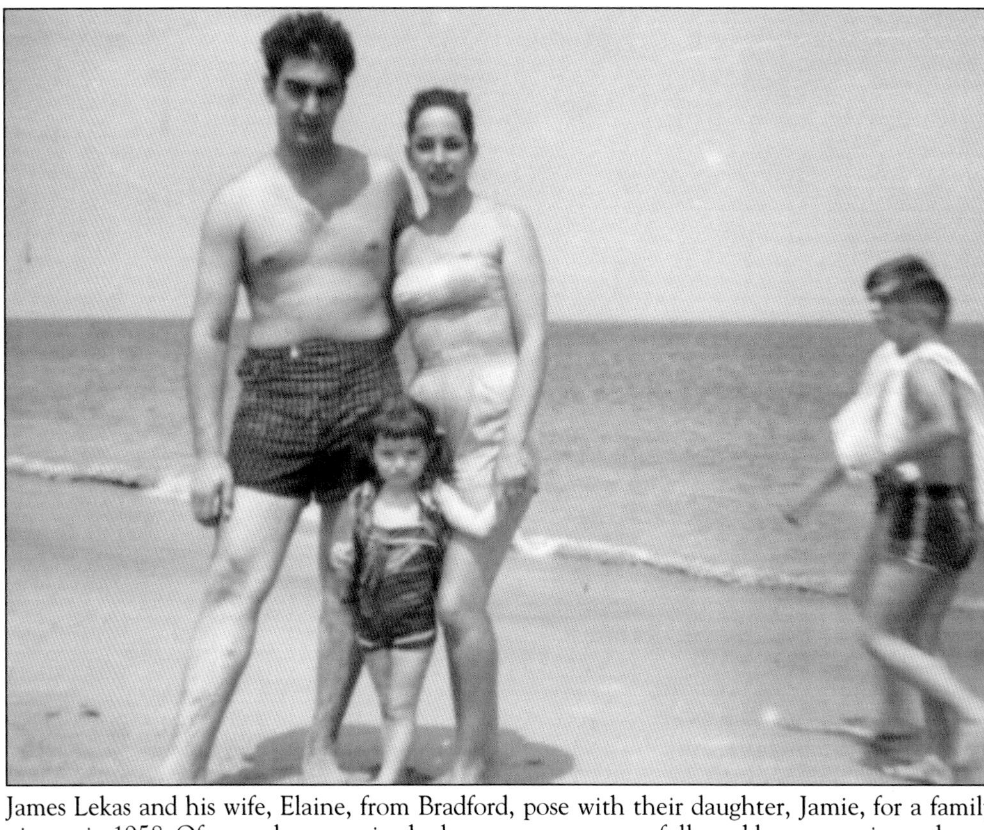

James Lekas and his wife, Elaine, from Bradford, pose with their daughter, Jamie, for a family picture in 1958. Often, a day spent in the hot summer sun was followed by an evening at home smothered in Noxzema, a 1950s treatment for a sunburn.

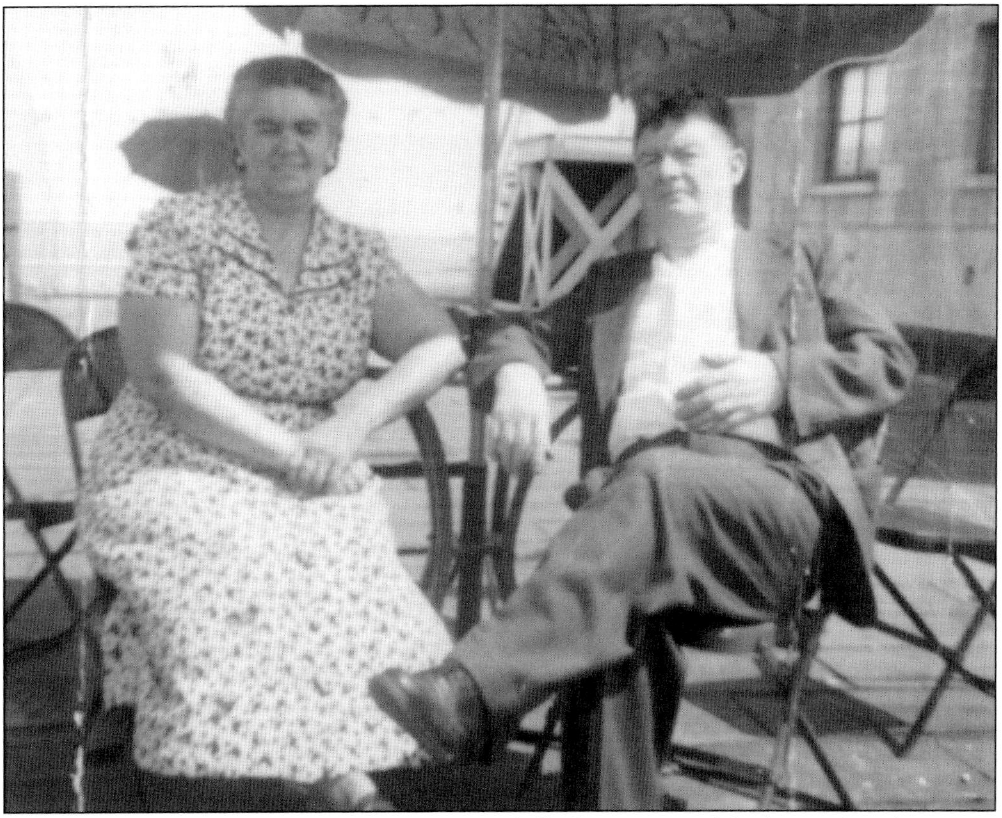

Anna Lekas and her husband, John, from Haverhill, share a spot of shade at a friend's cottage at Salisbury Beach. Both Anna and John came from Greece as children. Like most grandparents of the 1950s, they seldom sported a bathing suit at the beach.

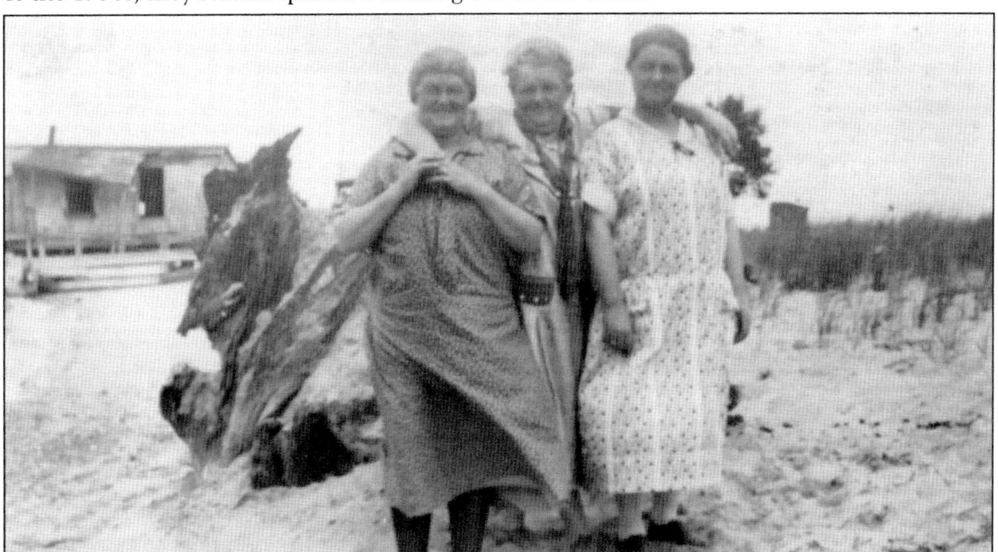

Matilda Pierce Merrill, Elizabeth Ward Pierce, and Gertrude Pierce Eaton take a position for a picture in front of a giant piece of driftwood at Black Rocks in 1920.

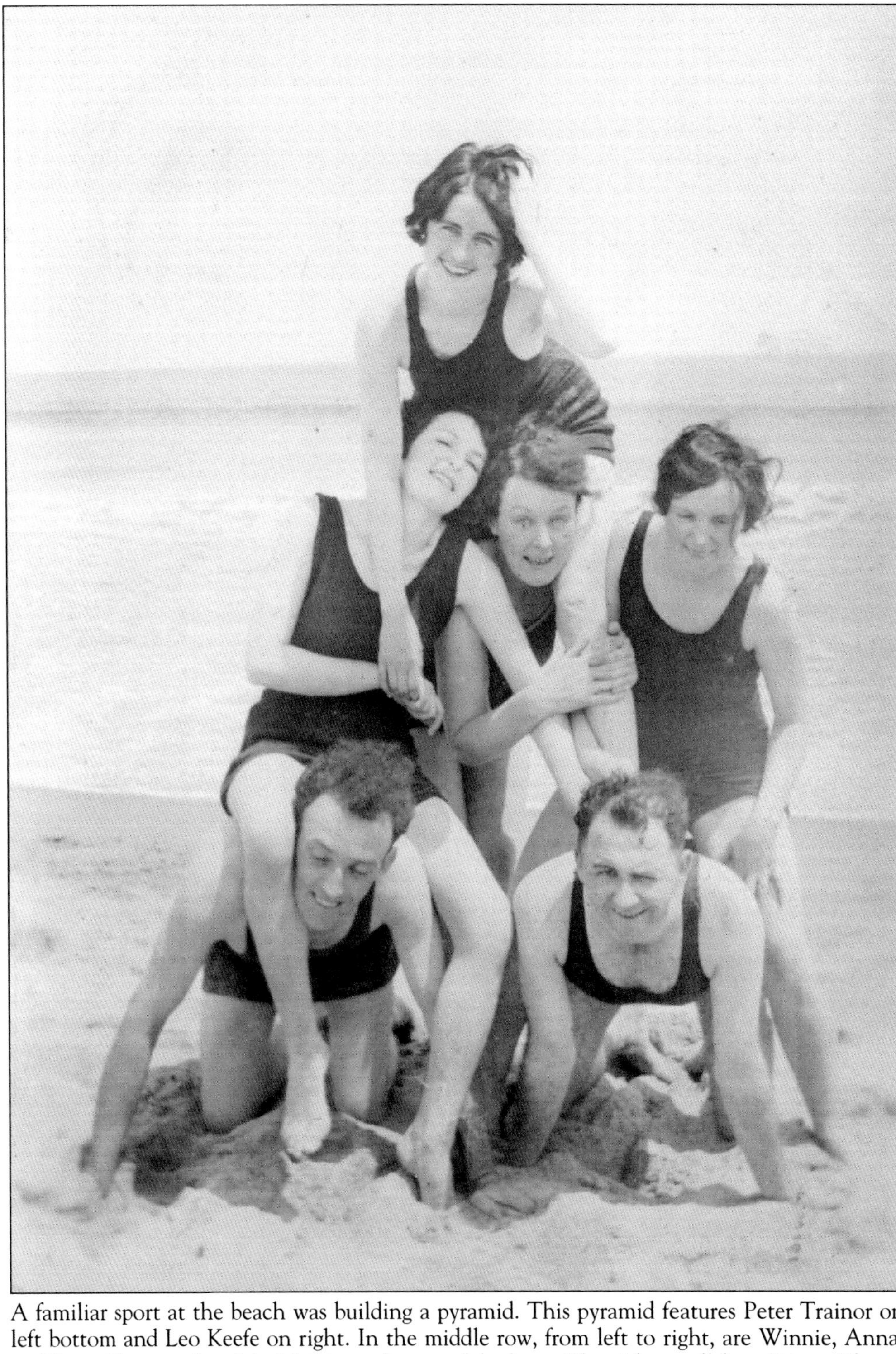

A familiar sport at the beach was building a pyramid. This pyramid features Peter Trainor on left bottom and Leo Keefe on right. In the middle row, from left to right, are Winnie, Anna, and Betty Trainor. Ann MacNeil is on the top of the heap. The girls are all from Prince Edward Island, Canada.

Six

If You Are Young at Heart

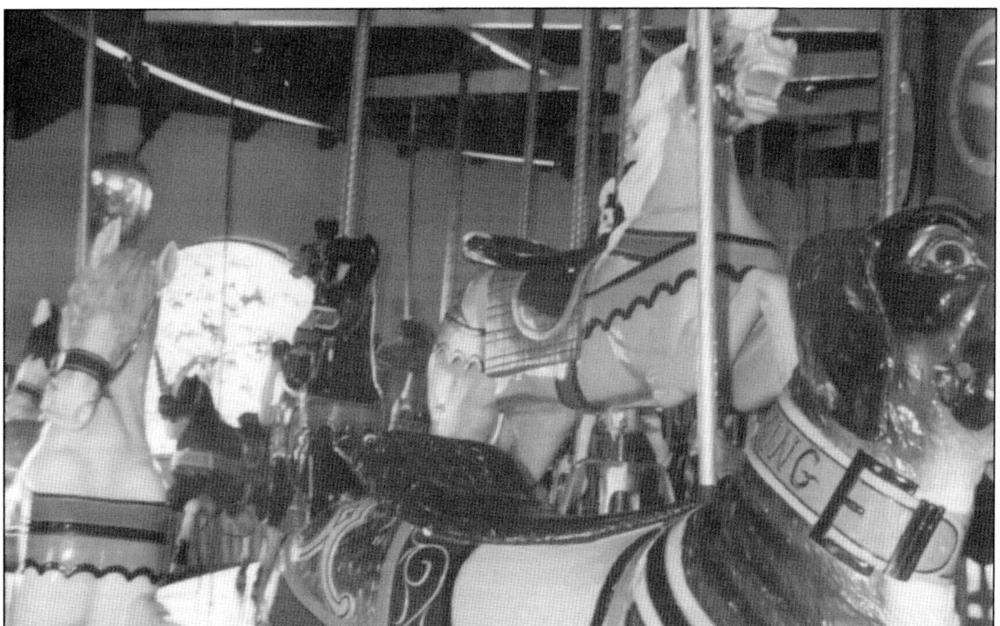

The Broadway Flying Horses carousel was built *c.* 1890. Is believed to have operated at Coney Island for several years before arriving at Salisbury Beach. In 1913, the original Culver Flying Horses were destroyed by the beach fire. The frame was then fitted with 46 animals carved by Charles Looff. A new carousel building was constructed in 1914, serving as a dance hall until the new Culver Flying Horses arrived later that year. The Rogers family bought the horses in 1933 and operated them under the name of the Broadway Flying Horses.

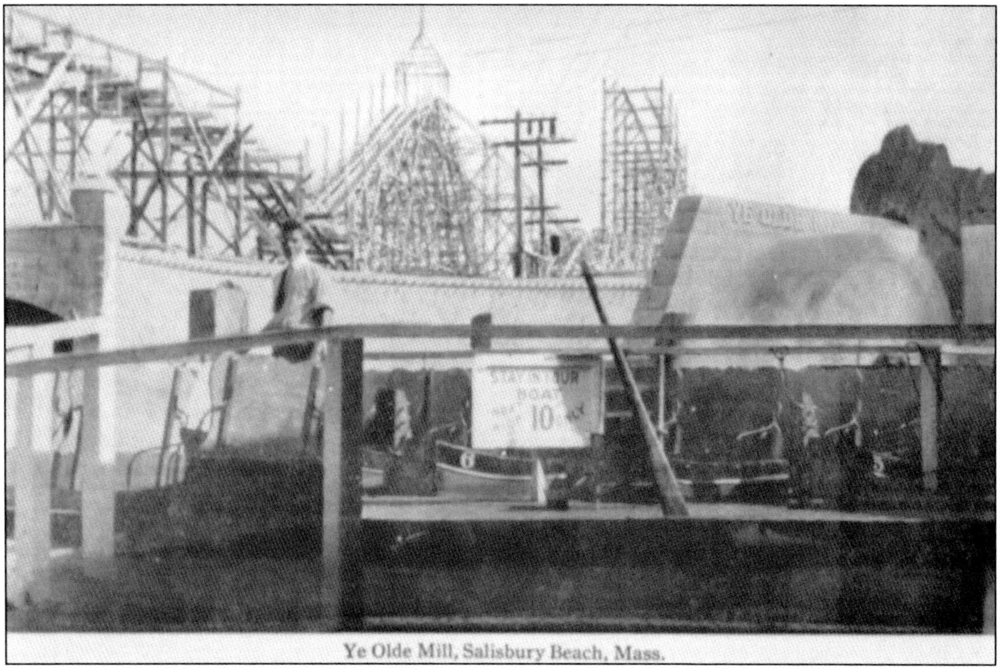

The Grand Thriller roller coaster is towering over Ye Olde Mill, which was damaged by fire on August 7, 1925. The Comet roller coaster was built in 1927 and was later rebuilt after the fire of 1948. The Ye Olde Mill ride seems to have featured a tunnel of love ride. The sign outside states, "Stay in your boat." (Courtesy Arnold Marookian.)

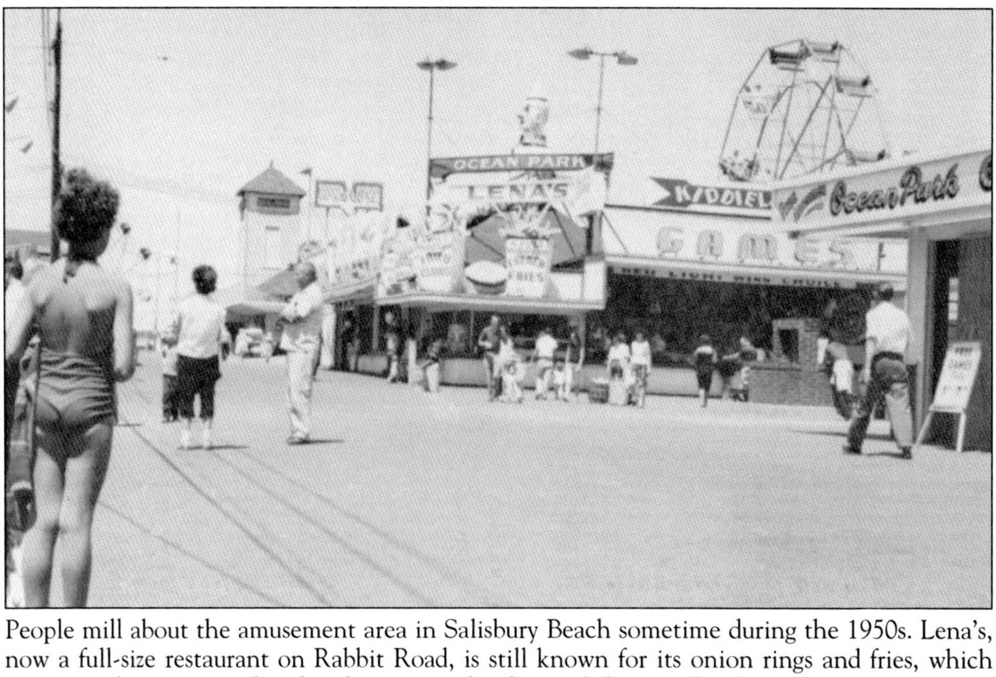

People mill about the amusement area in Salisbury Beach sometime during the 1950s. Lena's, now a full-size restaurant on Rabbit Road, is still known for its onion rings and fries, which appear in large size with a hamburger on the front of the stand. The author's family often headed to the beach for opening weekend in late winter to cure a yearning left unsatisfied all winter for some great fried food.

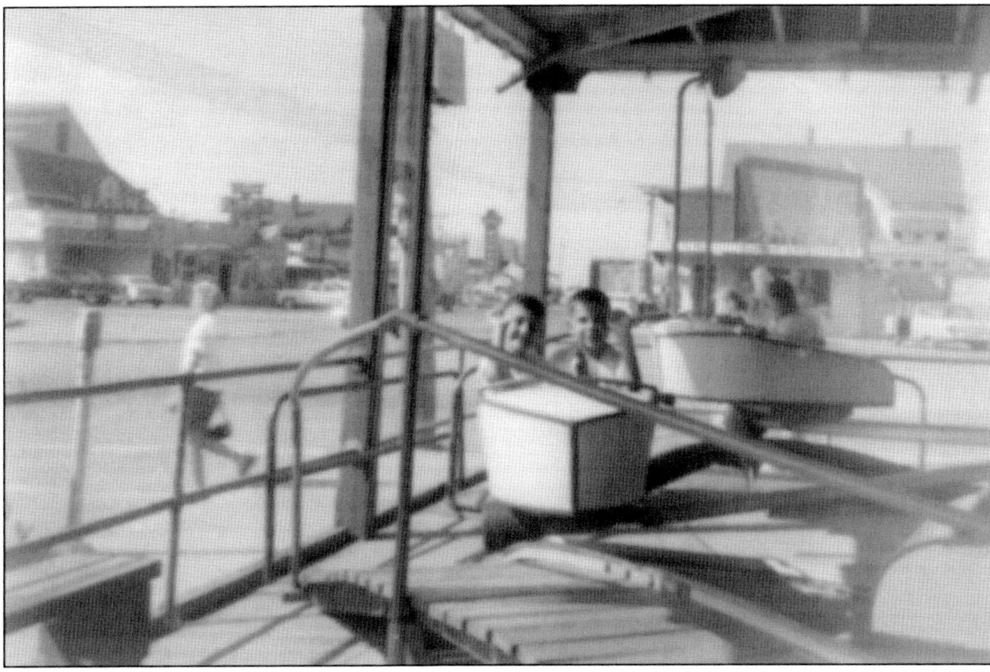

John Thomas, from Haverhill, Massachusetts, and James Grassi, from Metheun, ride the kiddie boat ride. Nobody could resist ringing the bell for the entire ride. Noise is what an amusement park is all about.

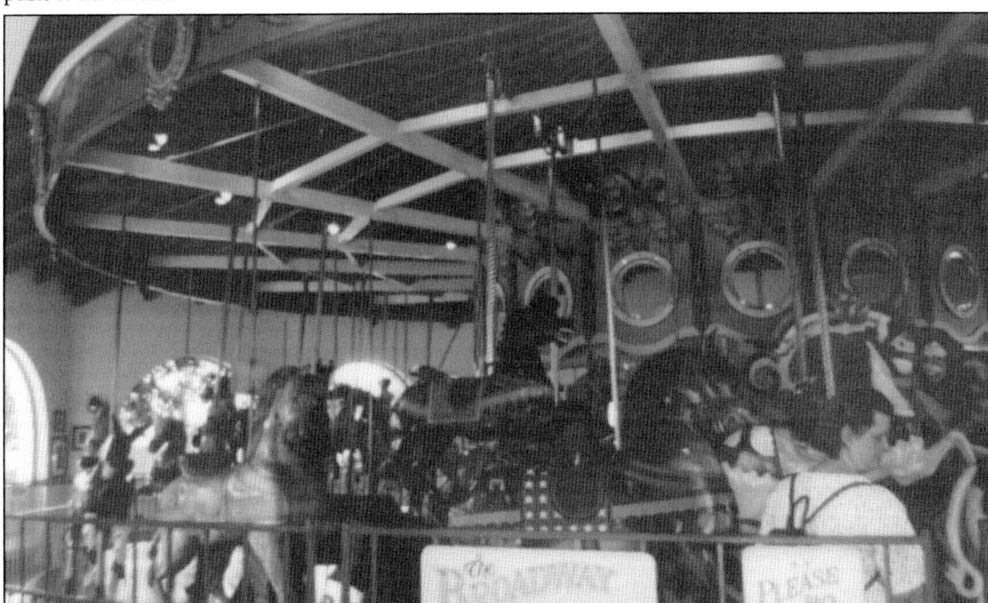

The famous Broadway Flying Horses ride was equipped with 46 animals, 4 chariots, and a 1914 Gebruders Bruder Band Organ. Looff, the animal carver known for his baroque style, created a total carousel environment using stained windows that cast a glow and mirrored jewels that created a kaleidoscope effect. Riders used to lean out and try to grab the brass ring. The ring was later removed due to safety hazards. The carousel, owned by Roger Shaheen, was sold in 1977 (in one piece) and is now in a San Diego mall.

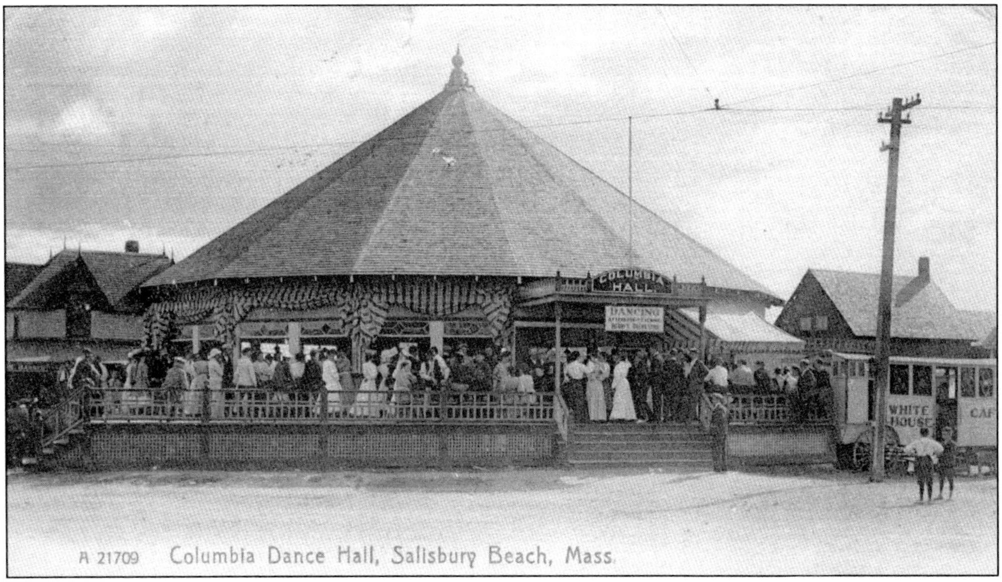

The Columbia Dance Hall is overcrowded with prospective dancers. The hall hosted dancing to an orchestra both afternoons and evenings. This same building once held the Culver Flying Horses (Broadway Flying Horses).

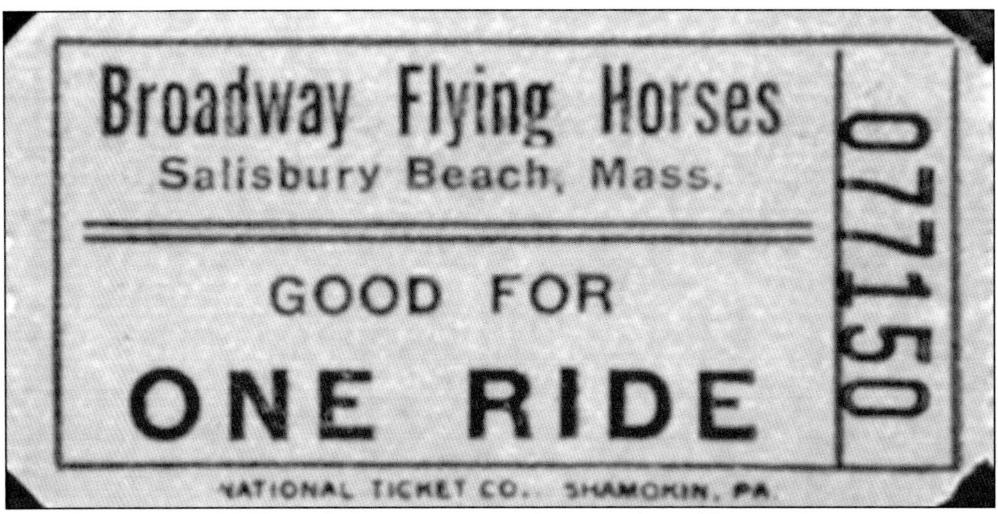

Old tickets for the Broadway Flying Horses are no longer redeemable.

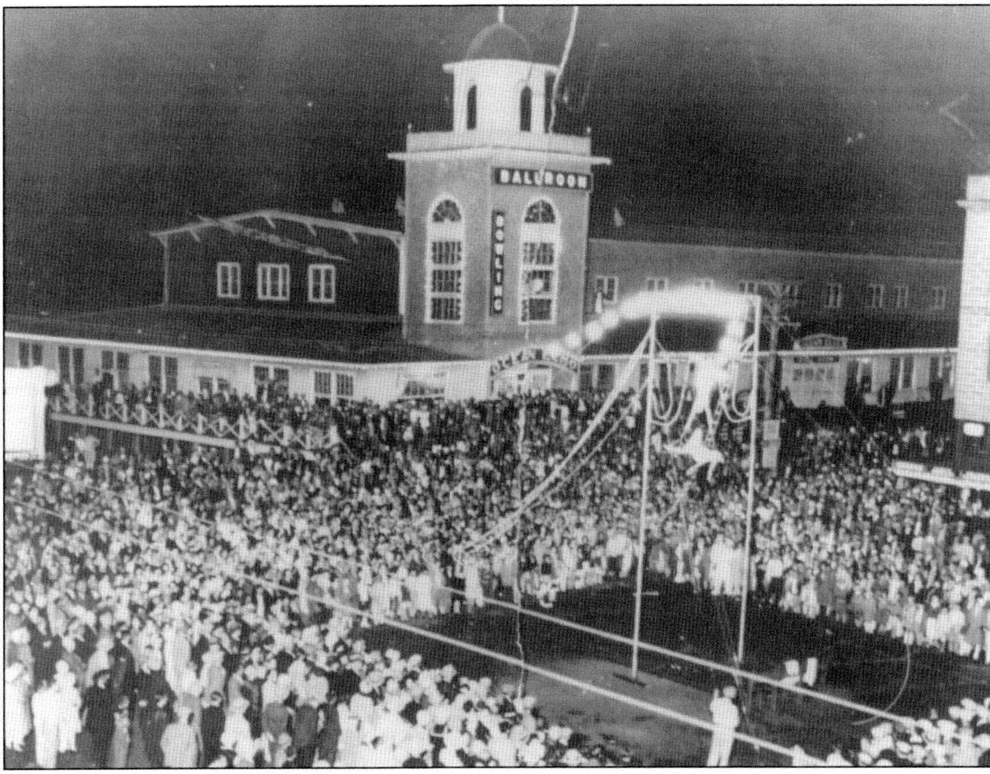

An aerial act is performed for an enormous crowd in front of the Ocean Echo. People arrived at Salisbury beach in droves with a yen for excitement. Ethel Merrill Rogers claims to have seen a performer killed after falling from the high wire with no net to break the fall. (Courtesy Joseph Callahan.)

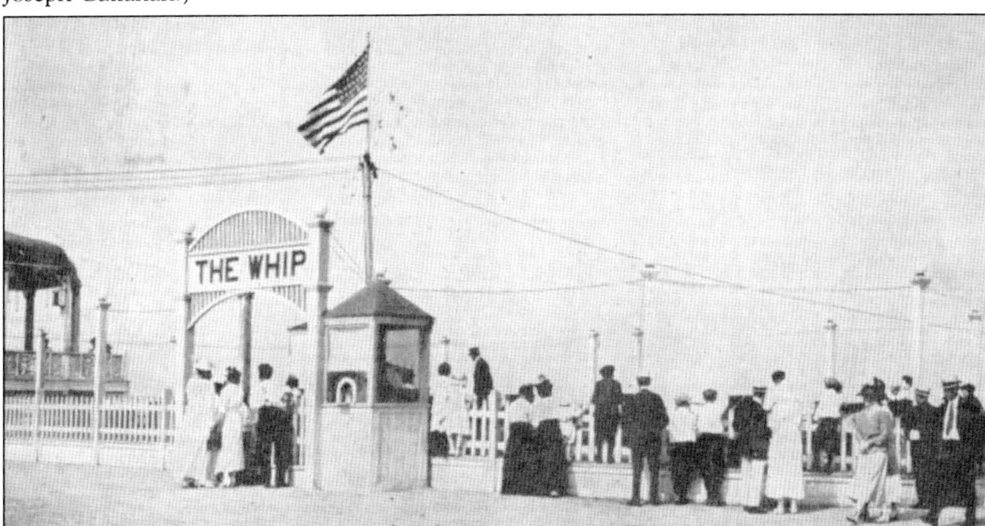

The Whip was a popular ride in the early 20th century. The ride was right next to the original Ocean Echo in front of the bathhouse. It was not until 1959 that Roger Shaheen converted his 300-car parking lot into an amusement area offering seven major rides, kiddie rides, miniature golf, and arcade games. (Courtesy Arnold Marookian.)

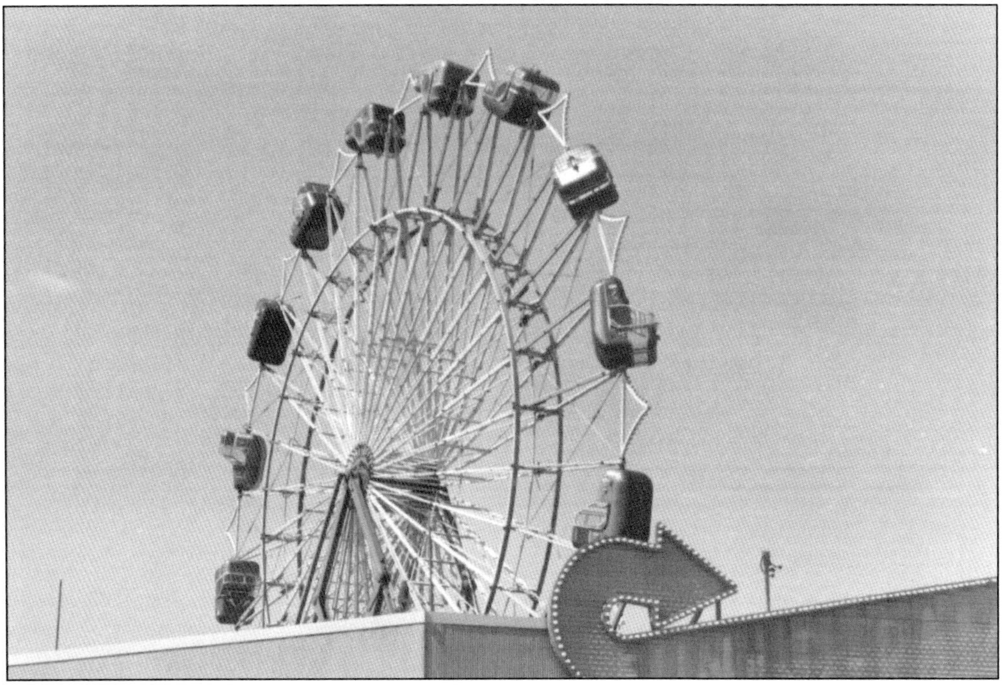

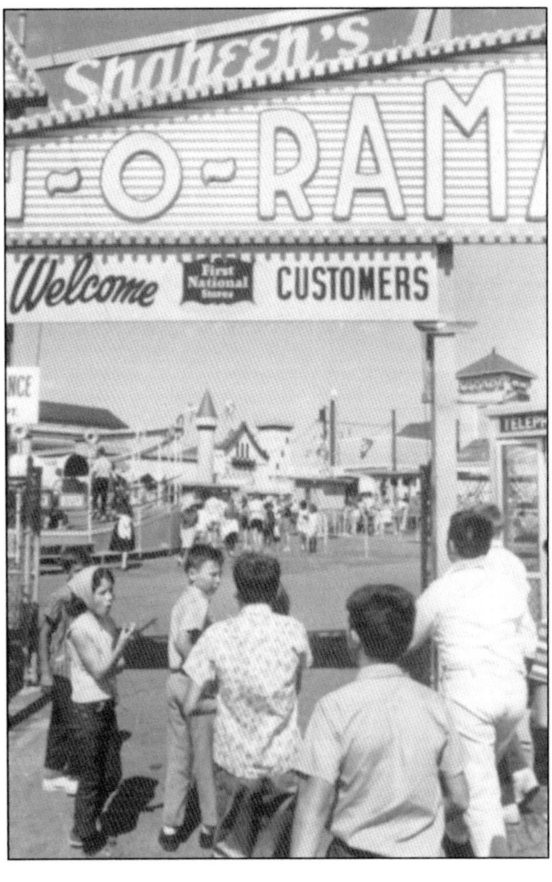

A strangely shaped Ferris wheel, this ride was known as the Sky Diver in the Shaheen's amusement park. The sign upon entering the ride states, "Secure all valuables." In June 1959, the local paper declared that as many as 200,000 people hit the beaches over that weekend, which was always good news for the amusement parks. (Courtesy Arnold Marookian.)

In the 1960s, employees and families from the First National Stores had a special day at Shaheen's Fun-o-Rama. Notice the young girl wearing the scarf very popular in the 1960s. This type of scarf is back today as a fashion accessory for young girls. (Courtesy Roger Shaheen.)

RECREATION FOR THE NATION
NATIONAL ASSOCIATION OF AMUSEMENT PARKS POOLS & BEACHES

National Association of Amusement Parks, Pools and Beaches

Code of Ethics

This Code of Ethics is hereby adopted by the National Association of Amusement Parks, Pools and Beaches at its 1950 Convention as the standard of practice for all its members who individually and collectively pledge themselves as follows:

1. To provide clean, wholesome and safe outdoor recreation for everyone.
2. To fill the hearts of children and all those young in spirit with joy while spending their hours of play and outdoor recreation in sunshine and fresh air.
3. To treat our patrons as our guests and by our courteous manner make them our friends.
4. To conduct our business on the highest plane of integrity so that all individual establishments will occupy places of honor in their communities and our industry may be respected in the nation at large.
5. To consider the ideal of service as one of our foremost requisites.
6. To foster and maintain a spirit of co-operation and fair dealing with our employees and concessionaires.
7. To establish and maintain intimate, cordial and friendly relations with our fellow members.
8. To establish and maintain a spirit of fairness and protection with amusement device builders.
9. We believe that these principles must be carried out by each member individually in order to foster and promote our industry which is a high and worthy one and also a vital and necessary part of our community life at all times.

The National Association of Amusements Parks, Pools, and Beaches adopted this Code of Ethics at its 1950 convention. (Courtesy Roger Shaheen.)

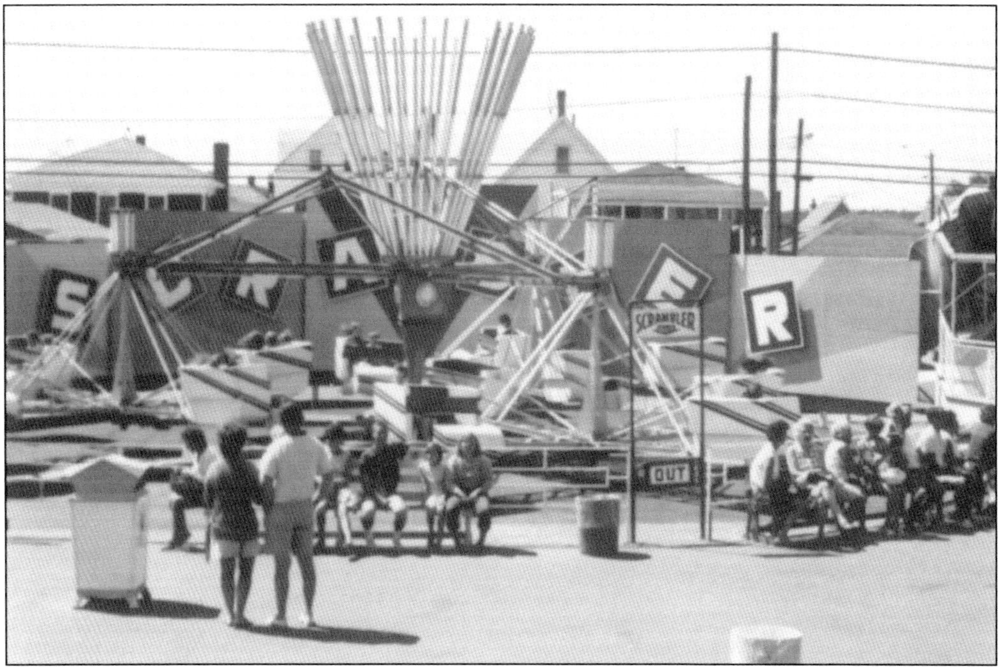

This throng of people is either resting or waiting to ride the Scrambler in the 1960s. In 1959, the Scrambler was the most popular ride on the beach. As many as 8,000 people rode the attraction in one day. Another constantly patronized ride that originated at Salisbury Beach was the Dodgem Cars. (Courtesy Roger Shaheen.)

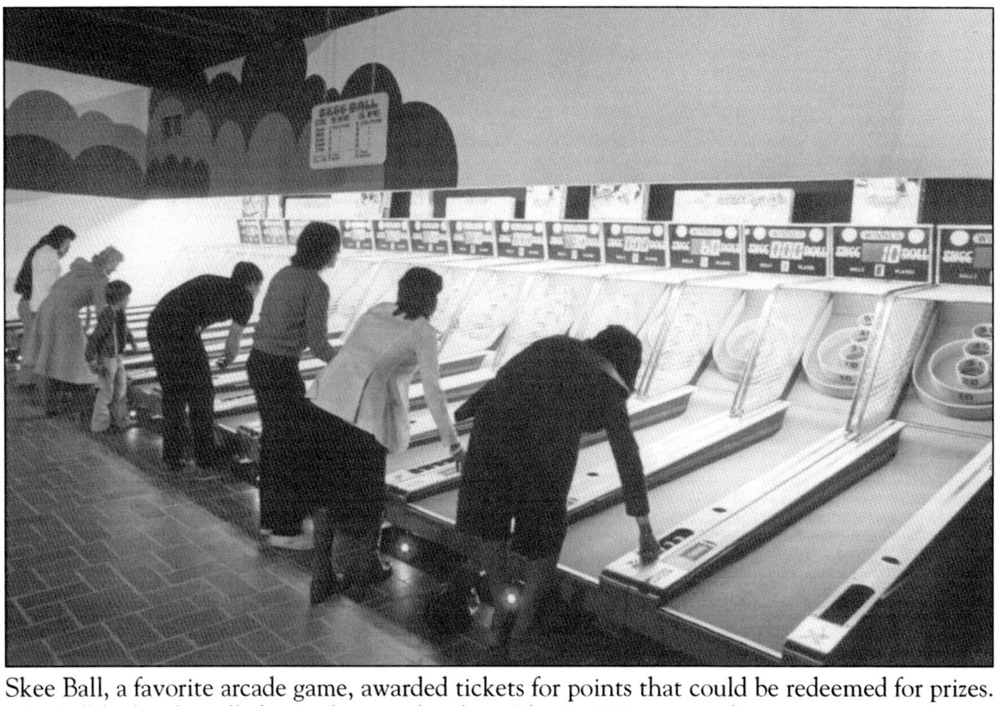

Skee Ball, a favorite arcade game, awarded tickets for points that could be redeemed for prizes. The ball had to be rolled into the circular slots. These 1970s contenders are intent on scoring big for a better prize. (Courtesy Roger Shaheen.)

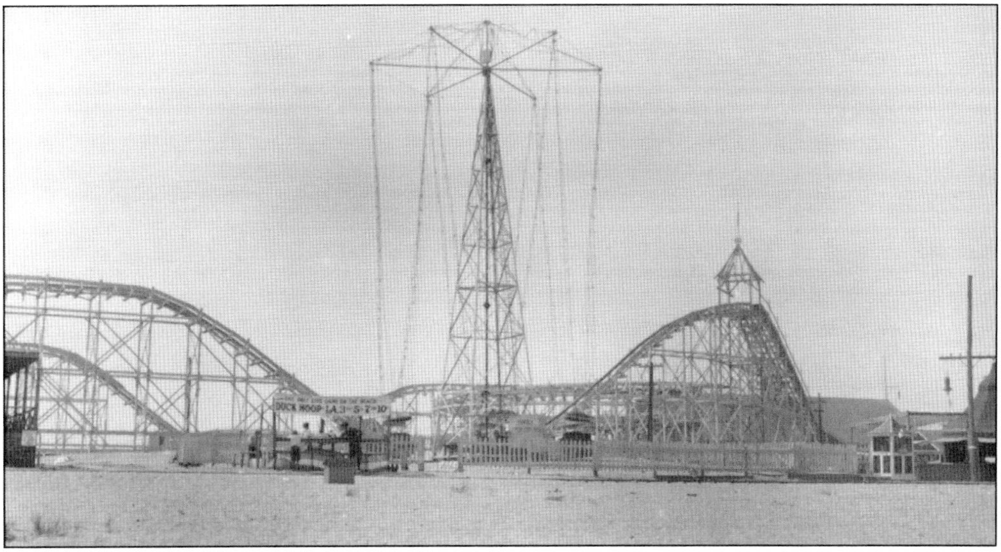

The Airplane ride faces the dance hall on the ocean while some people play Duck Hoop, which claims to be the only live game on the beach. (It is difficult to detect from this picture whether people looped real ducks. Those were the days that horses leaped into a pool of water, so anything is possible.) The second roller coaster appears in this picture.

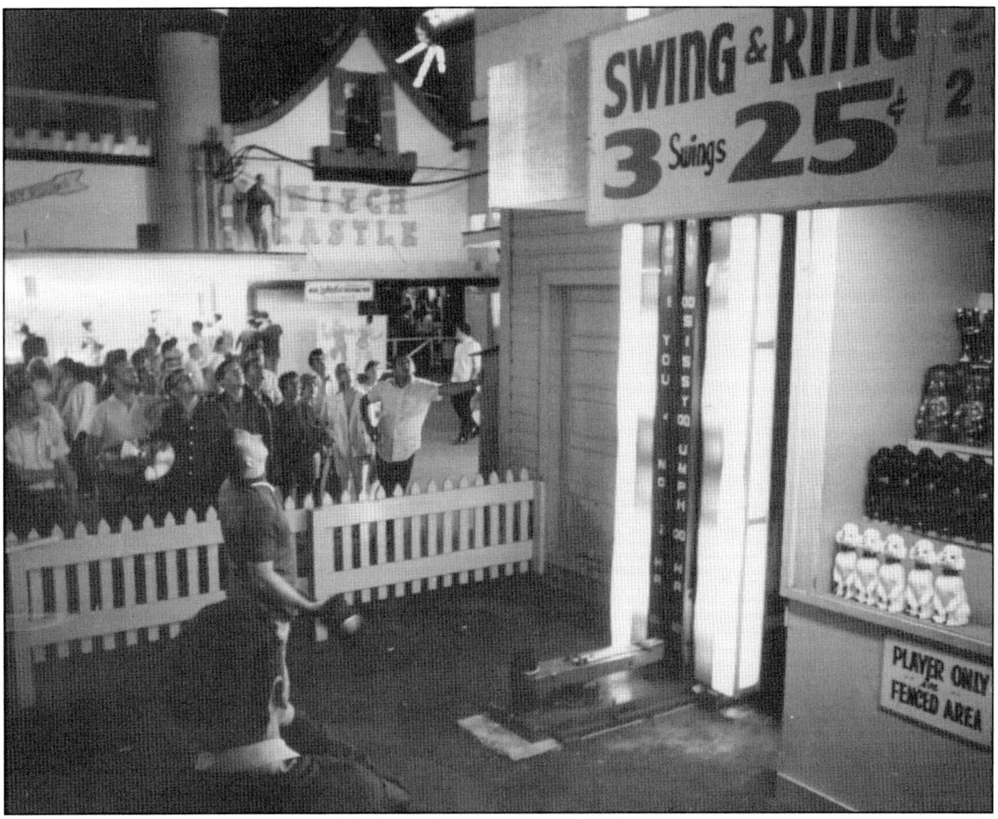

A man tests his strength as he watches the readout to see if he has won a prize. The Witch's Castle, a real beach favorite, appears in the left of the picture. (Courtesy Roger Shaheen.)

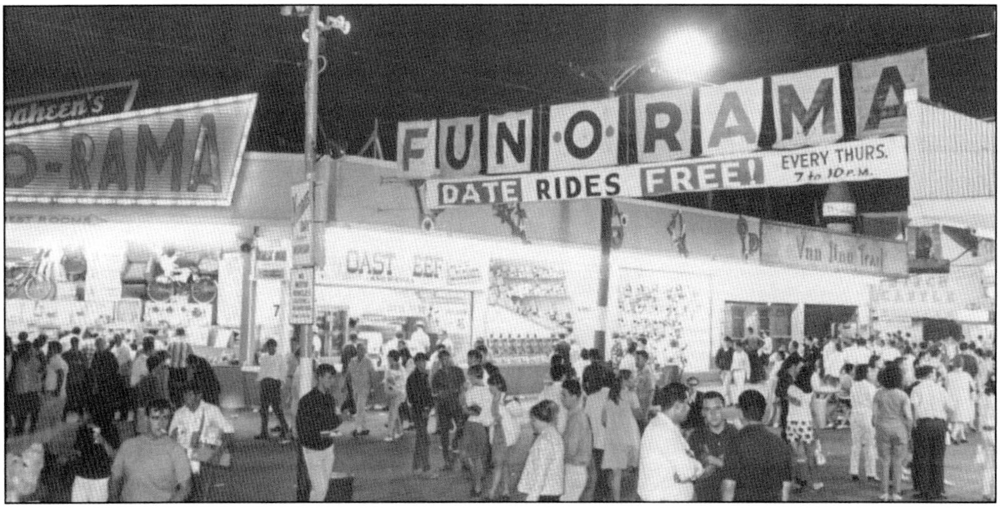

Shaheen's Fun-o-Rama allowed dates to ride free every Thursday night from 7 to 10 p.m. in the 1960s. Here, the beach looks in full swing on a typical summer night at the amusement park. Salisbury Beach has always been known as "the workingman's beach." Although people came from all over, the main population of the beach arrived from the Merrimack Valley.

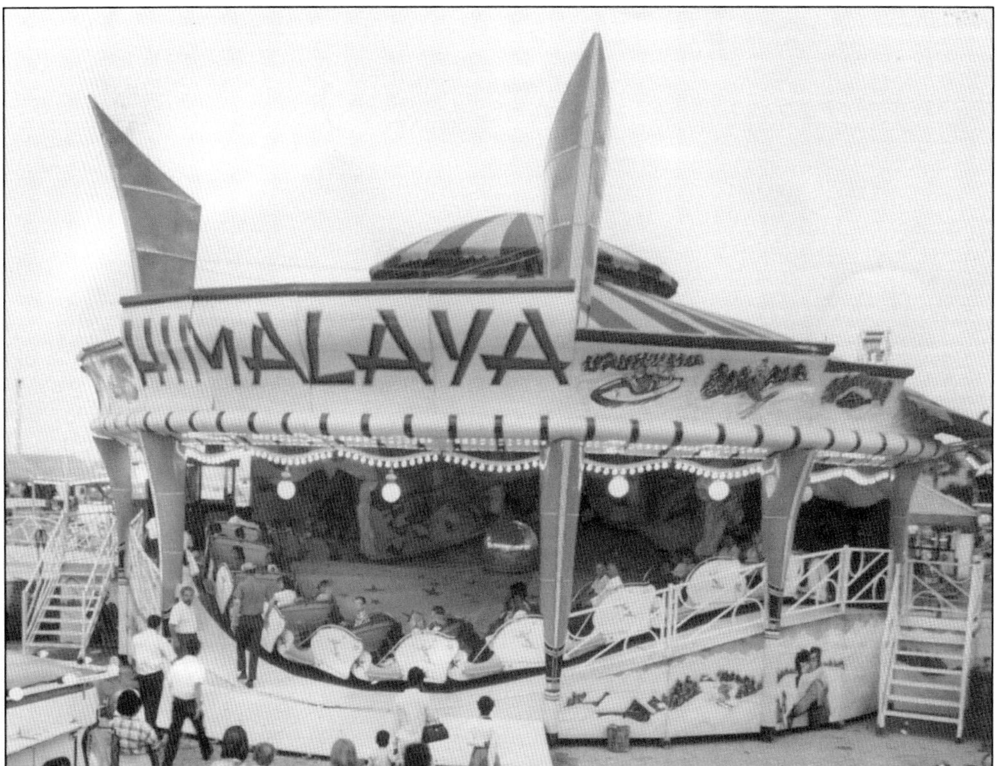

The Himalaya was one of the most frequented rides by teenage girls in the 1970s to 1980s. Loud popular music, played by a disc jockey who ruled over the ride and took requests, could be heard all over the amusement area. All of the men with charm and good looks who worked for the company were chosen to run this ride, a further inducement for attracting young women.

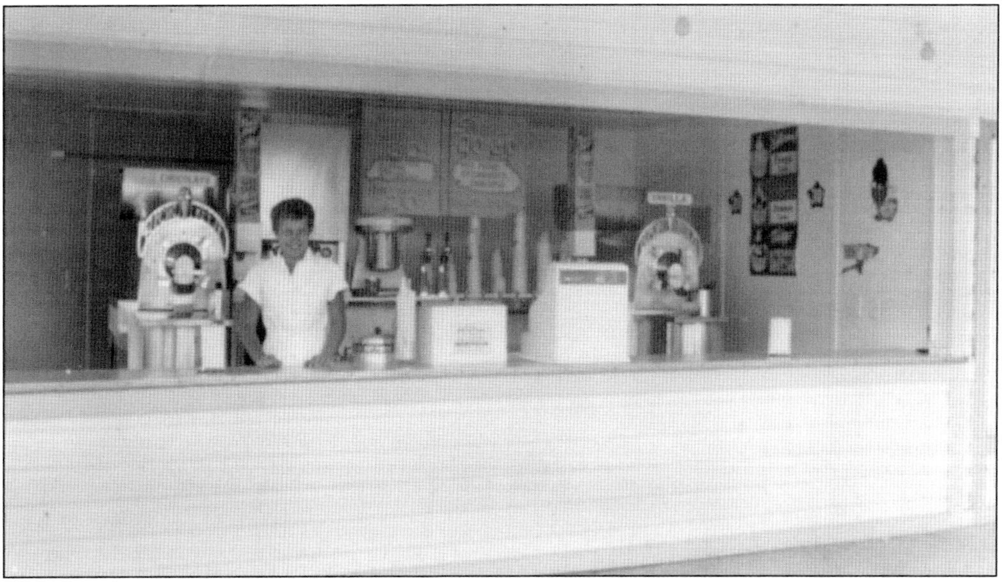

A woman named Carol stands behind the counter of the frozen custard stand in 1954 ready to serve up the delicious treat. Frozen custard is still very popular in some areas of the country, but according to Roger Shaheen it is no longer allowed to be served in Massachusetts due to the raw egg content. (Courtesy Roger Shaheen.)

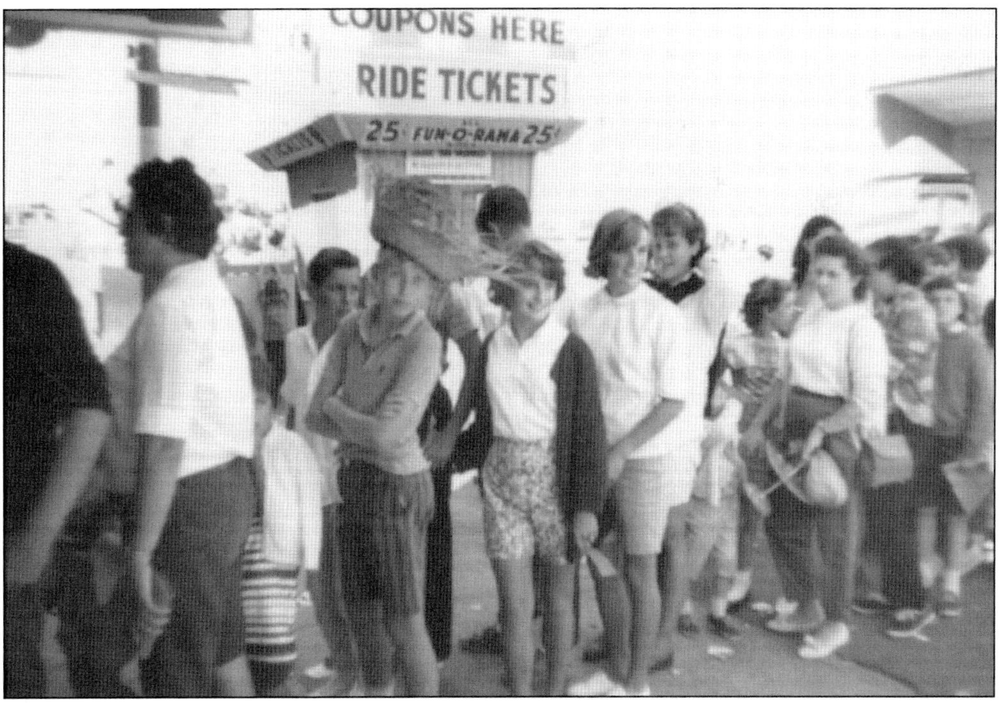

People wait in line to purchase ride tickets for the Fun-o-Rama in 1964. The boy with his hands crossed probably won the straw hat, which he wears tipped whimsically to the side of his head. (Courtesy Roger Shaheen.)

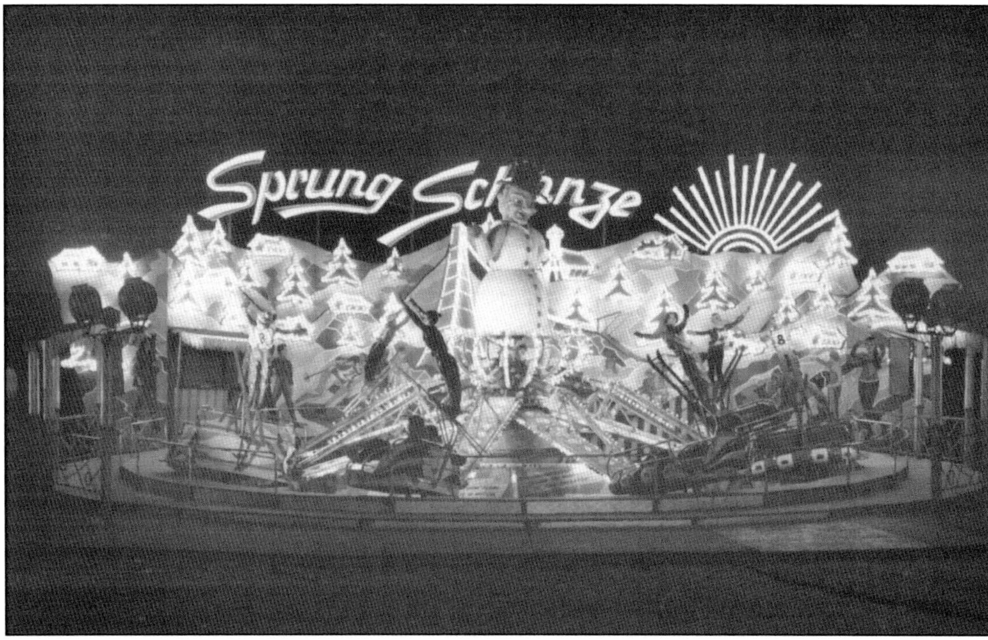

The Sprung Schanze ride had 7,543 light bulbs to create this visual experience.

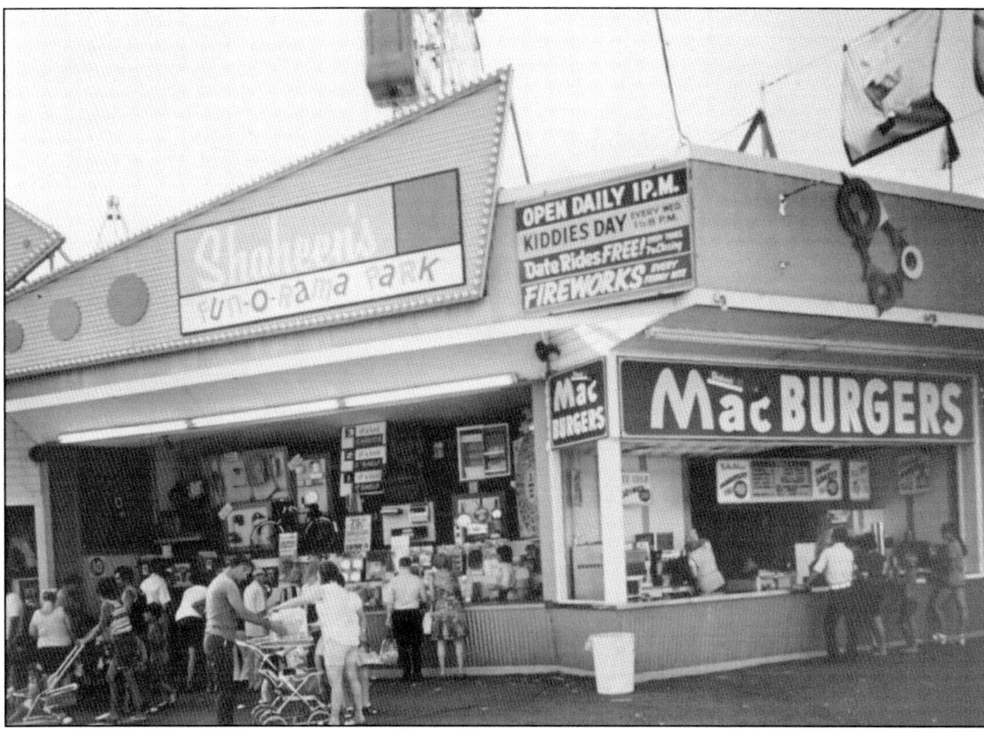

MacBurger only lasted a very short time at the beach. The owner, Roger Shaheen, was forced by McDonald's to change the name of MacBurgers to something more removed from the McDonald's name. Shaheen later owned two McDonald's franchises.

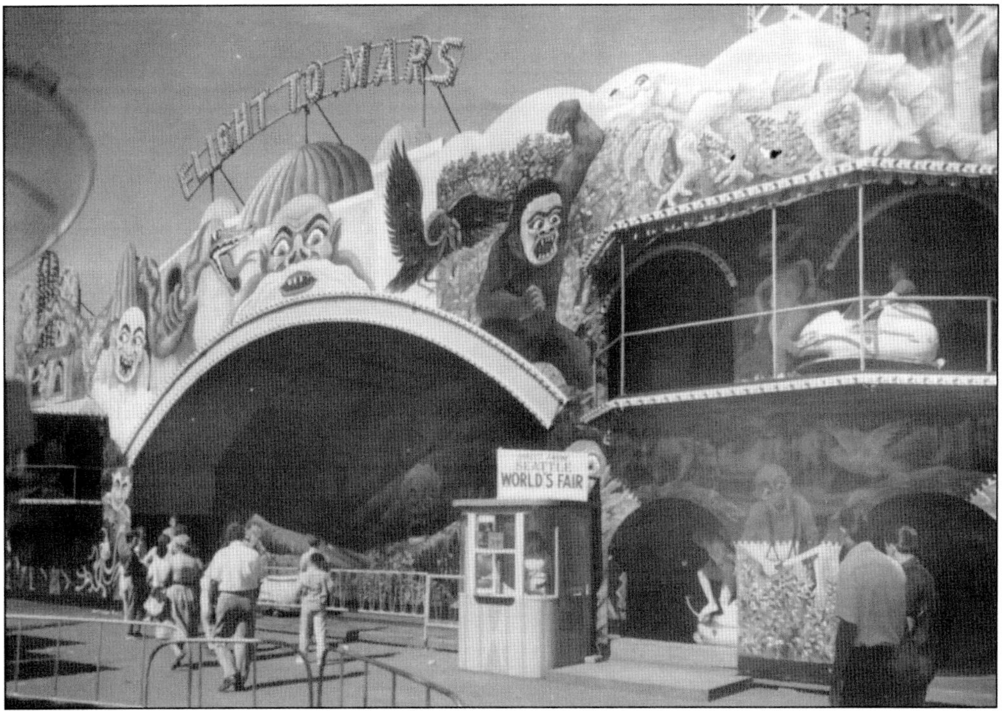

The Flight to Mars was purchased by Roger Shaheen at the Seattle World's Fair. In the 1980s, Shaheen's Pirate Park operated at Salisbury Beach along with other independent amusements. (Courtesy Roger Shaheen.)

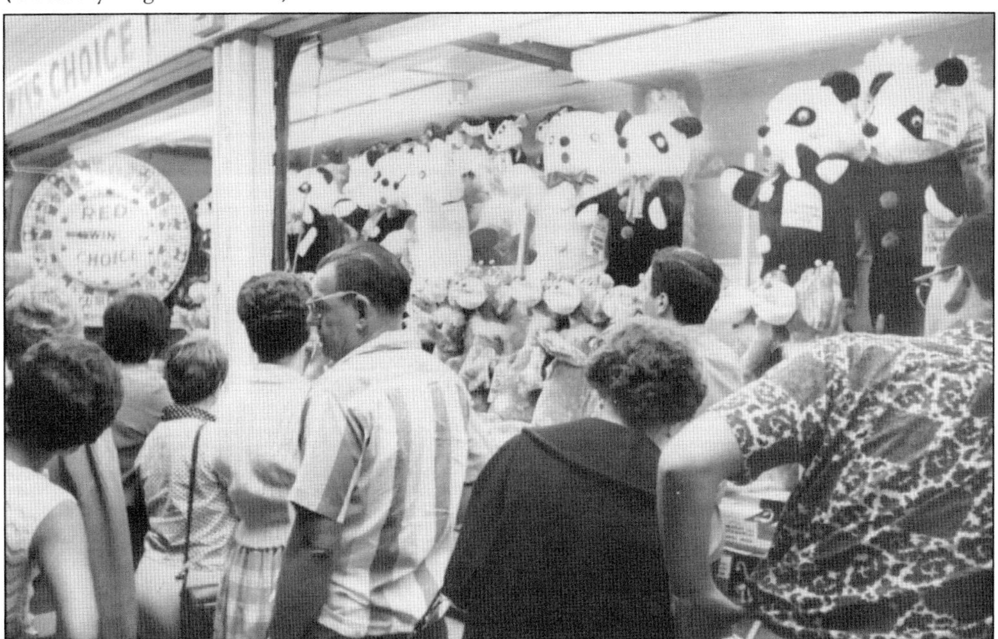

A line of stuffed bears wait to be picked by a winner of the Red Light Game. When the red light landed on the number that coincided with the number chosen on the board, the owner of that number won and could choose any prize displayed on the shelf.

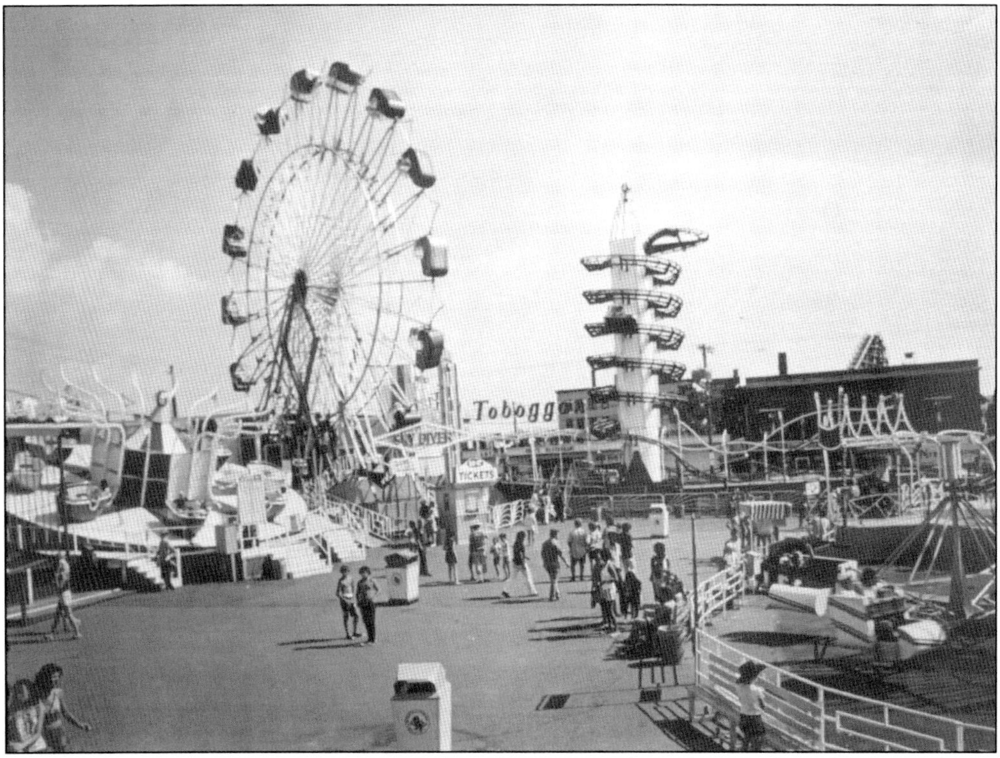

This is a great view of the amusement park in the 1970s. The Toboggan (possibly named after the original Jackman coaster), Sky Diver, and the Scrambler can all be seen in this picture.

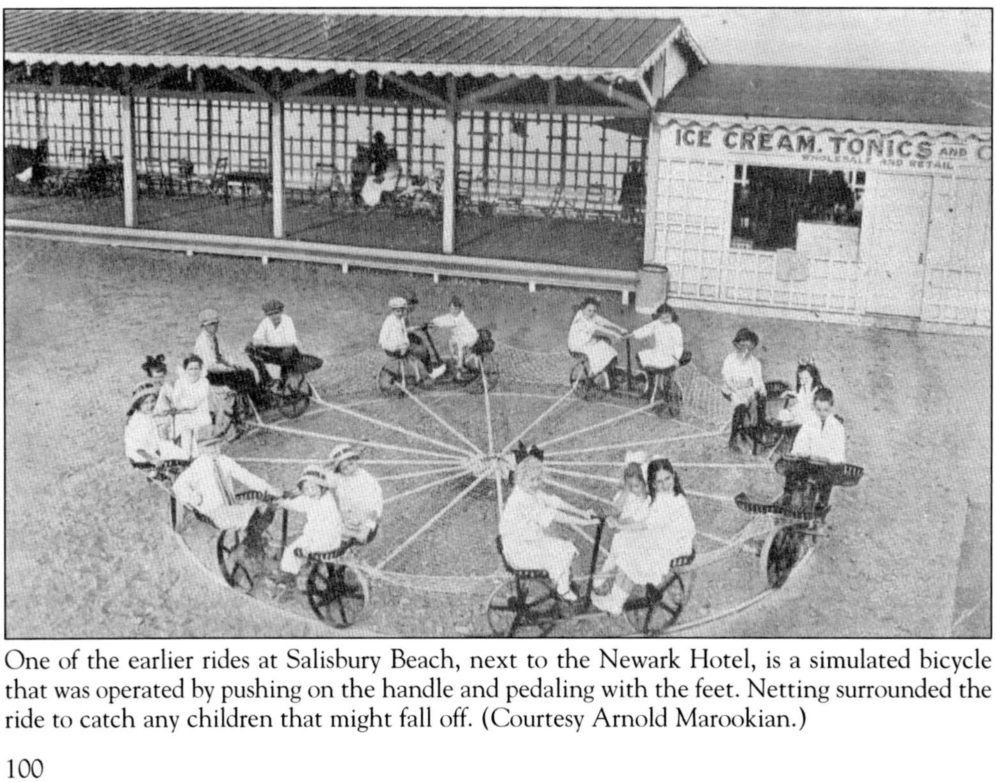

One of the earlier rides at Salisbury Beach, next to the Newark Hotel, is a simulated bicycle that was operated by pushing on the handle and pedaling with the feet. Netting surrounded the ride to catch any children that might fall off. (Courtesy Arnold Marookian.)

Seven

SENTIMENTAL JOURNEY

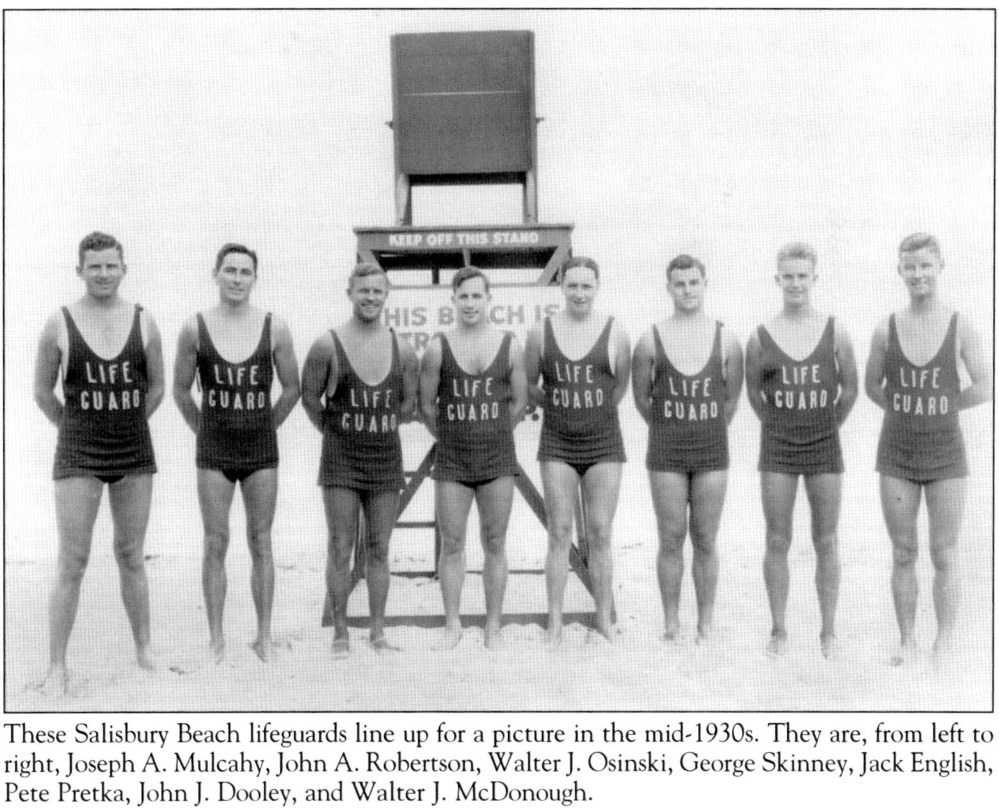

These Salisbury Beach lifeguards line up for a picture in the mid-1930s. They are, from left to right, Joseph A. Mulcahy, John A. Robertson, Walter J. Osinski, George Skinney, Jack English, Pete Pretka, John J. Dooley, and Walter J. McDonough.

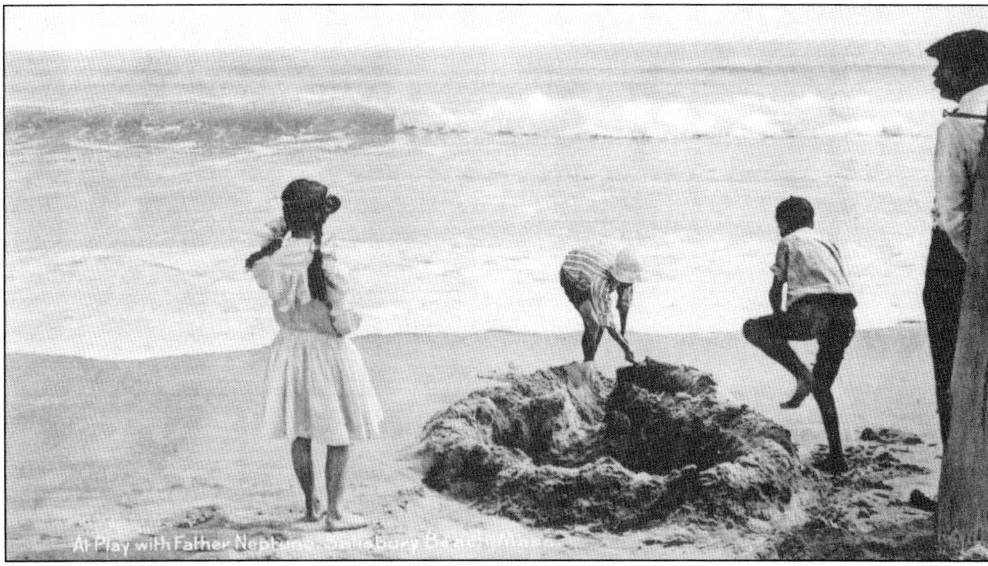

Children in the early 1900s build a sand castle at Salisbury Beach as their father looks on.

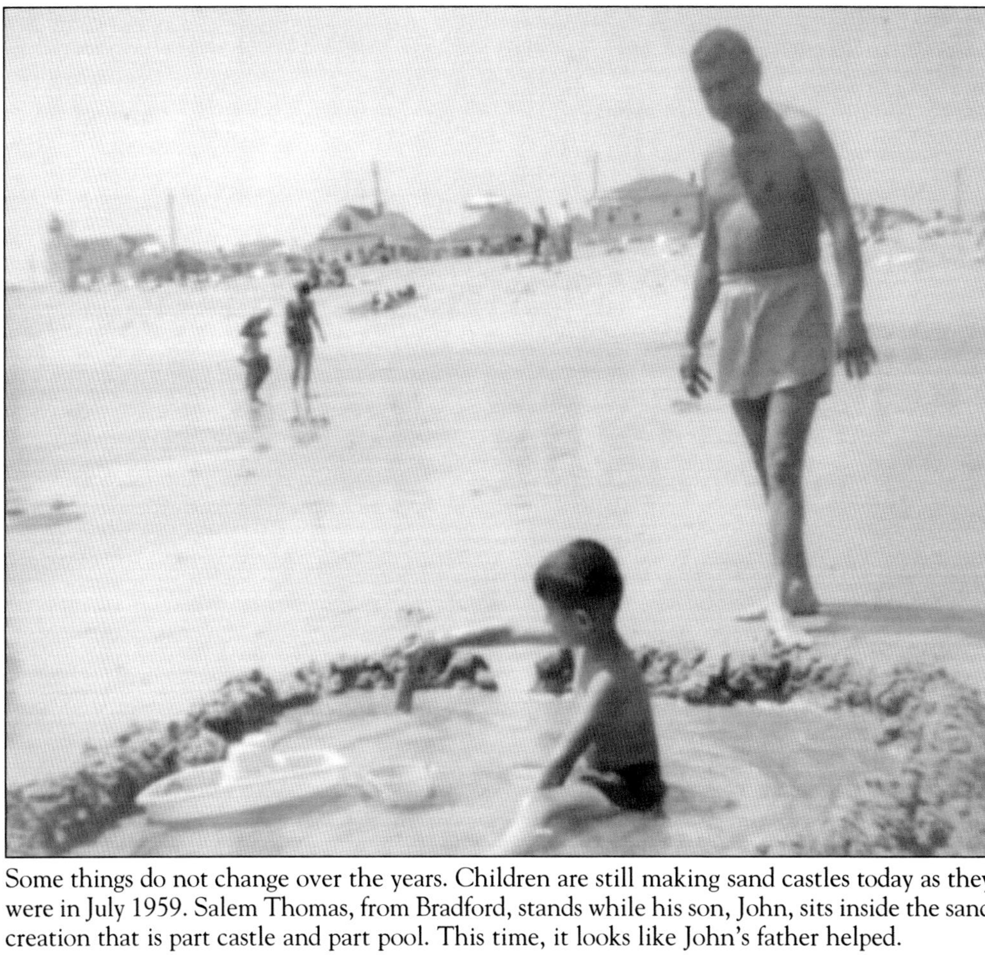

Some things do not change over the years. Children are still making sand castles today as they were in July 1959. Salem Thomas, from Bradford, stands while his son, John, sits inside the sand creation that is part castle and part pool. This time, it looks like John's father helped.

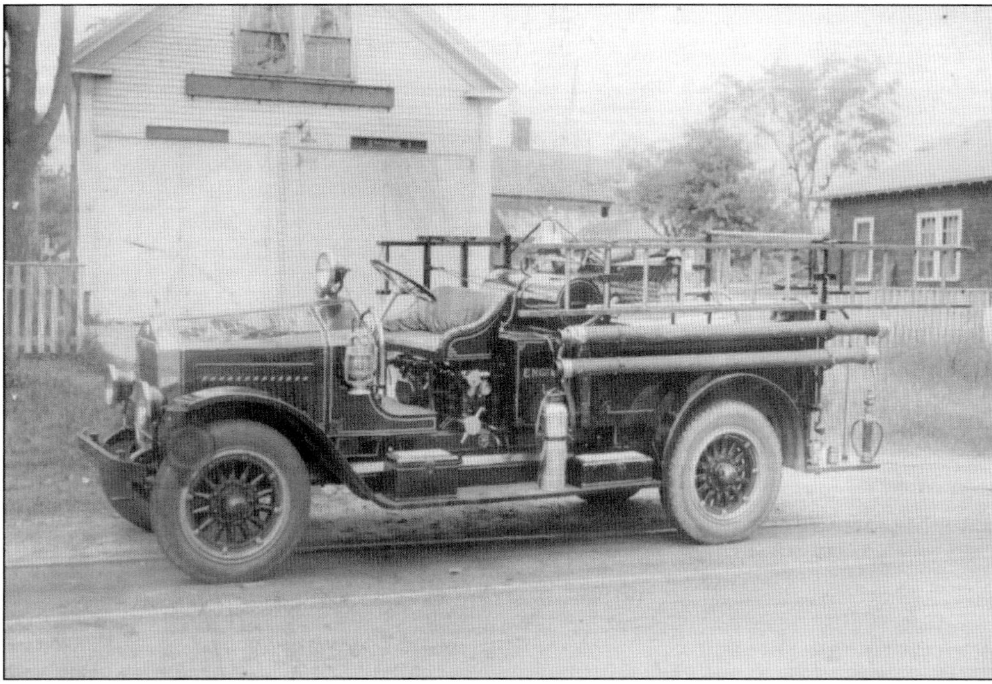

The town of Salisbury purchased two fire trucks in the mid-1920s, one for the beach and one for the town. Engine No.1 was the town truck. (Courtesy Joseph Callahan.)

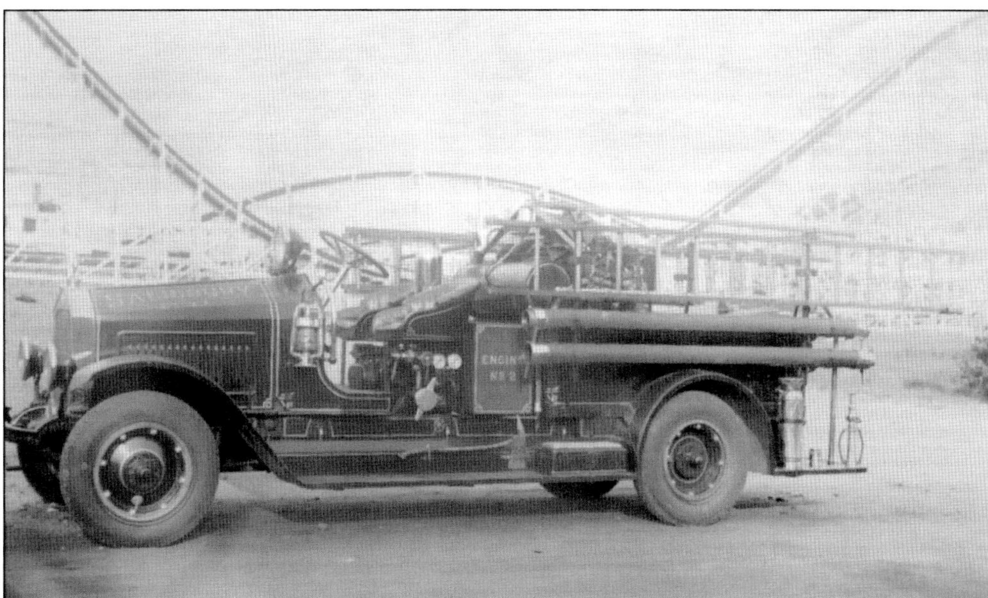

The beach fire truck, Engine No 2, is parked in front of the roller coaster in the mid-1920s. (Courtesy Joseph Callahan.)

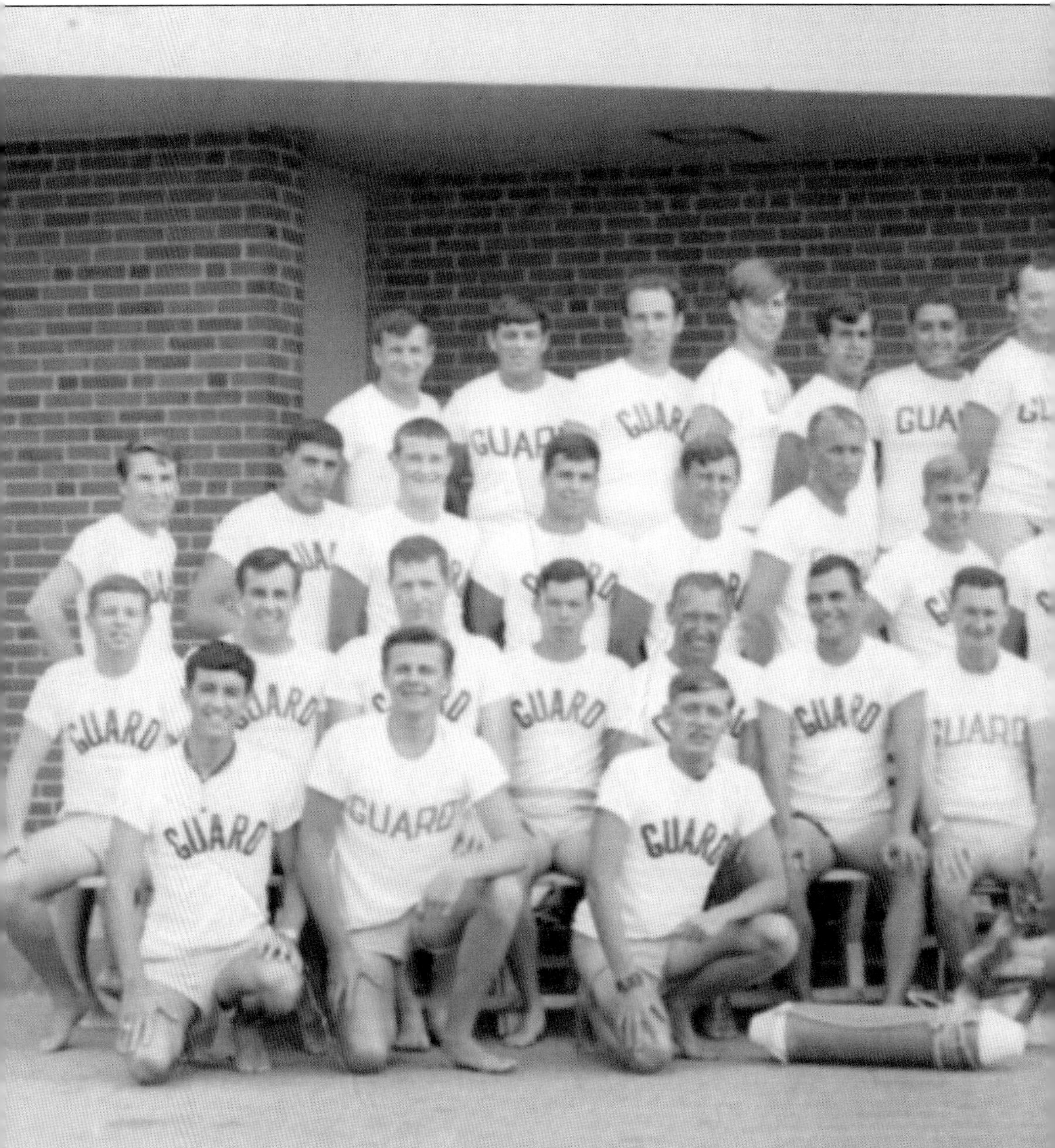

The Salisbury life guards of 1965 stand in front of the first aid room. They have increased in number over the years, as have the swimmers. No one has ever drowned while the Salisbury lifeguards were on duty. This was one of the most desired summer jobs for young men of the area. The 1965 lifeguards are, from left to right, as follows: (first row, kneeling) Joseph Kane, unidentified, Marty Fay, Duke the dog (mascot), J.B. McCarthy, unidentified, and Gary Little (later a local dentist in Amesbury at the offices of DiTolla and Little); (second row, seated) Doug Stoddard, Dennis Merchant, Steve Boxer, Gary Guptil, John McCormick, John Kalil, John Heggarty, nurse Estelle Kezer, beach superintendent Jesse Parino, head lifeguard

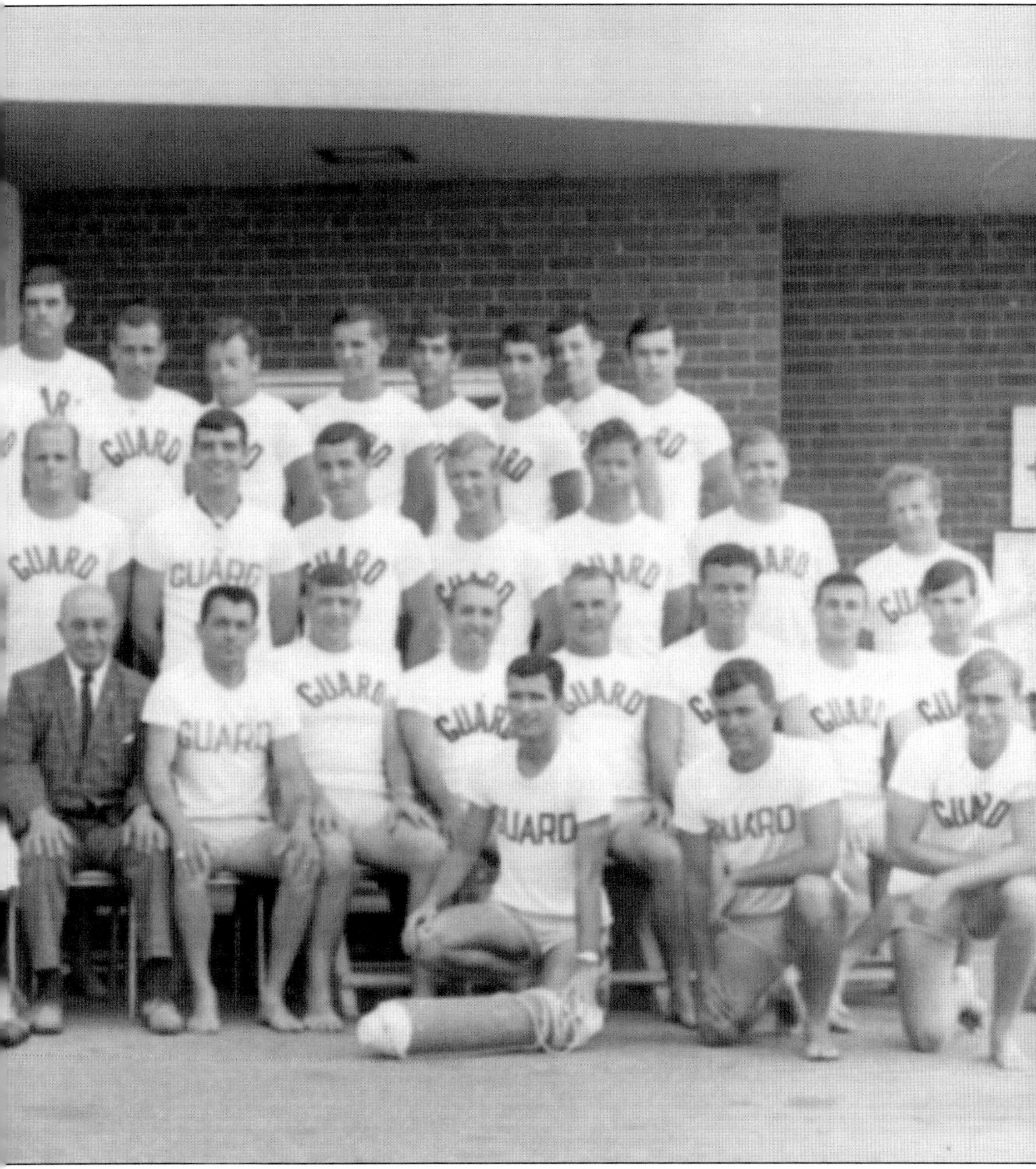

Leon "Dedo" Deroian, Pete Gulazian, Jerry Grasso, Charles U. Foley III, Dennis Mulcahy, unidentified, and Bill Murphy; (third row) J.J. McCarthy, Frank Zito, Ernest Carroll, Steve Richardson, Bernie Parent, Paul Keenon, Mickey McLaughlin, unidentified, Roger Farrar, James Mooney, unidentified, Bernie Morrison, unidentified, Howard Daigle, and Doug Morse; (fourth row) Paul Le Maitre, Dennis Fitzgerald, Larry Petorutto, Tony Parino, Randy Hiller, Jim Pialtos, unidentified, Roger Duscharme, Jim McNeil, Frank Pappalardo, Bill Carey, Rick Tobacco, Ron Rosietti, Judd Lavin, and Pete Scanlon. (Dr. Gary Little is responsible for the identification of the guards and the spelling of their names.)

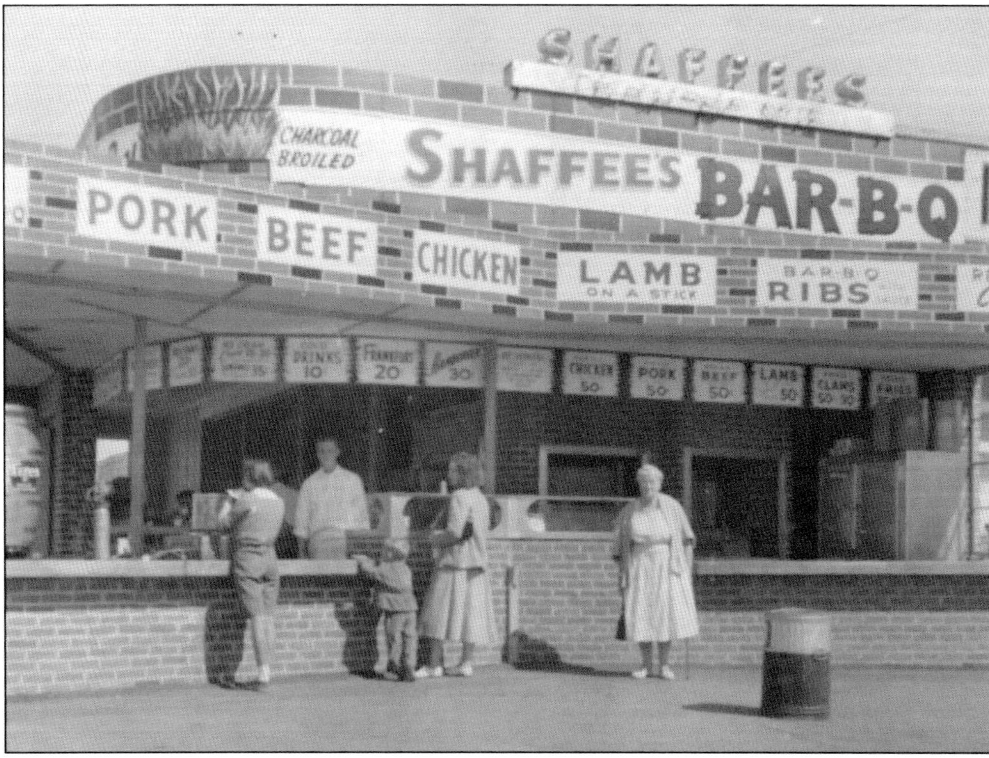

Schaffee's Barbecue was a very popular spot on the beach, located on the oceanfront off the north end of the Frolics building. Notice the prices in 1957 and the Hires root beer barrel to the left of the picture.

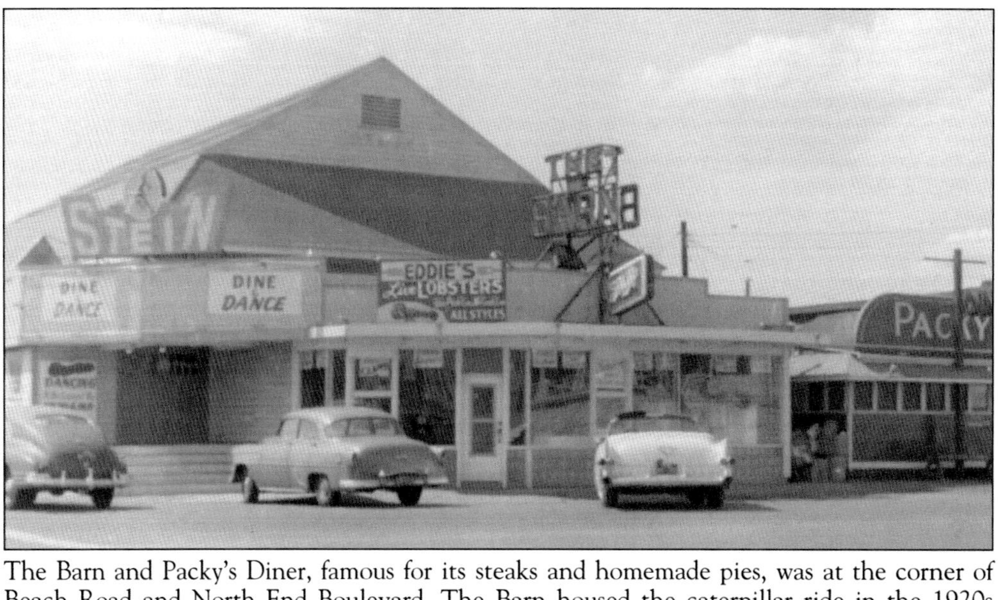

The Barn and Packy's Diner, famous for its steaks and homemade pies, was at the corner of Beach Road and North End Boulevard. The Barn housed the caterpillar ride in the 1920s and dance marathons during the Great Depression. Both buildings were destroyed in the fire of September 1959, fought by fire trucks from 11 neighboring towns. One fireman, Wilfred Richards, who was 51 years old, died from a heart attack brought on by battling the inferno.

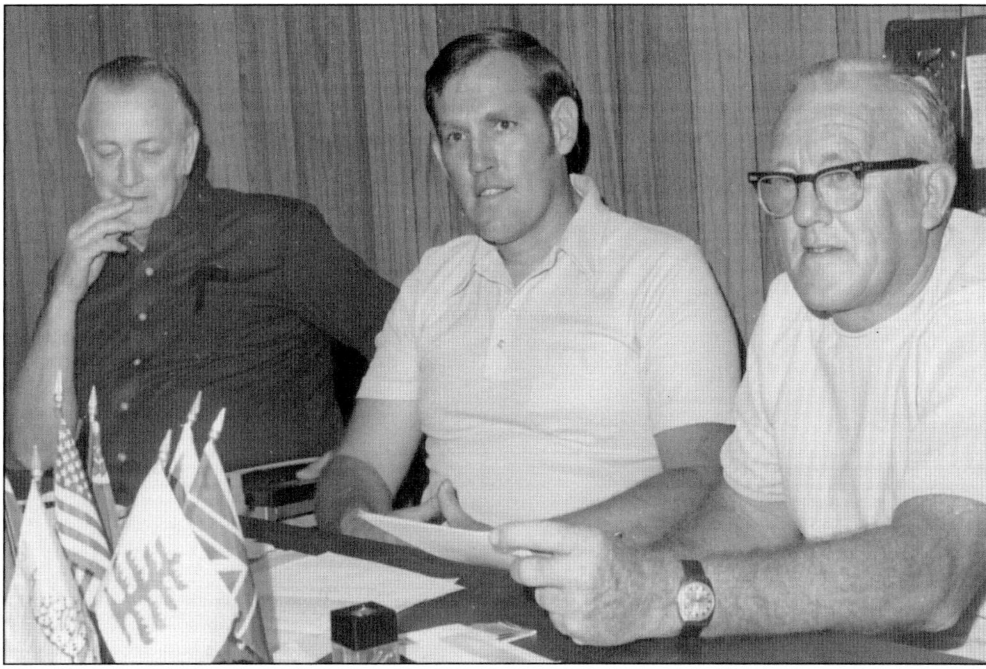

The Salisbury Board of Selectmen ran the town and the beach before the introduction of a town manager. This picture was taken in the bicentennial year of 1976. The selectmen are, from left to right, James Hunt, Carl LeSage, and Walter Morse.

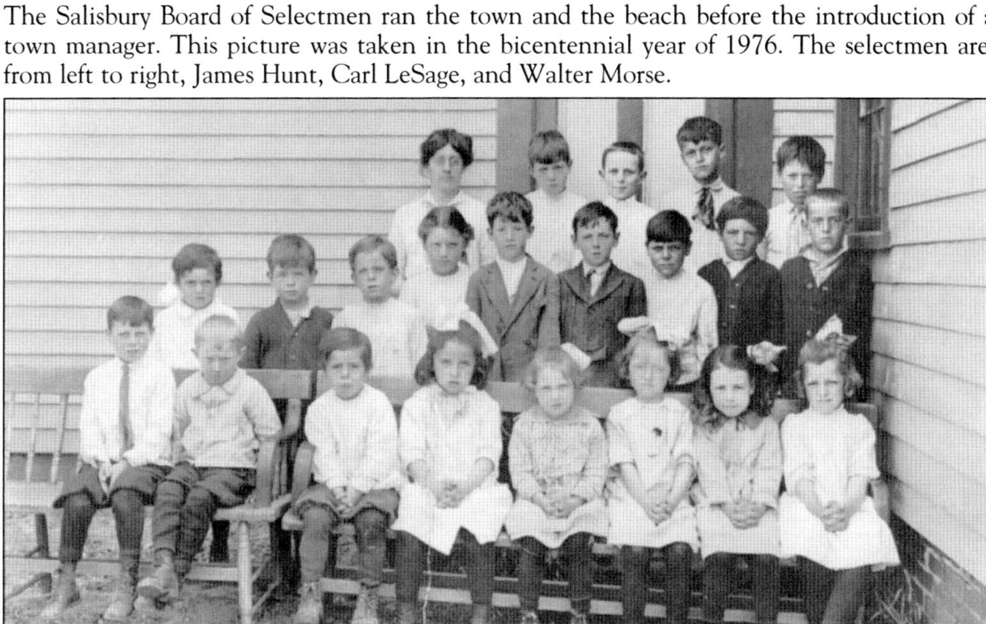

Children at the Plains School pose for their first-grade class picture in 1916. They are, from left to right, as follows: (front row) Donald Brown, Bill Peel, Roby Felch, Gertrude Hunt, Hazel Lamprey, Dorthea Norward, Henrietta Wimont (Kent), and Dorthea Sanborn Evans; (middle row) Norman Felch, two unidentified students, Elizabeth Sanborn, Robert Wilmont, one unidentified student, Wibur Congdon, Elbridge Felch, and Donald Brown; (back row) teacher Miss Knowles (Brown), one unidentified student, Teddy McFarland, Steven Cutter, and one unidentified student. Hazel Cote (in the front row) claimed she had to wear boys shoes because they lasted longer.

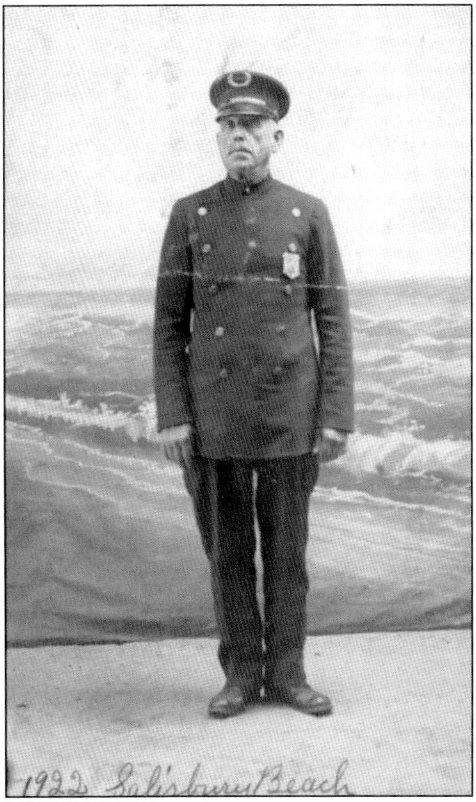

No flappers allowed! A flapper is described in the dictionary as a young woman in the 1920s who showed disdain for conventional dress and behavior. This police officer's job was chasing flappers off the beach in 1922. He does look like he could be easily charmed by one of these unconventional women, but took his job seriously.

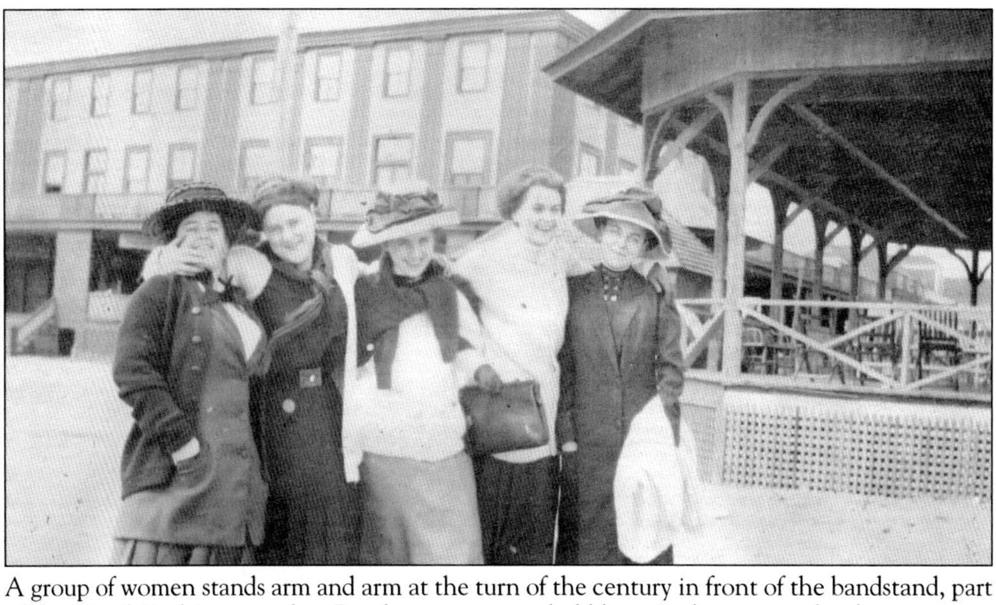

A group of women stands arm and arm at the turn of the century in front of the bandstand, part of the Hotel Cushing complex. Band concerts were held here in the summer by the ocean.

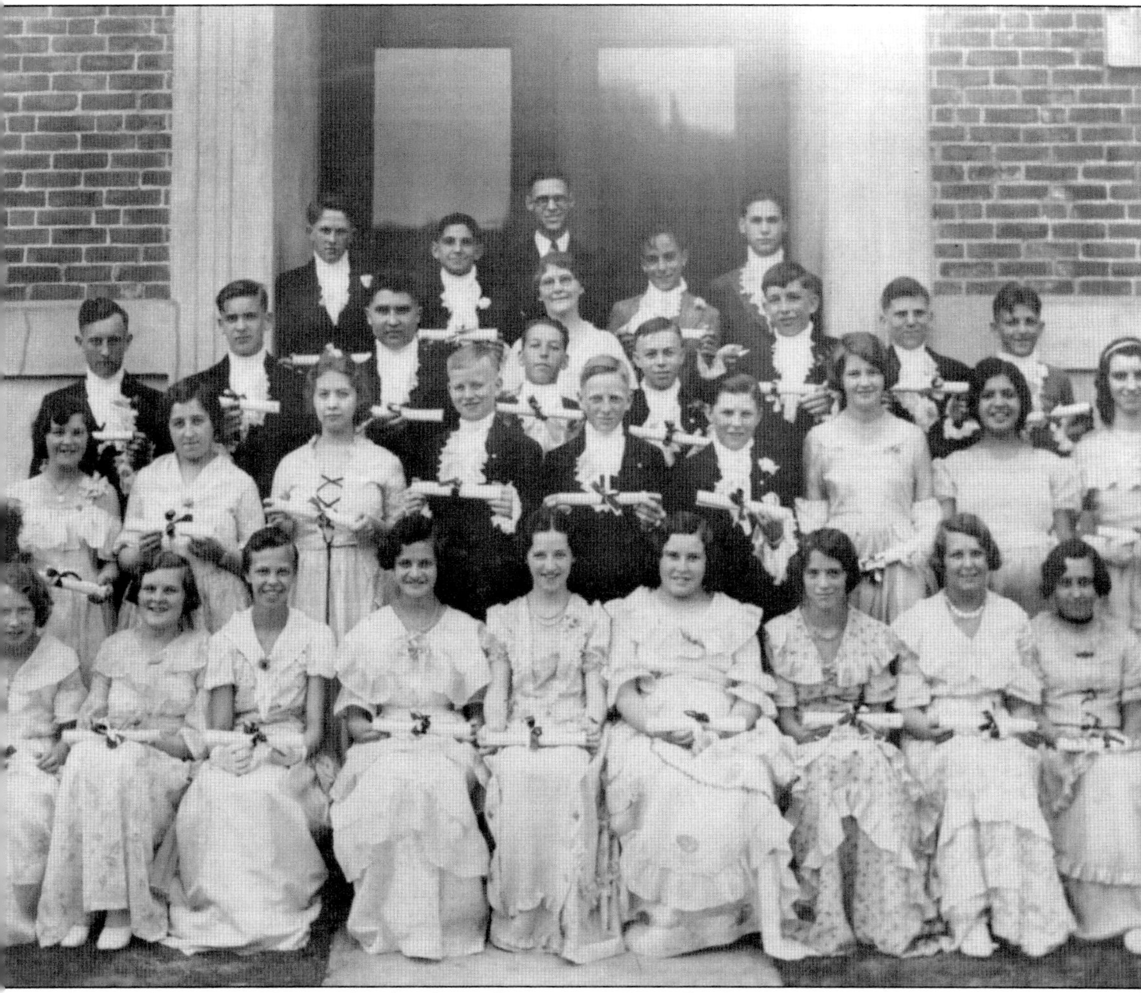

The Jacob F. Spaulding School Class of 1932 are formally dressed as they hold up their diplomas. They are, from left to right, as follows: (first row) Elsa Robblee, Ethel Merrill, Thelma Weston, Mary Burns, Rita ?, Lia Moore, Marion Merrill, Carrie Janvrin, and Norma Carr; (second row) Edith Decie, Helena Borin, Laura Krone, James Patton, Clifford Patterson, George Smith, Georgia Cockran, Nancy Papoulious, and Ruth Woodard; (third row) Raymond Kellett, Edward Lane, William Moore, Duane Marden, Charles Danielson, Robert Pickard, Lloyd Oliver, and one unidentified student; (fourth row) Donald Morrisette, Chalmus Alison, Mrs. Chase, Jackie Stevens, and Harry Sears. Principal Roland Gibbons is at the top.

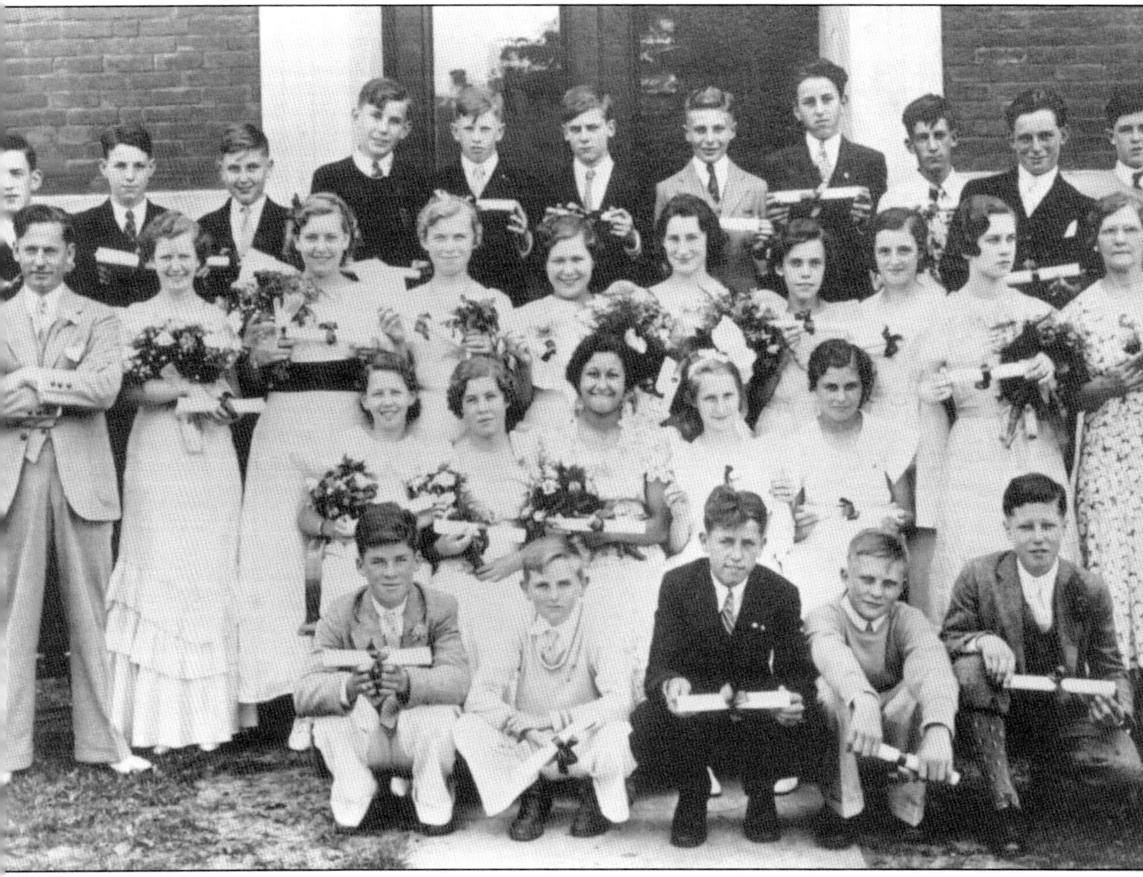

Members of the 1934 eighth-grade graduating class of Jacob F. Spaulding School hold tight to their diplomas with mixed expressions on their faces. They are, from left to right, as follows: (first row) Roland Thomas, Warren Lord, John Kearney, Leland Danielson, and Robert Smith; (second row) Frances Bartlett, Jane Grayton, Vivian Moghabghab, Bertha Robblee, and Charlotte Moore; (third row) teacher Philander Mann, Eleanor Dow, Caroline Downs, Mabel Bartlett, Virginia Hayes, Muriel Arthur, Betty Stone, Zofie Borin, Carol Congdon, and Bernice Chase (teacher); (fourth row) Albert Gagnon, Charles True, George Fowler, Robert Antell, Everett True, one unidentified student, Roger Shaheen (who later became owner of the beach amusement park), Homidas Peters, one unidentified student, Clarence Pickard, and one unidentified student.

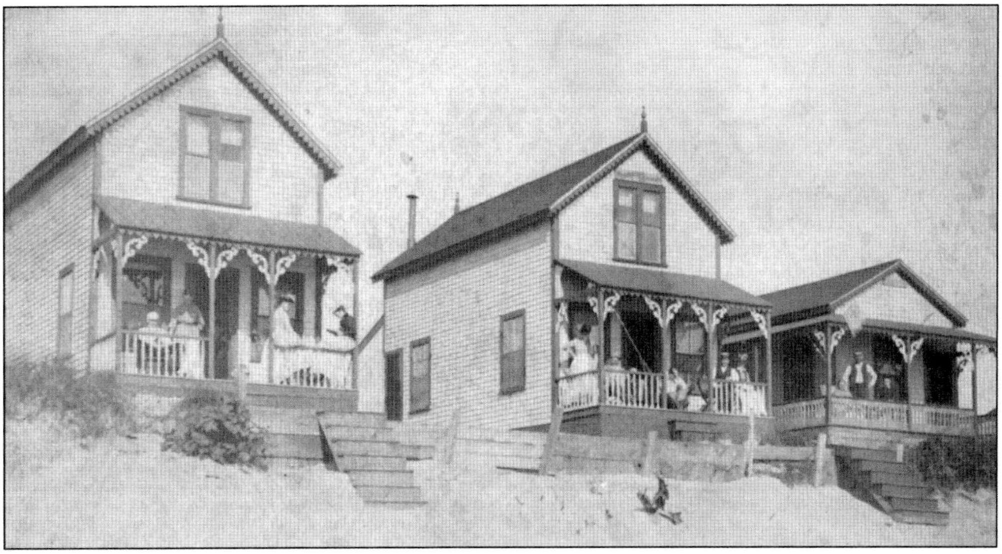

These gingerbread-decorated cottages are located at the south end of the beach. They look like cottages found at Oak Bluffs on Martha's Vineyard. These adorable buildings must have been burned or razed.

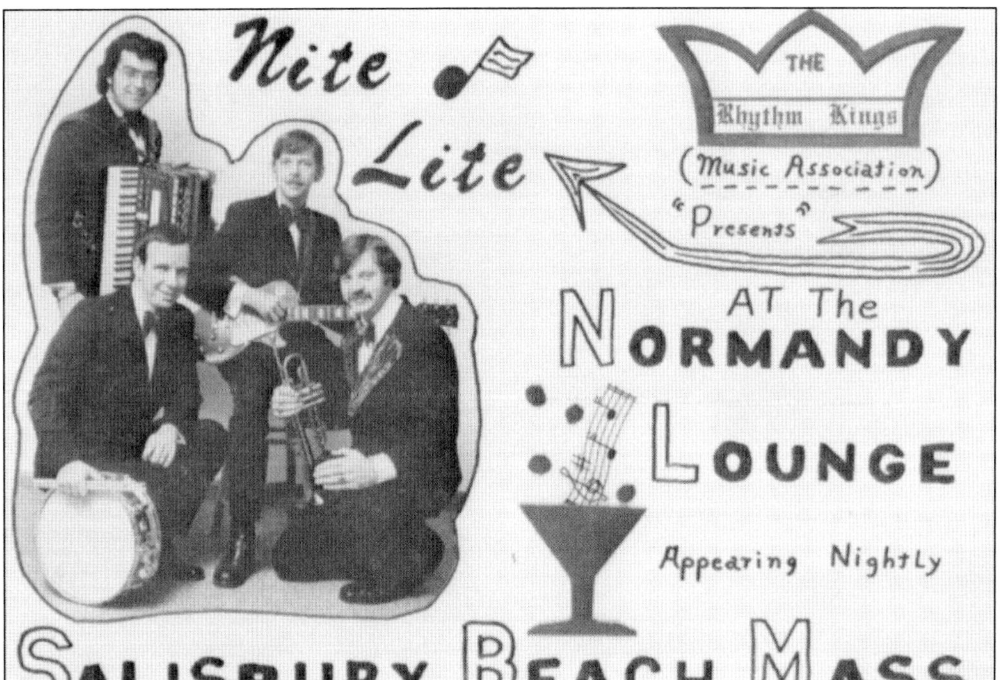

A local group known as the Rhythm Kings played at the Normandy Lounge at Salisbury Beach in the 1970s. (Courtesy Arnold Marookian.)

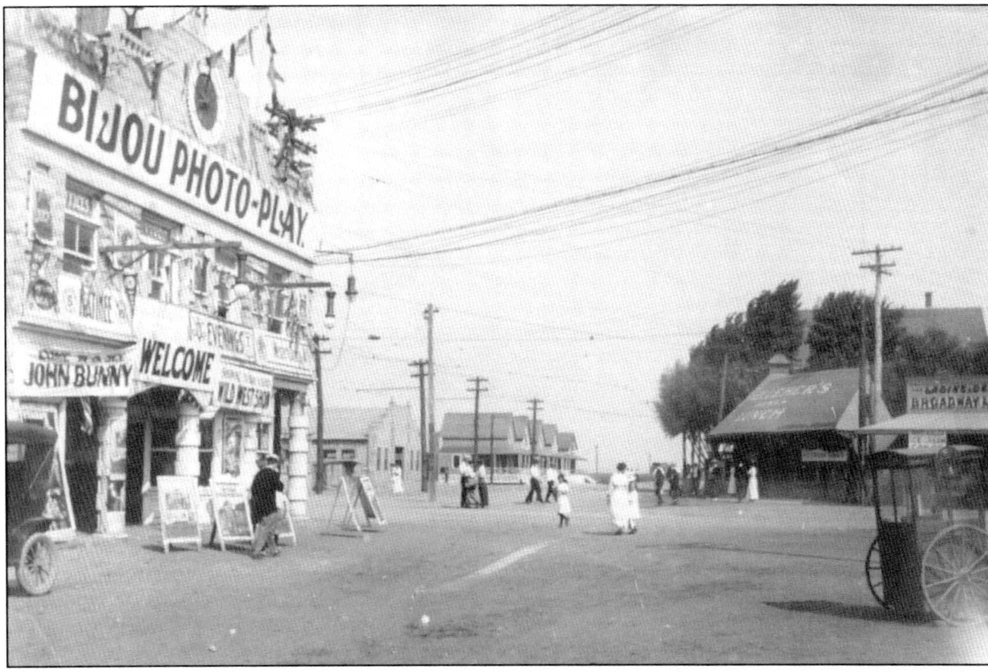

This turn-of-the-century picture was taken looking north toward Hampton Beach. The road on the corner of the building where people are walking is Broadway. The Bijou Photo-Play showed silent pictures. It was located at what now is the center of the parking lot access area. The theater did not burn in the fire of 1913 and was used as a temporary police station. Across the street is Kelleher's Wigwam Lunch. The garage in the center left is Cooks Garage. The stand with hand-rolled ice-cream cones was owned by Fuller Littlefield.

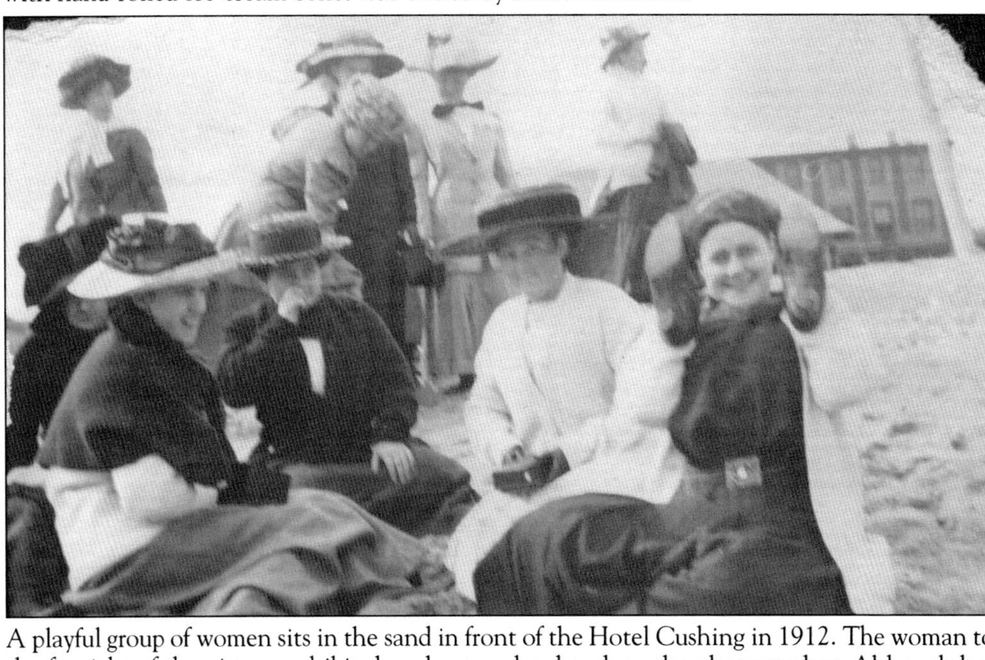

A playful group of women sits in the sand in front of the Hotel Cushing in 1912. The woman to the far right of the picture exhibits her shoes on her hands to the photographer. Although her feet are hidden under her skirt, her friends seem to be laughing at this daring behavior.

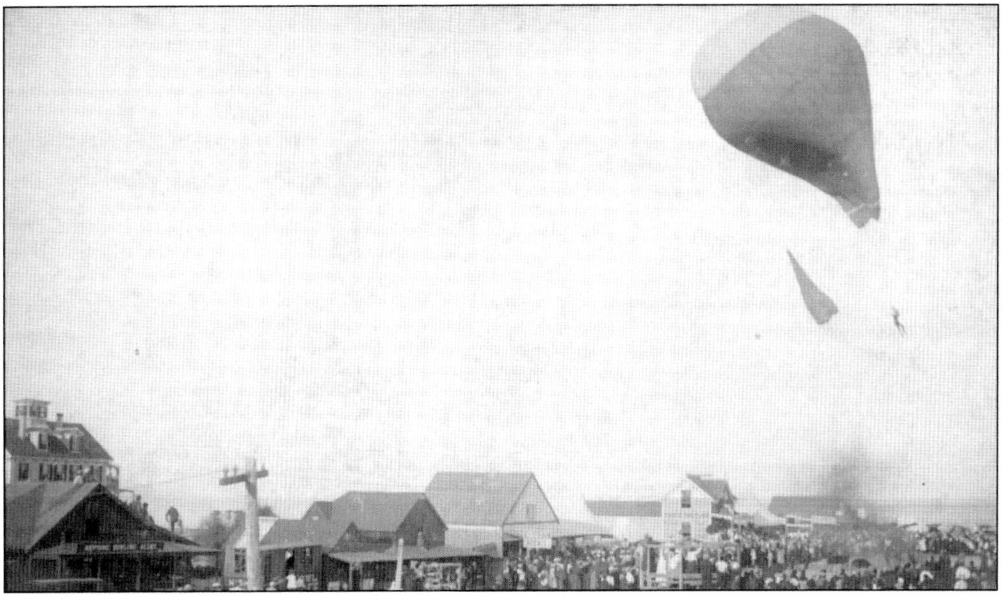

A big attraction at Salisbury Beach was a balloon ascent. These ascents originated as early as 1885. A fire was started in a sandpit and a crowd held the balloon over the fire to catch the gas. The balloon was released and often a trapeze man was alighted with the balloon and dropped into the ocean. This event had its share of disasters. One man was tangled in the rope and drowned, and another balloon caught fire.

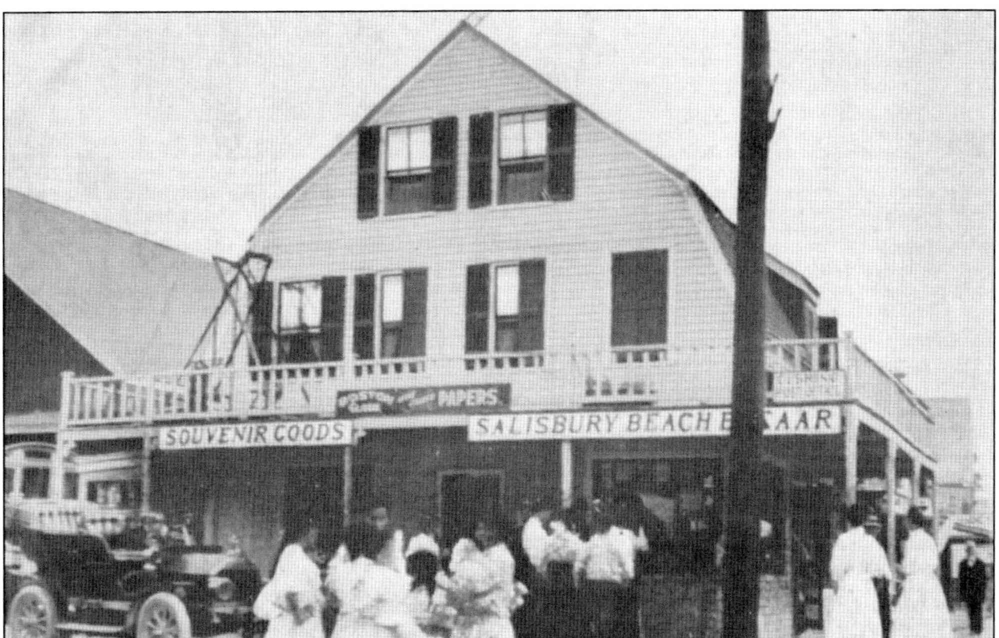

The Salisbury Beach Bazaar advertised souvenir goods. The *Boston Globe* and other papers could be purchased at their store. The Cushing post office was located on the right side of the building.

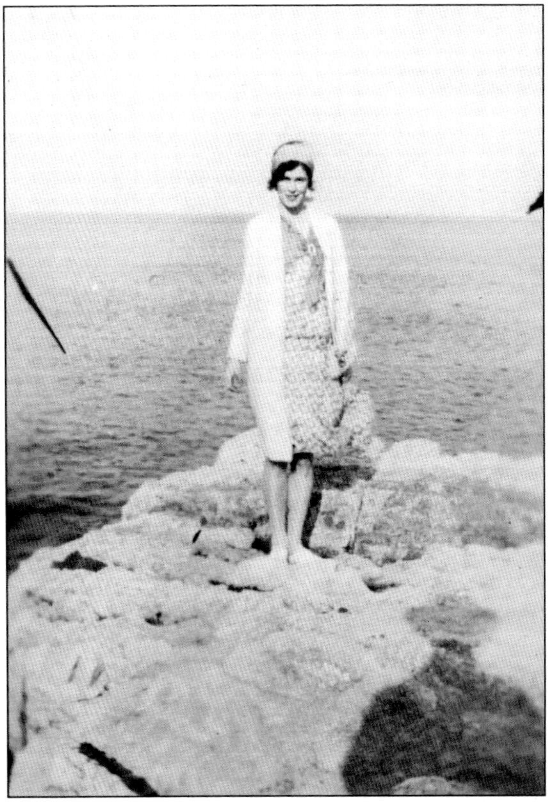

Marie Donovan from Haverhill stands on the jetties at Salisbury Beach while the breeze ruffles her 1920s outfit.

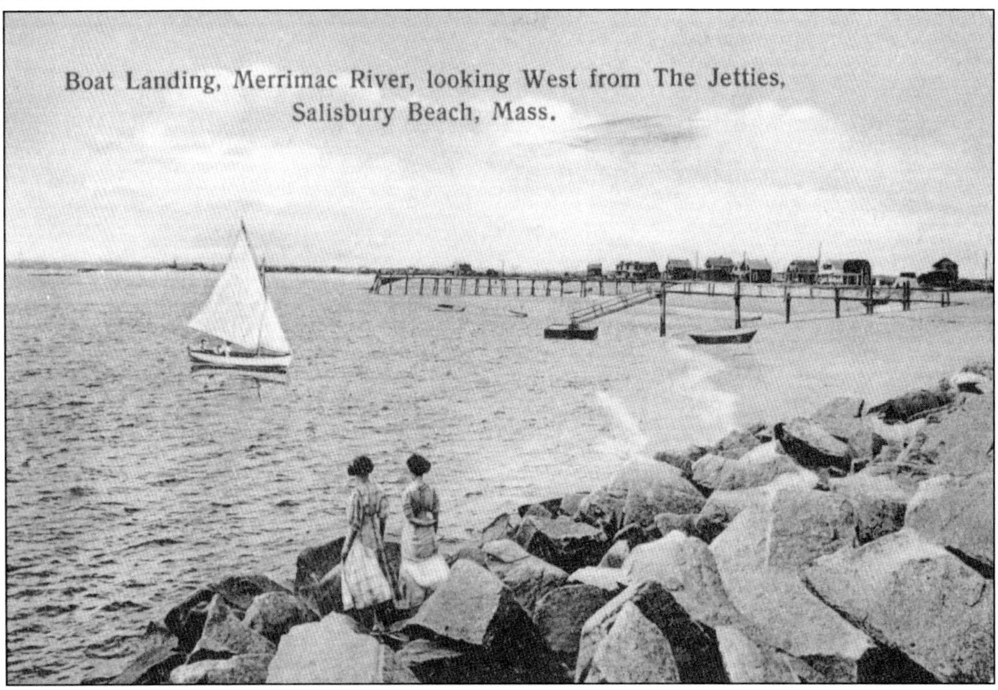

Two women on the jetties stare out to sea. The boat landing on the Merrimack River is visible looking west from the jetties. (Courtesy Arnold Marookian.)

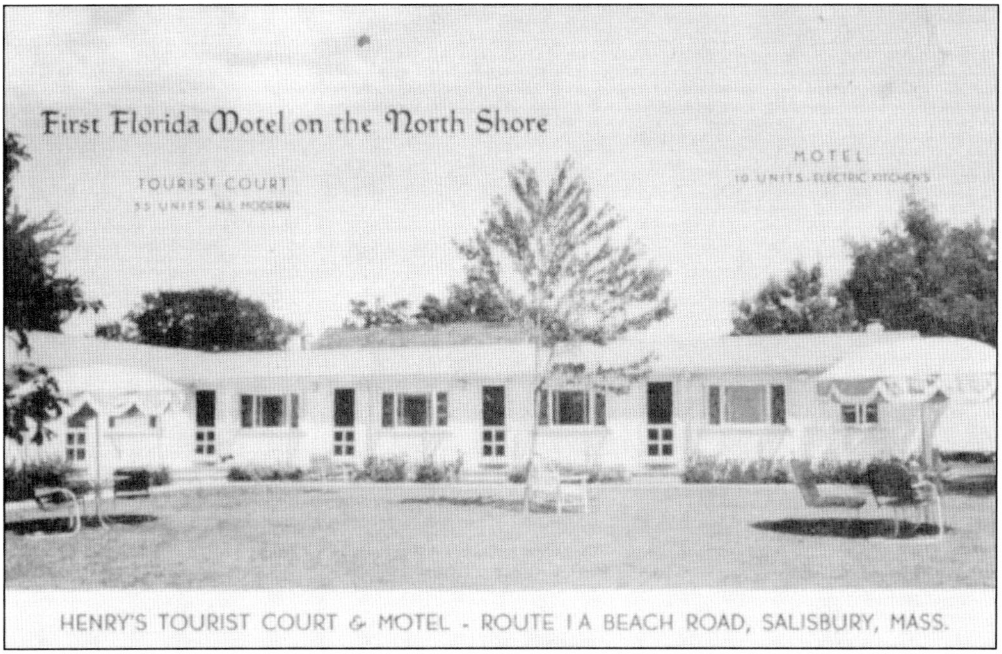

Henry's Tourist Court promotes its modern motel units with all-electric kitchens. The motel claims to be the first Florida motel on North Shore. The 44 units and 37 cottages could accommodate 250 people. A pool was installed in 1959. It was the trend in the 1950s for a family to spend their entire vacation in a motel. A family of six could stay comfortably in the Florida motel units. (Courtesy Arnold Marookian.)

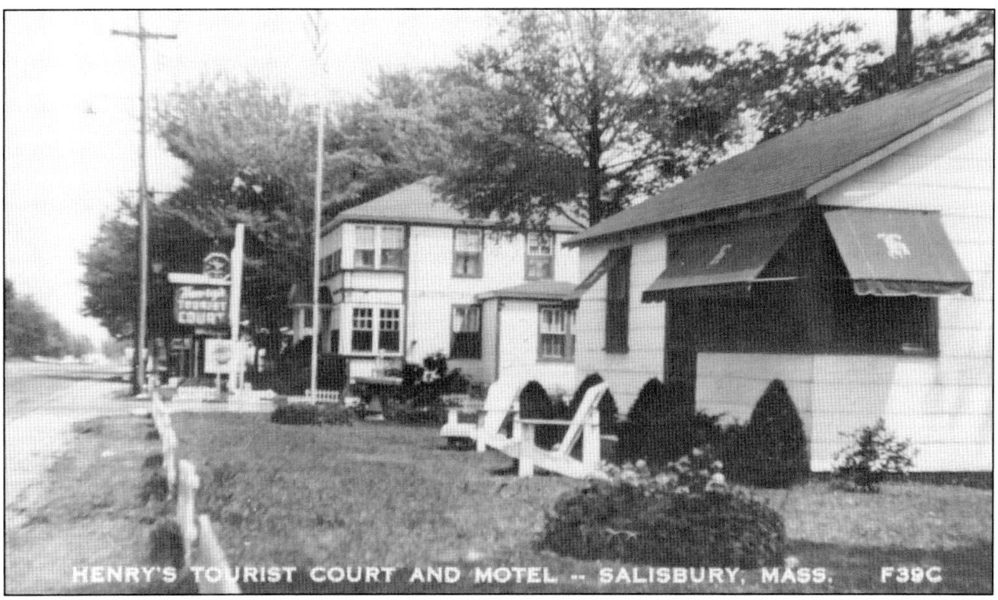

Henry's Motel was the home away from home for many entertainers who played at the Frolics and the Ocean Echo. The motel had been operated by Lil and Henry Patty since 1929. They were hosts to Louis Armstrong, Ella Fitzgerald, Red Buttons, Patti Page, Theresa Brewer, Sam Levenson, Martha Raye, the Four Aces, Connie Francis, and Jimmy Dean among others. (Courtesy Arnold Marookian.)

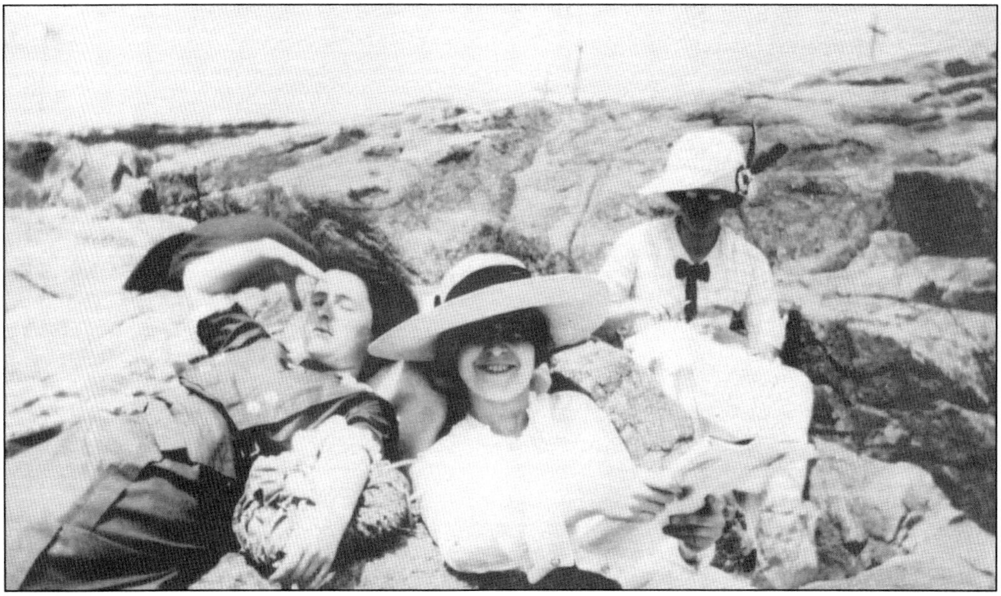

Jean Ditto Bauer, Bradford College Class of 1911, poses in the center with her friends on the jetties. Tanning did not come into vogue until the 1920s, so most women kept their skin covered up with the use of large hats.

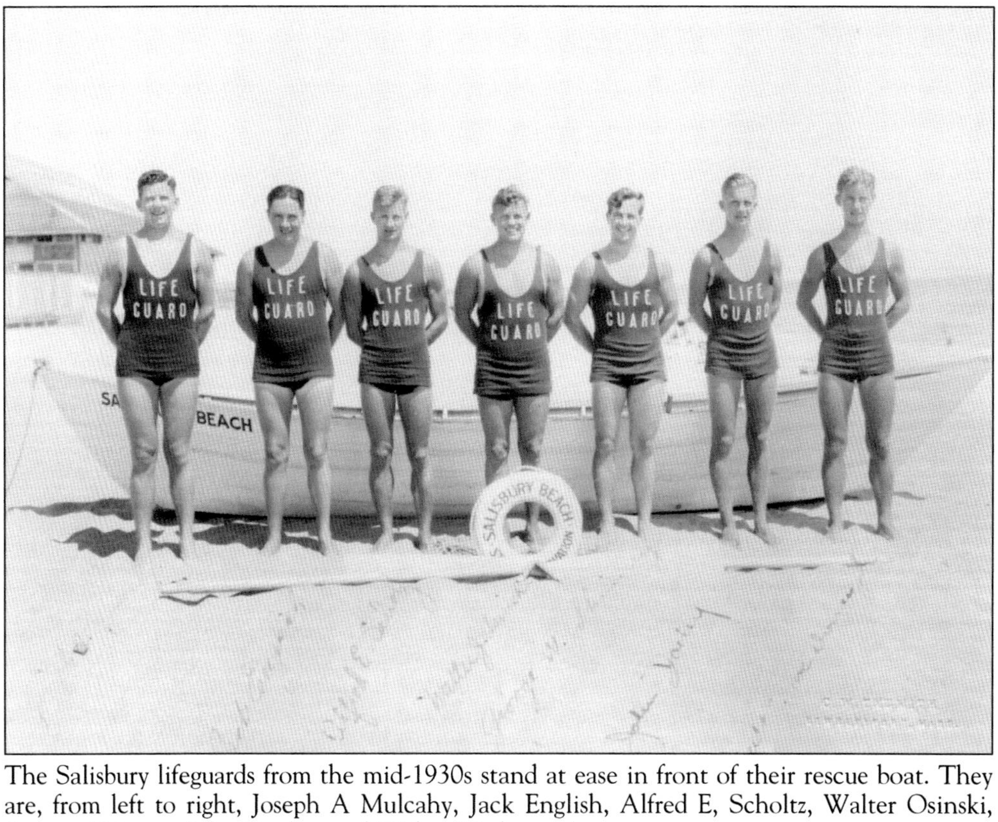

The Salisbury lifeguards from the mid-1930s stand at ease in front of their rescue boat. They are, from left to right, Joseph A Mulcahy, Jack English, Alfred E, Scholtz, Walter Osinski, George Shinney, John Dooley, and Walter Mcdonough.

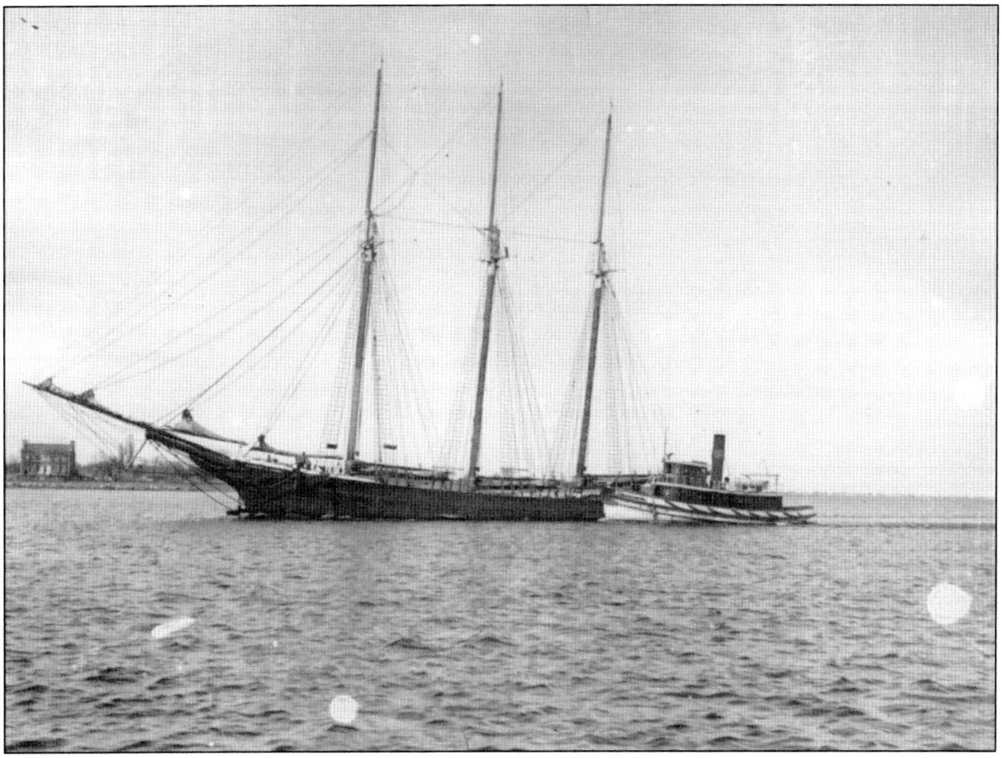

The ship named *Samuel S. Thorpe* is being escorted by a tugboat. It is passing by Rings Island and has just come from the ocean through the mouth of the Merrimack River. (Courtesy Arnold Marookian.)

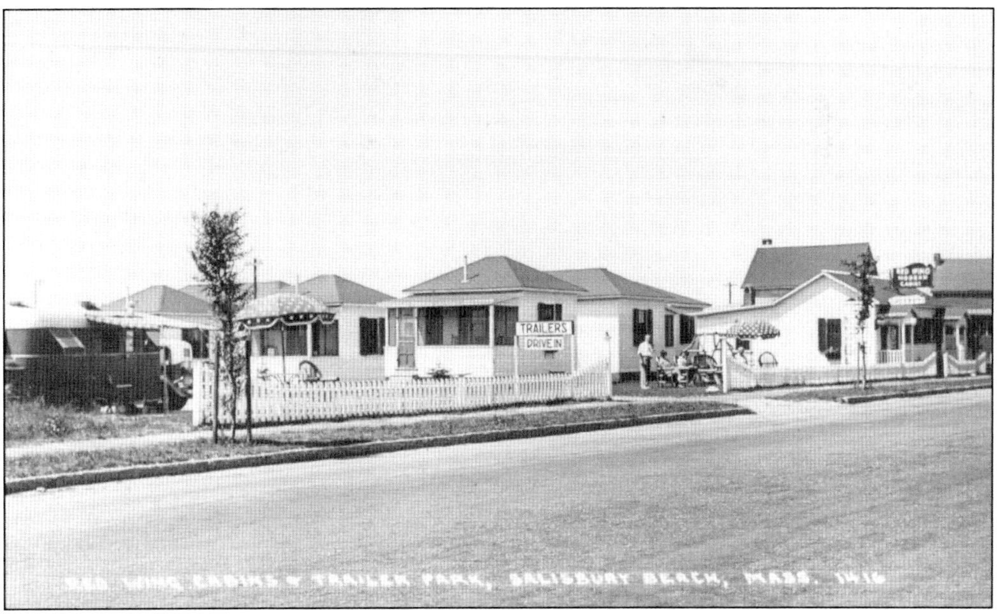

The Red Wing cottages as they appear in the 1940s at Salisbury Beach welcomed trailers. It must have been a combination cottage and campground. The cottages were rented by the week, month, or season. (Courtesy Arnold Marookian.)

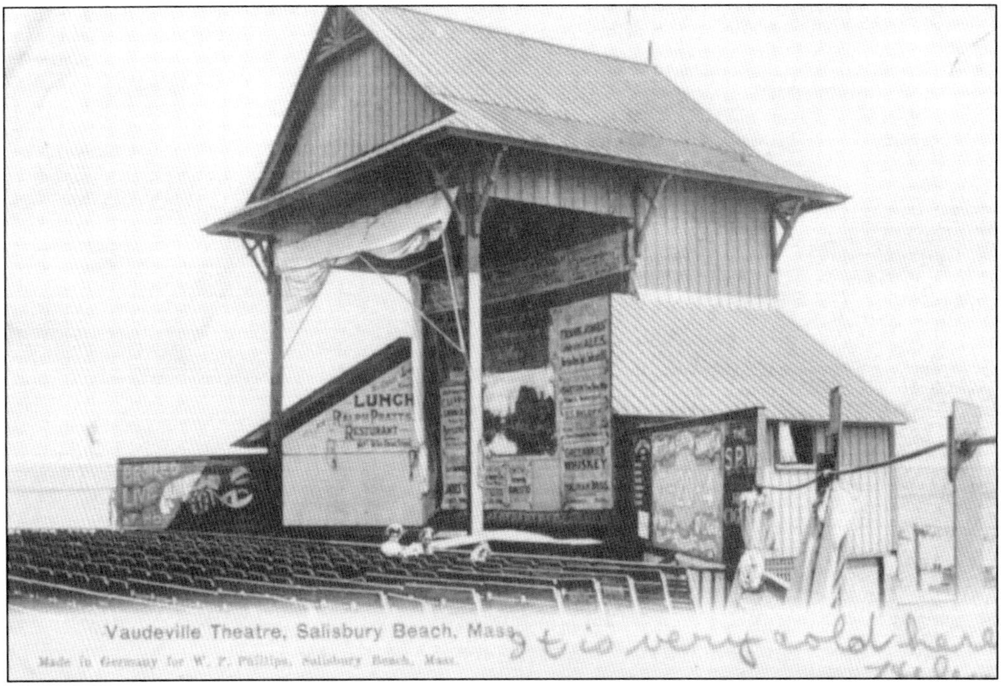

The Vaudeville Theatre was a later addition to the Hotel Cushing. Entertaining the masses was the main goal of Salisbury Beach.

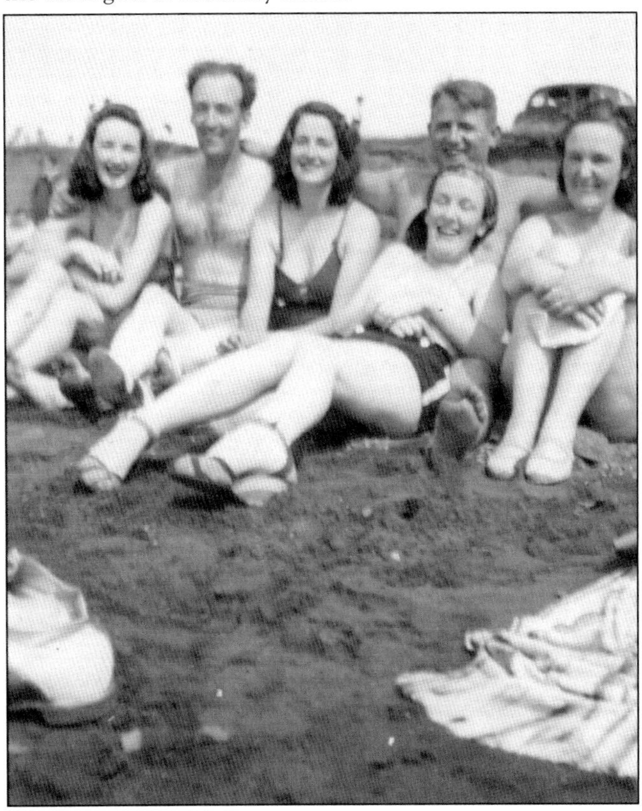

A group of young people enjoys the beach in the 1940s. They are, from left to right, one unidentified person, Peter Trainor, one unidentified person, Etta Trainor (displaying her ankle-strap shoes and more leg than the 1920s beachwear), Rudy Kohler, and Betty Trainor Keefe.

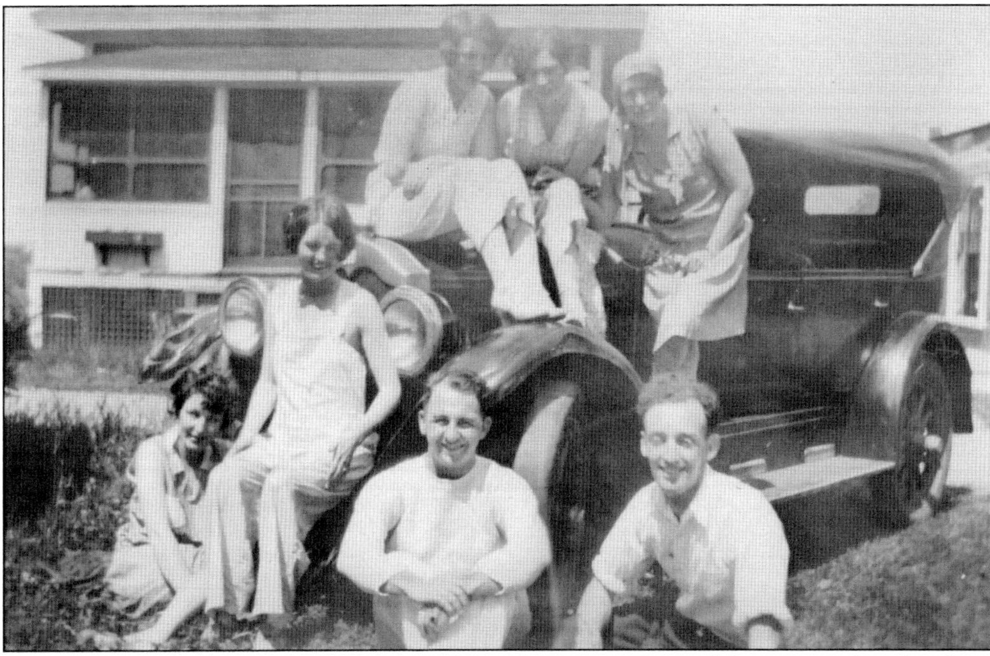

A gang from Prince Edward Island sits on their 1920s car in front of the cottage that they have rented in Salisbury Beach. They are, from left to right, as follows: (front row) Anne McNeil (under headlight), Winnie Trainor (on bumper), Leo Keefe, and Peter Trainor; (back row) Etta Trainor, Marie Donovan, and Betty Trainor. Leo Keefe and all of the women in this picture with the exception of Marie Donovan worked at Bradford College.

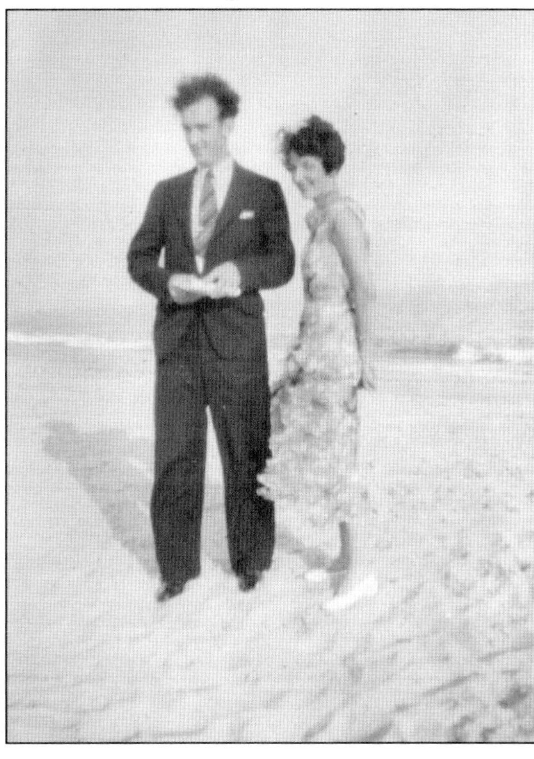

Peter Trainor and his sister, Winnie, stand on the beach. They are festively dressed for an evening of dancing at the Ocean Echo.

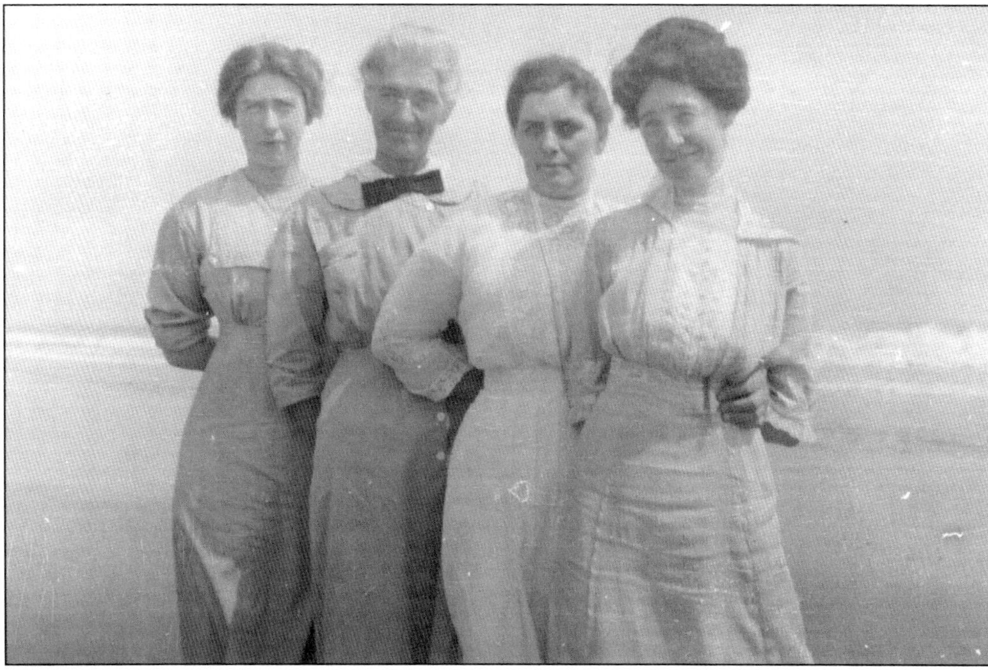

Agnes Donovan, from Bradford, at the far left of this picture lines up with three of her friends from Lawrence. Many people from the Merrimack Valley remember the long-anticipated annual beach trip to Salisbury with their families.

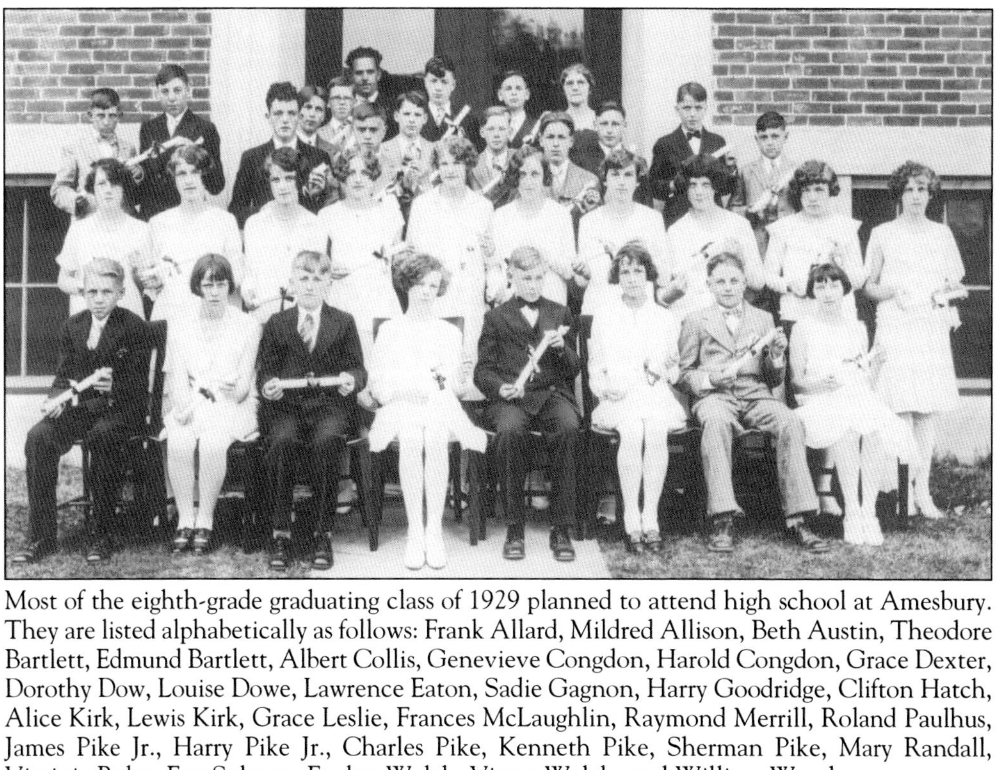

Most of the eighth-grade graduating class of 1929 planned to attend high school at Amesbury. They are listed alphabetically as follows: Frank Allard, Mildred Allison, Beth Austin, Theodore Bartlett, Edmund Bartlett, Albert Collis, Genevieve Congdon, Harold Congdon, Grace Dexter, Dorothy Dow, Louise Dowe, Lawrence Eaton, Sadie Gagnon, Harry Goodridge, Clifton Hatch, Alice Kirk, Lewis Kirk, Grace Leslie, Frances McLaughlin, Raymond Merrill, Roland Paulhus, James Pike Jr., Harry Pike Jr., Charles Pike, Kenneth Pike, Sherman Pike, Mary Randall, Virginia Ruhp, Eva Solmon, Evelyn Welch, Victor Welch, and William Wood.

Etta Trainor, who was from Prince Edward Island and worked as a waitress, is shown in a revealing bathing suit that exposes both her arms and legs. In the late 1920s, as people became interested in exercising, healthier food, and sun worshipping, showing more flesh at the beach became the fad.

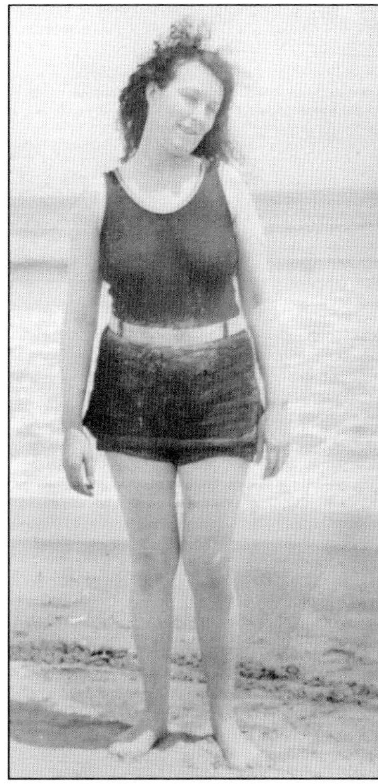

The Seaside School, built in 1893, was a one-room schoolhouse at Salisbury Beach and was moved from its original location. When the tide was high, the school had to close due to flooding. The school was eventually abandoned in 1917 because of its rickety condition. The young people at the beach later attended school in Salisbury center. The group includes, from left to right, the following: (front row) Eddie Foote, Herbert Beevers, Randolph Frothingham, Donald Greenlaw, Jacob Beevers, and William Brown; (middle row) Nellie Lake, Mildred Brown, Mary Beevers, Marguerite Evans, Isabelle Foote, Melissa Brown, and Melissa Brown's sister; (back row) Franklin "Red" Randall, teacher Katherine Rowe, Spalding Beevers, and Norman Greenlaw.

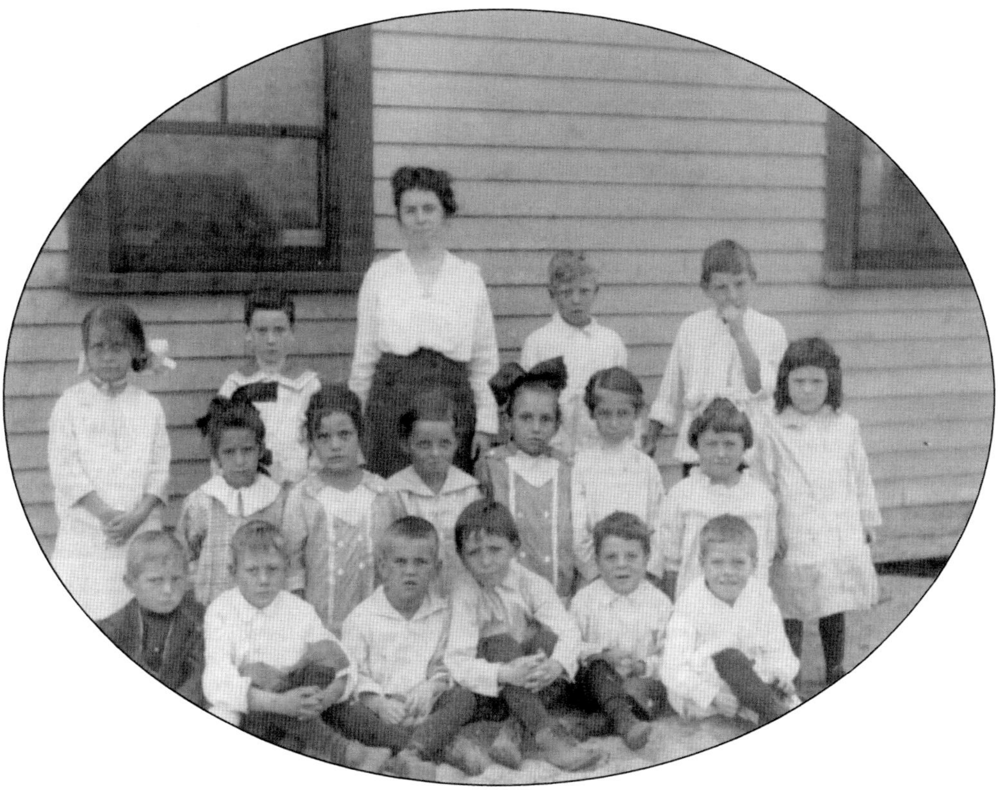

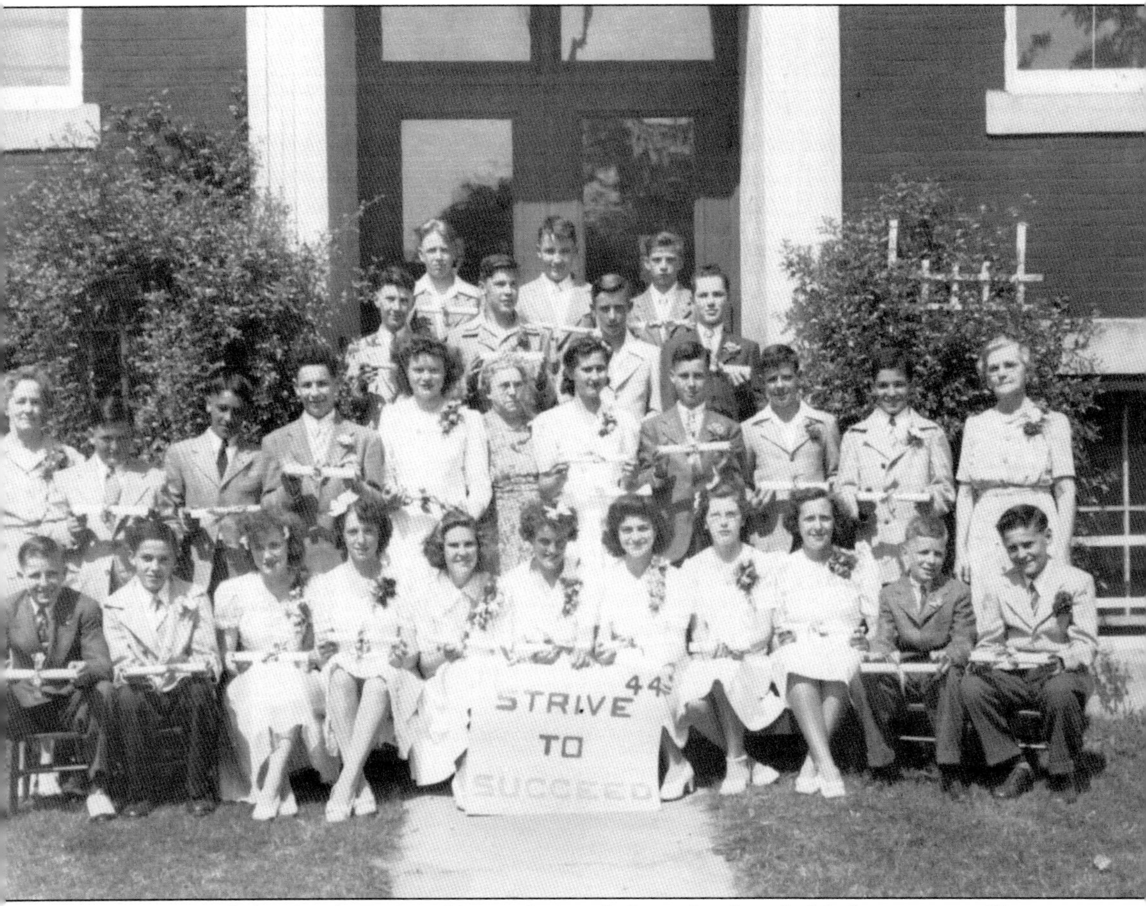

Members of the Jacob F. Spaulding 1944 eighth-grade class hold their motto, "Strive to Succeed," for their graduation picture. The list of the graduates, in no particular order, is as follows: Stewart Ackerman, James Beckwith, Lidwine Beevers, Helen Blaisdell, William Coffey, Claire Dutton, Erdine Eaton, George Eaton, Elsie Fowler, Herbert Fowler, Edith French, Leonard French, Raelene Helfrich, Ronald Hogan, Jaques L'Heureux, Peter Merluzzi, Freeman Morehouse, Donald Nichols, Anthony Papoulias, Shirley Pierce, David Pike, James Rizzi Jr., Julia Romeo, Walter Ross, Delbert Sawyer Jr., T. Buswell, Jean Dow, Raymond Flanders, Barbara Gormley, Vilma McNeil, Georgianna Meek, George Miller, Jennie Orechwo, and Wesley Patterson.

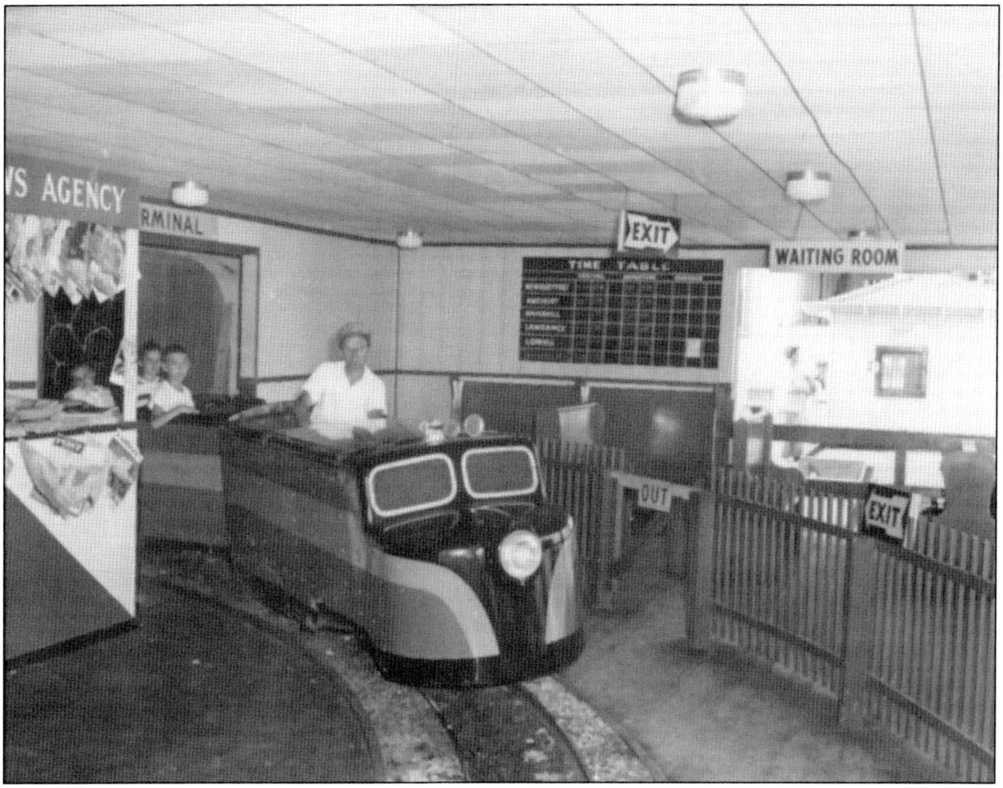

A miniature train takes passengers for a ride around the beach. This picture was taken by William B. Coltin for the *Daily News* in 1940. (Courtesy Roger Shaheen.)

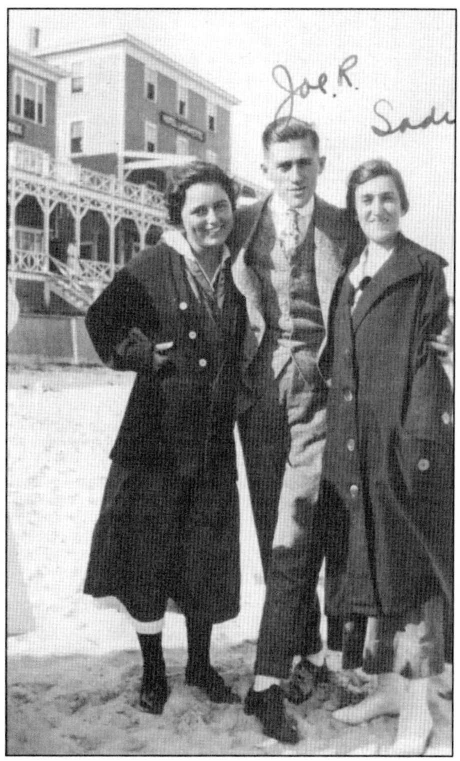

Three friends from New York City stand in the sand in front of the Vinton Villa. The first girl to the left is unidentified, and the other couple is only identified only as Joe and Sally R.
So many people have enjoyed the beach over the years that many of their names have been long forgotten.

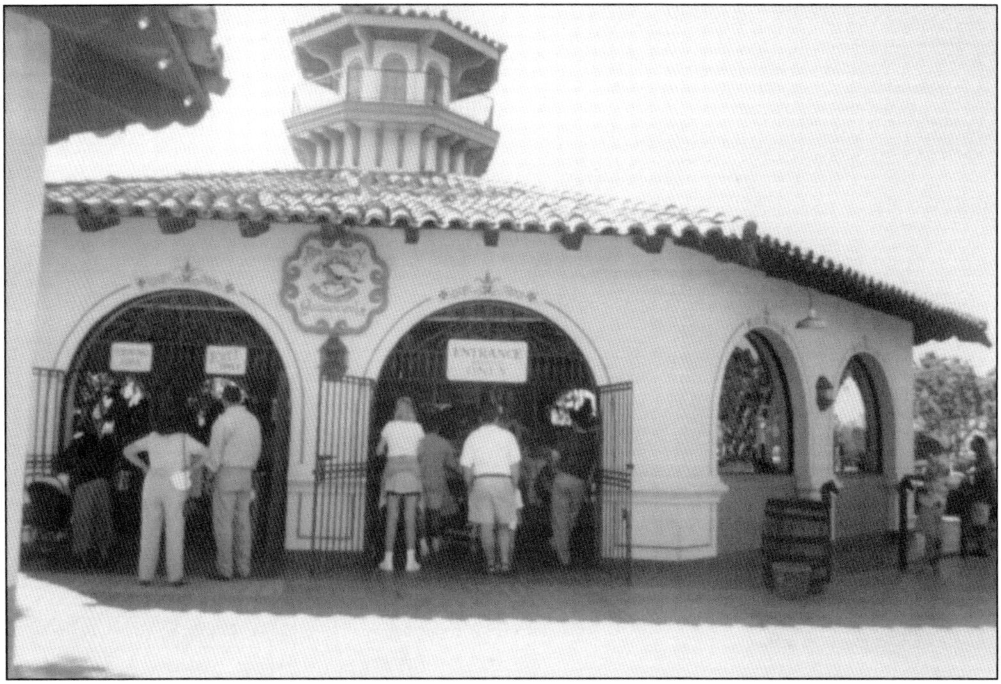

People gather around the attractive present home of the Salisbury Beach Broadway Flying Horses in San Diego, California. Although sadly missed at the beach, the vintage carousel was sold as one unit, preserving its historical value. Unlike the Whalom Park's Looff horses, which were just auctioned off piece by piece like so many memories of the past, the Broadway carousel will maintain its historic integrity in San Diego.

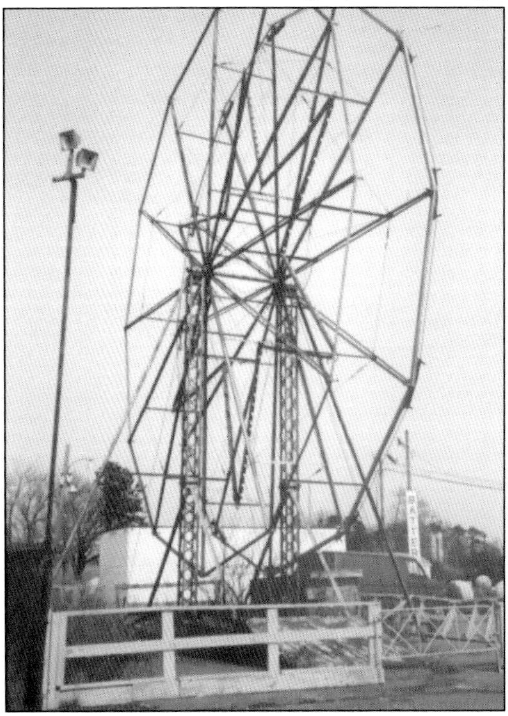

An abandoned Ferris wheel at the entrance of the beach is stripped of its former splendor. Once, people would thrill to be stopped at the top with a panoramic view of the beach below. When the Ferris wheel was introduced at the 1893 World's Colombian Exposition, it was one of the most popular rides.

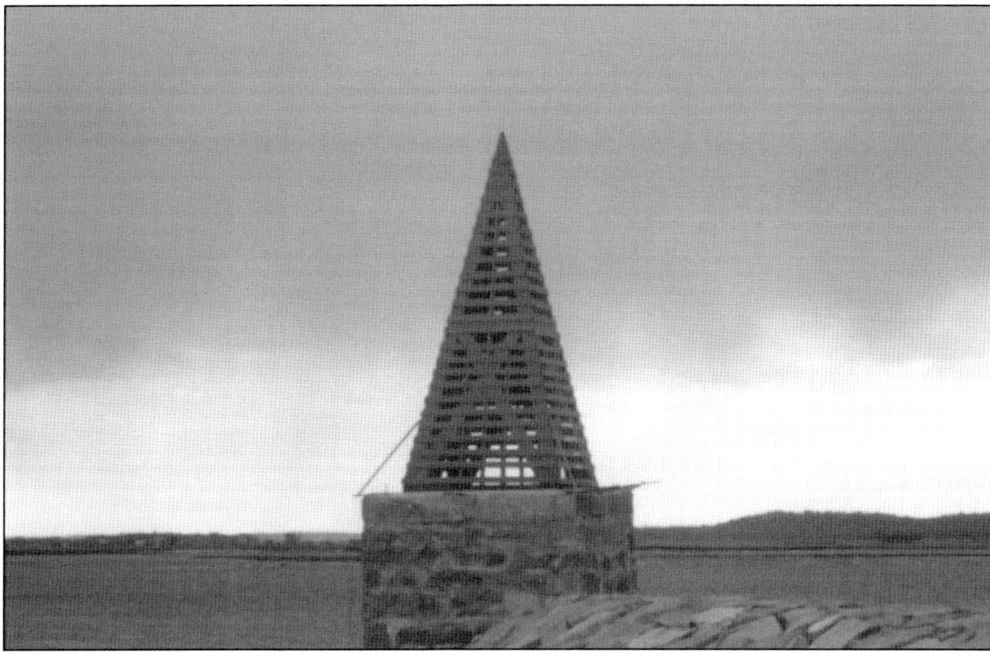

Shown is Butler's Toothpick today. The top is now an orange metal construction.

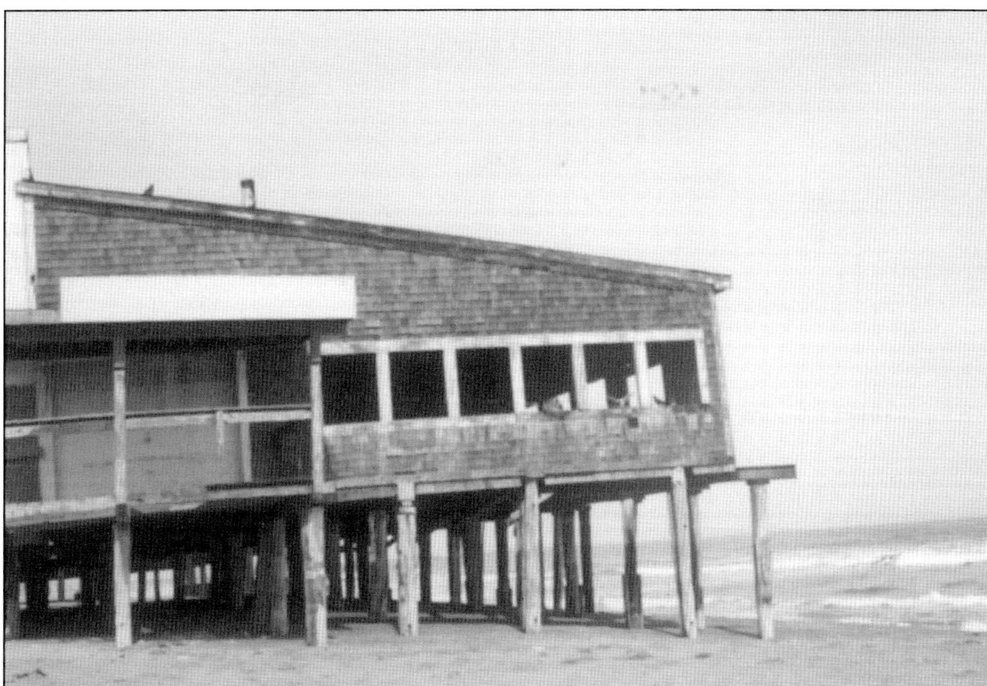

Lonely sea gulls perch on an empty building jutting out to the sea. The empty space to the front of the picture is where the Ocean Echo–Frolics stood until its demolition in 1999. Much of the midway area has lost the luster over the years.

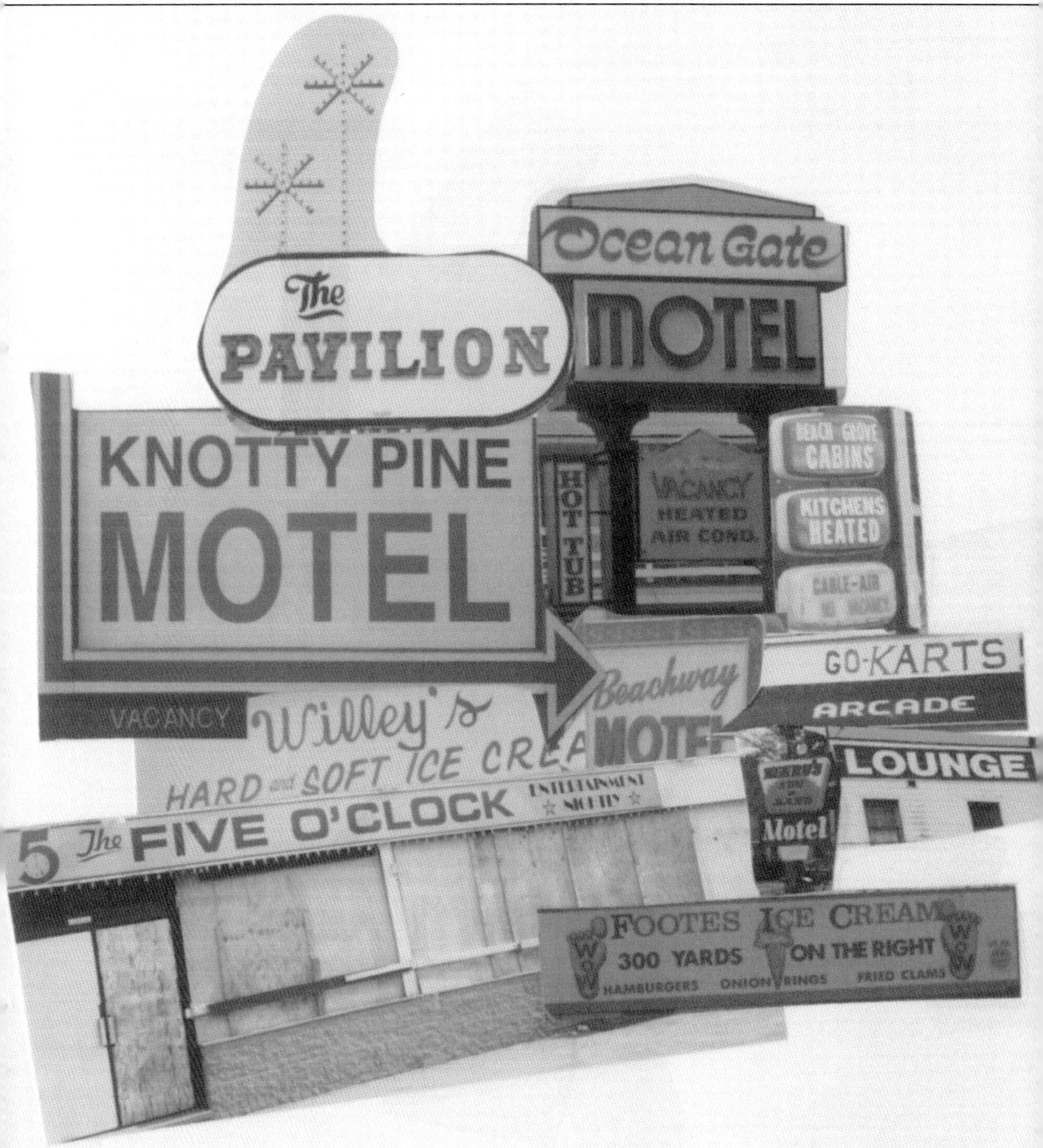

This collage shows some of the present-day signs on Beach Road and at Salisbury Beach center.

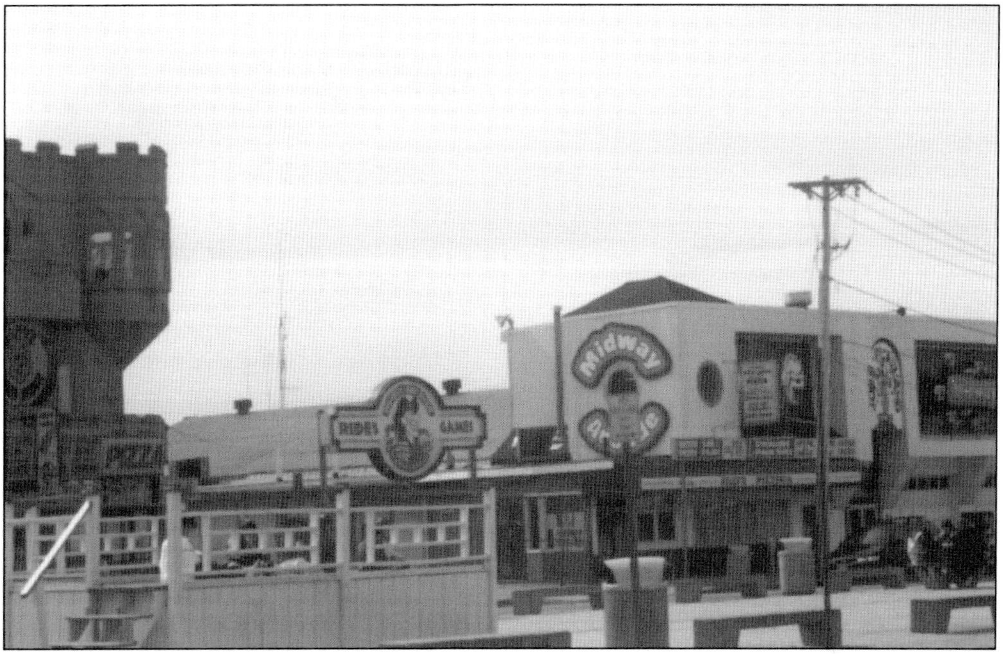

The center of Salisbury Beach today holds no remnants of its romantic Victorian days. The fashionable hotels no longer grace the oceanfront. It has changed considerably since the days of dances at the Ocean Echo and the early days of the spectacular Frolics. At the beach today, the bawdy has replaced the beauty.

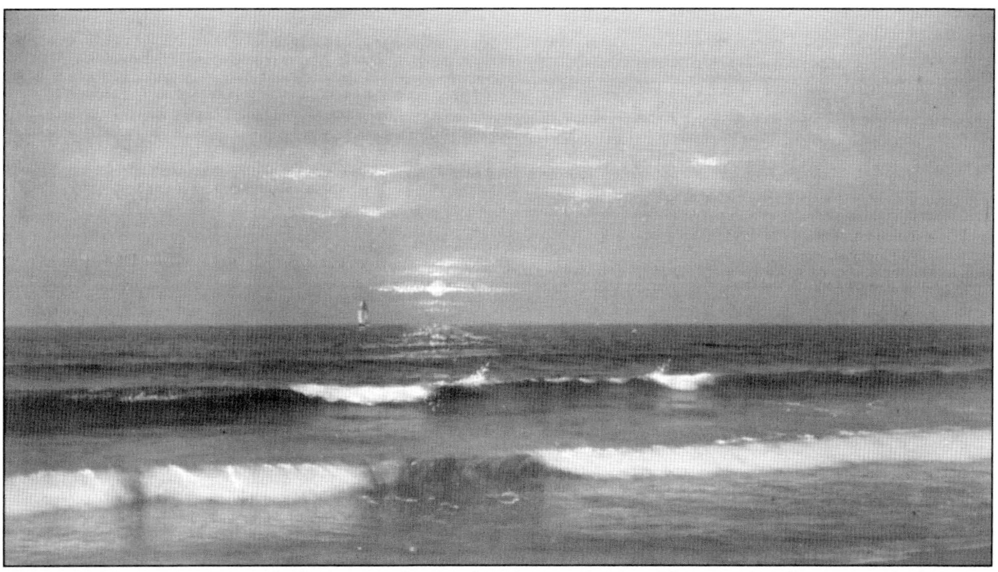

As the moon rises over Salisbury Beach, maybe that path, sparkling with silver moonlight over the ocean, will appear and we can walk across and bring back some of the glamour that was once Salisbury Beach if only in our memories.

Dedication and Acknowledgments

I wish to dedicate this book to my Uncle Phil Walsh, who tried to teach me to dance but instead taught me to fly, and to Bradford College, where I learned to soar.

Special thanks to my husband, the Honorable John C. Stevens III, for the great advice and all his patience, proofreading, and editing.

And to my editor, Amy Sutton, for allowing me the honor of presenting the history of Salisbury Beach.

I would like to thank my advisor, history professor, author, and friend Dr. Patricia Trainor O'Malley for sharing her great family albums with me.

Many thanks to Larry Streeter, Salisbury chief of police, for giving me wonderful leads; to Arnold Marookian, for sharing his postcard collection and memories of Salisbury Beach; to Roger Shaheen, for letting me delve through and use his wonderful collection of beach pictures; to Ruth Harden, for the use of the great scrapbook, stories, and pictures; to Ethel Rogers for sharing her Aunt Bessie's scrapbooks and spending hours telling me long-forgotten Salisbury Beach lore; to Joseph Callahan, first full-time fire chief in Salisbury, for lending pictures and information; to Scott Nason, for trusting me with his valuable stereoscopic pictures even though I misplaced them once; to Hazel Cote, for wonderful stories and pictures of the old beach; to Karen French, for sharing her lovely grandmother; to Gary Little, a great boss and the ultimate Salisbury lifeguard, for lending his lifeguard picture and facts; to Edna Mulcahy for pictures of the original Salisbury lifeguards; to Ruth Gagnon for her leads, encouragement, and her living history group; to Mary Sherman for the great Frolics picture; to Jamie Thomas (we made it!) for sharing her family pictures and her friendship; to Flora Grassi Thomas for coffee and my first beach pictures; and to Suzanne Cote, reference librarian at Amesbury, for always being available to help me. Thanks also to Kathy O'Malley and the Haverhill Historical Society for my internship.

A very special thanks to my niece, Courtney Stevens, for taking the pictures of the Broadway Flying Horses in their new home in San Diego.

Last of all, thanks to the staff of the Salisbury library for their help and cooperation: Gail Lyon, library director; Marsha Fowler, local history and genealogy; Terry Kyrios; and Joan Bomba.